# THE BRITISH CONSERVATIVE PARTY AND ONE NATION POLITICS

*David Seawright*

continuum

NEW YORK • LONDON

2010

The Continuum International Publishing Group Inc
80 Maiden Lane, New York, NY 10038

The Continuum International Publishing Group Ltd
The Tower Building, 11 York Road, London SE1 7NX

www.continuumbooks.com

Library of Congress Cataloging-in-Publication Data
A catalog record for this book is available from the Library of Congress.

ISBN: 978-1-4411-2369-5

Typeset by Newgen Imaging Systems Pvt Ltd, Chennai, India
Printed in the United States of America

# Contents

# Acknowledgments

As is often the case, the work on a book such as this incurs a multitude of debts. Thus, there is the obvious obligation on my part to express my gratitude to all those who have helped and assisted, in a variety of ways, with the completion of this research monograph. With this in mind I would like to begin with an acknowledgment of the assistance of the British Academy, for the research grant SG 35058 which enabled me to undertake the research for this project and to the staff of the various libraries and archives for their generous help and assistance.

I would like to take this opportunity to thank Sheridan Westlake of Conservative Central Office for permission to consult and quote from the Conservative Party Archive (CPA) at the Bodleian Library Oxford and also to Emily Tarrant, the archivist and Colin Harris and Oliver House for their generous help and guidance in the use of this resource. I am grateful to the British Library of Political and Economic Science and to the archivist, Sue Donnelly, for permission to consult and quote from the papers of Sir Gilbert Longden and for access to the British Oral Archive of Political and Administrative History (BOAPAH). For the work gleaned from the papers of Sir John Rodgers, at the Centre for Kentish Studies, Kent, a thank you to Sir Piers Rodgers for his permission to view and quote from his late father's papers. I would like to thank Robert Butler, the Librarian and Nigel Cochrane, from the University of Essex, for all their help and for their permission to consult the papers of Lord Alport and I would also like to thank the Master and Fellows of Trinity College Cambridge for their permission to consult and quote from the papers of Richard Austen (RAB) Butler. I am grateful to Lord Howard of Rising who, on behalf of the trustees of the Enoch Powell papers, gave permission to quote from this archival resource and in particular to Katherine Thompson of the Churchill Archives Centre, Churchill College, Cambridge, for all her generous help with regards to the Powell papers.

For granting helpful and informative interviews I would like to thank, Alistair Burt MP; Lord Mark Carlisle; Sir Philip Goodhart; Damian Green MP; David Heathcoat-Amory MP; Lord David Howell; Jacqui Lait MP; Andrew Mitchell MP; Caroline Spelman MP; Sir Michael Spicer MP and David Willetts MP. I would also like to thank Robert Jackson and members of the One Nation

Group for permission to consult the "attendance book" for 1992–2004 and Keith Simpson MP for his correspondence with regards to updates on the membership of the group.

I would also like to take this opportunity to thank the many colleagues and friends at the University of Leeds for their unstinting encouragement and advice over many years and for their comments and advice regarding this project: especially Geoff Fry, Ed Gouge, Clive Jones and Kevin Theakston; and in particular Stuart McAnulla who has consistently offered guidance and constructive criticism and who speedily alerted me to the "Responsible Society context" when it was in its initial development by David Cameron. I owe a debt of gratitude to Joe Organ, then a research student at Leeds University, who coded all the One Nation pamphlets and the housing sections of the Campaign Guides and in this context I would also like to thank Andrea Volkens, of the Wissenschaftzentrum Berlin, for her generous help and her advice on understanding the Manifesto Research Group coding procedures. My thanks also to Chris Wylde for his help in constructing the excel graphs for Chapter 3. I am indebted to Katie Gallof and in particular to Marie-Claire Antoine at Continuum for their patience and for their support of this project. I must pay a special tribute to Andrew Gamble for his support and guidance over many years and for his generous help and encouragement with this particular project. Of course, and no doubt to the immense relief of many of those mentioned, the usual disclaimer applies, that the interpretation of this work, its inaccuracies and mistakes are mine and mine alone.

During the course of the research and writing of this work there has been much personal and family support to which I must give a special mention. My neighbors are acutely aware of this work as an excuse for my shortcomings with regards to such necessary maintenance and gardening activity. So for their generous help and understanding with this I thank Paul and Jane Hyman and Colin and Jean Glasby; with particular thanks to Colin and Jean for the concomitant supply of the "water of life." There have been many happy family events that also need mentioning. It was special to see Joanne, Craig and Sarah again after so many years and the marriages of Craig and Tracey, Robert and Elizabeth and Aaron and Joanne were wonderful events but it is with particular delight that I mention the arrival of the newest generation: Ava, Reuben and my own little Zachary. Family is just so important and I thank them all for the support they have given me over the years and I am sure they will all join with me in thanking my sister Tricia for all her longstanding selfless work on our behalf and to whom this book is dedicated.

# Foreword

The British Conservative Party has been one of the most successful political parties in any modern democracy. Between 1915 and 1997, the Conservatives were never out of government for more than six years. They were in government either alone or in coalition for 62 of those 82 years, or 75 percent of the time. In its long period of success, the party became strongly identified as a party of the nation, promoting a particular national idea, and seeking to appeal to all citizens. In one sense it had no choice. Once the suffrage began to be extended the Conservatives could not rely on the votes of the country areas to return them to office. In a country so urban and industrial as Britain had become, the Conservatives needed to be a party of the whole nation, and to seek to represent the cities as well as the shires. The genius of Conservative statecraft was to adjust to the demands of the new democracy, and find a way to create a genuine national appeal. Disraeli had understood much earlier that if politics in modern Britain became a contest between the two nations, the rich and the poor, the Conservatives would lose.

The One Nation approach has been associated at times with a particular ideological tendency in the party, but David Seawright is correct to point out that the approach does not belong to any one faction. It is what every Conservative leader must seek to follow. Margaret Thatcher may not have used the term, One Nation, but she famously declared after her third election victory in 1987 that her next task was to win the votes of the citizens of the inner cities, declaring that she wanted them as well. It was not enough to rely on the votes of the bankers and the comfortable suburbs. Margaret Thatcher was often accused of shattering national unity and creating two nations, but her own view was very different. She believed that only her policies could recreate a true national community again. In that sense she was acting as many Conservatives before her, seeking to unite the classes rather than to divide them and to stress the principles and values which were shared in common.

One Nation has been threatened however not only by the two nations of the social classes, but also by the four nations of the territorial politics of the United Kingdom. Being a national party in the multinational United Kingdom of Great Britain and Northern Ireland has sometimes been difficult, because within this state, the British identity has always been to some extent contested, and considered by some as subordinate to the primary loyalties of being Scottish, Welsh,

Irish, or English. The Conservative Party has always drawn its main strength from England, and although a quintessential English party, it has never believed it could prosper by being only an English party. In recent years, when at times it has appeared as little more than a southern English party, with no significant representation in many parts of Northern England, or in Wales, or in Scotland, let alone Northern Ireland, fears were raised for the survival of the party. The true One Nation tradition was when the Conservatives proclaimed themselves a Unionist party and won significant representation through the United Kingdom, not least in Scotland. In the 1950s, the party was still able to win half of the Scottish seats. At the core of this Unionism was a particular conception of Britain as an empire, an expanding power, which incorporated other nations and territories within its rule.

Central to Conservative statecraft has been the aim of finding the policies and the symbols through which both the two nations and the four nations might be transcended in One Nation. The Empire played a major role in this, but after 1945, the Empire went into retreat, and at the same time new forms of social citizenship in the shape of universal welfare and health programs became an alternative focus for national unity. Fresh thinking was needed by the Conservatives, and the One Nation Group was an important source. It is the history of this group, and the importance of its thinking to the development of the subsequent evolution of party thinking which David Seawright seeks to demonstrate. In the first half of the twentieth century, the Conservatives had become a collectivist party and an interventionist party. One Nation was interpreted to mean that the government should protect citizens, especially in hard economic times like the 1930s. The Conservatives imposed imperial preference, encouraged industrial cartels, and protected small businesses from competition. The One Nation Group in the 1950s attempted to move the party in a very different direction, drawing increasingly on the tradition of economic liberalism, which had never gone away, but which had become rather muted.

David Seawright brings out very well the different emphases within this new One Nation approach, and its considerable influence within the party. He shows how it appealed strongly to David Cameron, who has set himself the task to revive both Unionism, while accepting devolution, and social justice, while avoiding too great a reliance on the state. His espousal of green ideas and his promotion of the third sector are distinctive aspects of his particular adaptation of the One Nation approach. The importance of civil society in Britain, the dense web of voluntary, not-for-profit organizations has always been one of the things which has made Britain distinctive. The failure in the 1990s to prevent most of the building societies from abandoning their mutual status and becoming banks was from this perspective a failure of One Nation Conservatism. By signaling his determination to rely on the third sector to a greater extent than ever before in the delivery and design of public services and the development of the green agenda, David Cameron seeks to revive the spirit of One Nation thinking. If the Conservatives as expected return to government in 2010, they will confront very difficult economic circumstances, and this new One Nation approach will face a stern test, but it is now once again central to Conservative strategy and will not be lightly abandoned.

Andrew Gamble
University of Cambridge

# CHAPTER ONE

# Introduction: One Nation, Food for Thought

In 2006, just months after winning the Conservative Party leadership contest, David Cameron launched a process that he termed "Built to Last." Included in the process was a statement of aims and values that were to be the essence of Cameron's modern compassionate Conservatism: setting out the general political platform for the Conservative Party under his leadership. Such aims and values were debated in a series of countrywide road shows before being endorsed overwhelmingly by members of the Conservative Party in a ballot in September 2006.[1] The front page of this *Built to Last* document declared:

> We are a modern, compassionate Conservative Party. Our enduring values mean we believe in trusting people, sharing responsibility, championing freedom and supporting the institutions and culture we share as one nation. Conservatives are not ideologues. That is why in each generation we change, applying our values to new challenges.[2]

This image of enduring values applied to new challenges, the derivative of which is generational change, but within the context of the institutions and culture of one nation is one of the most abiding myths[3] of the Conservative Party. What at first appears as an oxymoron is found to be paradoxically central to Conservative Party politics. What the Conservative opponent views as the political maneuvers of an opportunistic and unprincipled party are, for the Conservative, the necessary actions to be taken on behalf of the entire nation. The use of the term One Nation clearly matters for Conservative Party politics; for nigh on 200 years, an impression has been disseminated that only the Conservative Party puts "Nation" before any sectional interest and that, only the Conservative Party, as *the* national party, has the ability to assuage and balance the plurality of competing interests on behalf of the whole nation. Thus, the power and longevity of such a concept as One Nation is crucial to any understanding of the success of the Conservative Party, and as we shall see it is because of this long and successful utilization of the term One Nation that so many within the party are so keen to lay claim to it.

This book examines such competing claims to One Nation Conservatism while emphasizing the centrality of One Nation to any fundamental understanding of Conservative Party politics. In so doing, it analyzes both the conceptual use of the term and, with the formation of the One Nation group of Conservative MPs in 1950, its incarnation. This dual analytical approach delivers the theoretical insights and the empirical focus that facilitates an exposition of how and why a party that makes such emphatic claims to enduring values has such a proclivity to generational change.

## The Chapters and the Thesis

Students of Conservative Party politics are no doubt well aware of Lord Kilmuir's (David Maxwell-Fyfe) dictum of loyalty being the "secret weapon" of the Conservative Party.[4] Indeed, Andrew Gamble in the 1970s could state that "the Conservative party is renowned for its unity and cohesion, the absence of factions in its ranks and loyalty to its leaders."[5] Gamble made this assertion with regard to his explanatory thesis of Conservative Party politics, namely, how the politics of support is successfully converted to the politics of power. Although Gamble was well aware of the differing ideological positions within the party— "this babel of conflicting voices"—he emphasized the construction of a party organization, which could successfully compete in the political market; in reality, this meant maintaining the support of the party in Parliament and in the country while marketing itself to the mass electorate. Gamble correctly identifies Conservative success with the "need to develop a politics of the nation," the process by which the Conservative leadership's electoral policy not only reflects the politics of the *Conservative Nation* but ensures that this politics of the nation becomes coterminous with the politics of the state, that is, ensures success for the party in the mass electorate.[6] Of course, after three electoral defeats since 1997 and "factional" infighting over the issue of Europe, the above objects of renown are now rather questionable. However, it may well be that this absence of factions and loyalty to the leader per se were never the party's "secret weapon." It is the claim of this book that this is to be found elsewhere, and that it is through the examination of the politics of One Nation Conservatism that we identify where the real "secret weapon" of the party lies.

R. J. White in his book, *The Conservative Tradition*, examines the thoughts of Conservatives in relation to the centuries-old discussion "which has ranged over the whole field of political thought and experience . . . the relation of the State to the individual."[7] But crucially, with this age-old discussion in mind, students of Conservative Party politics should be aware of R. J. White's maxim that "parties are forever in need of refreshment at the springs of doctrine."[8] Focusing on the conceptual use of One Nation and the One Nation group of Conservative MPs as a microcosm of postwar Conservative Party politics allows us not only the opportunity to rule out the assertion that loyalty was ever the secret weapon of the party but to identify the real secret weapon in the manner in which the party refreshes itself at such springs of doctrine. We shall see in the following pages that the Conservative Party is more of a doctrinal party than is commonly thought and through examining the composition and actions of the One Nation group we see how a "creative tension" over doctrine leads the party to perpetually consider that very refreshment of which White spoke. This claim for doctrine challenges the self-proclaimed image of the party as non-ideological. Indeed, in the "Built to Last" document, we find the abiding shibboleth that "Conservatives are not ideologues." But, however much the ideological approach is to eschew the notion of ideology itself, in the chapters that follow, we appreciate just how widespread the debate and tension over doctrine is within the party and over that age-old question in particular—the optimal level of state intervention? Thus, the real secret weapon of the party is revealed in the way it utilizes One Nation as an ethos and the way in which competing debates over doctrinal trajectories are facilitated within such an ethos. And, it is groups like One Nation who help promote and enable these debates on change: cognizant, of course, of those enduring values as affirmed by David Cameron.

The remainder of this chapter sets out the historical use of the One Nation term and the enduring claim of the party to be truly the party of the Nation. It also introduces the reader to the, now almost as "mythical," backbench group of MPs, which formed under the label of One Nation in 1950. The history of the group and its composition is analyzed, stressing its diverse membership in terms of Gamble's "babel of conflicting voices," and an assessment is made of its "influence" within the party and, more importantly, of its contribution to policy debates and to the idea of "adaptation to new challenges." Chapter 2 examines One Nation in the context of ethos and doctrine in the Conservative Party. Building on the ideological tension and diversity found in this chapter, it places such "debate" in the historical and ideological context of Conservatism. The dual nature of Conservative Party politics is examined, and the resultant tension from such doctrinal positions is analyzed to show that this need not be detrimental to the electoral success of the party. Indeed, it is argued that this "tension" is the essence of that Conservative Party success, but it can (and usually spectacularly when it does) malfunction, with a commensurate adverse effect on electoral performance.

With the dual nature of Conservative Party politics in mind, Chapter 3 analyzes the work of the One Nation group in greater depth utilizing the methodological approach of the Manifesto Research Group (MRG), now based at the Wissenschaftzentrum, Berlin (WZB), on computerized analysis of political texts. The significance of this approach is that it allows us to establish if the publications from the One Nation group can be classified as "extended state or limited state" Conservatism and more importantly, when the manifestos are used as a "comparative base," whether we can ascertain the relative policy proximity of these One Nation publications to Conservative policy per se throughout the postwar years until the 1990s. This is important as Chapter 4 focuses on and challenges a certain portrayal of One Nation as a group exclusively on the left of the party, because in any effective exposure of the great myths of British politics, it is important to demonstrate just how distorted and pervasive such a view has become. Chapter 5 then looks at the role of the One Nation dining group relative to other party groups and offers a reinterpretation of the "factions and tendencies" approach to explaining Conservative Party politics.

Chapters 1 to 5 will leave us with the realization that there is indeed a paucity of consensus to be found within the ranks of the Conservative Party on doctrine. But, we find in Chapters 6 and 7 that there is a similar lack of consensus on the increasingly important issues of territorial politics, race, and Europe. Although the One Nation group never produced a formal policy document on devolution or race relations, we find in Chapter 6 that its members were deeply involved in those debates, leaving us with a conundrum to address: "One Nation, but which?" And then, in Chapter 7, we see that such debate and tension is not confined to the domestic realm. Thus, in "One Europe or no nation?" the One Nation members play a significant role in the prevailing debate about Britain's place in the world, especially concerning its relationship with Europe and the global market place; in addition, it allows for that other pervasive myth to be comprehensively exposed: One Nation is equivalent to "One Europe." With David Cameron "elected" to One Nation membership relatively recently, Chapter 8 explores the future trajectory of Conservative Party policy and the extent to which we can discern and accept such generational change in line with those enduring values: in light, of course, of what we have learned by that stage from this study of One Nation. In short, this book offers the first book length in depth study of One Nation Conservatism[9] and shows us how such an examination of the One Nation group is an invaluable exercise in any analysis of the politics of the British Conservative Party, but we now begin by a brief but necessary summary on the origins of the "One Nation myth" itself.

## Mythical Origins: Disraeli on England

Conservatives have a certain predilection for establishing for themselves a line of party ancestry, hardly surprising one might think in a party, which eulogizes a "partnership" between "those who are living, those who are dead, and those who are to be born."[10] One of the foremost of those ancestral lines is that of Disraeli, "it has been the habit of Conservatives to go to Disraeli as to a sacred flame."[11] And Disraeli is commonly held to be the source of the One Nation theme.[12] He incorporated the rhetorical flourishes of the Young England movement into his romantic novels in the first half of the nineteenth century and later in his famous Manchester and Crystal Palace speeches of April and June 1872, respectively. In these works, Disraeli outlined his trio of objectives, which would enable the party to transcend the divisive sectional interests in society by appealing to the electorate as *the* party of the nation.

Gentlemen, the Tory party, unless it is a national party, is nothing. It is not a confederacy of nobles, it is not a democratic multitude; it is party formed from all the numerous classes in the realm—classes alike and equal before the law, but whose different conditions and different aims give vigour and variety to our national life.[13]

In a conjunction between the defense of established institutions and a eulogy to the British Empire, Disraeli espoused as his third great object, the elevation of the condition of the people.

It must be obvious to all who consider the condition of the multitude with a desire to improve and elevate it, that no important step can be gained unless you can effect some reduction of their hours of labour and humanise their toil.[14]

But, crucially, Disraeli offers an immediate qualifying sentence, "[t]he great problem is to be able to achieve such results without violating those principles of economic truth upon which the prosperity of States depends."[15] In these two sentences, we find then an encapsulation and an anticipation of the postwar debates concerning affordable social services. These were, of course, predicated upon a much wider parallel debate within the party between the protagonists of the extended state and the limited state on the best way to actually achieve the goal of elevating the condition of the people. But, economic reality was never allowed to get in the way of the rhetorical benefits of myth and for Southgate Disraeli in his 1845 novel *Sybil*, subtitled *The Two Nations*, "coined a phrase that will live for ever and was immediately arresting" when describing the early-nineteenth-century relations between the rich and the poor: "Two nations; between whom there is no intercourse and no sympathy . . . ."[16] The solution, of course, lay with "the Young England conviction that there could be an alliance between the 'nobs and snobs.'"[17] This symbolic union takes place in *Sybil* in the marriage of the aristocratic young hero with the beautiful but penniless heroine.[18] In reality, Disraeli then never used the term One Nation (however much he echoed the romantic sentiments of Young England). Furthermore, Smith stresses that the "gulf between the 'two nations' was not bridged" when Disraeli was in power or later in the *Tory Democracy* of Lord Randolph Churchill, who pursued supposedly the Disraelian tradition but in reality merely presented "a collection of postures and slogans, rather than policy . . . ."[19] This interpretation is echoed by O'Sullivan believing Disraeli to have "invented" a new political myth, as early as 1835 and that this "one nation idea" revealed:

above all, great polemical ingenuity . . . [and that the] crucial distinction in the myth was obviously that between class and nation, with the Whigs being branded as a class, and the Tory party being elevated to the true representative of the nation as a whole.[20]

O'Sullivan had Disraeli looking back himself for similar inspiration to the eighteenth century Tory, Bolingbroke, "whom Disraeli regarded as the principal defender of the ideal of 'one nation' during the eighteenth century."[21] Such an opinion we see delineated also in the work of Geoffrey Butler on *The Tory Tradition*:

> Bolingbroke saw that while the game was Hanoverian against Jacobite, the latter could not hope to win. So long as the Tories were wedded to a fad, they could not make a fight against the Whigs. Only by becoming a national party, not the party of a clique, had they any chance of playing their due part in English political life.[22]

Thus, through the work of Disraeli, both in his novels of the early nineteenth century and in his famous speeches of the last quarter of that century, we have sketched out for us an outline of the One Nation myth. However, we should also note with interest here that Peel, the object of Disraeli's and Young England's merciless criticism,[23] echoed similar sentiments in the early nineteenth century to those found subsequently in Disraeli's Manchester and Crystal Palace speeches. Indeed, in Chapter 2, we look in greater detail at this long-standing contention about "Conservative principles" and, more importantly, how such disputes on future doctrinal policy can be resolved, as this is crucial to any understanding of the secret weapon in the Conservative armory. But, for now, we should note that Peel, at the Merchant Taylor's Hall in 1838, speaking on "Conservative principles," gave a similar outline to that found in Disraeli's trio of objectives above:

> . . . the duty prescribed by our principles—is the maintenance of the ancient institutions of the country . . . that society, and those habits and manners which have contributed to mould and form the character of Englishmen, and enabled this country, in her contests and the fearful rivalry of war, to extort the admiration of the world, and in the useful emulation of peaceful industry, commercial enterprise, and social improvement, have endeared the name of England and Englishmen in every country in the world . . . .[24]

This example of Peel and Disraeli highlights the extent to which there is a tendency to exaggerate the scale of difference rather than continuity in the core Conservative message, and such an emphasis upon "the great divide" is examined further in Chapter 4. Crucially, this is an early example of the outcome of intraparty tension when it malfunctions spectacularly, as mirrored in the Conservative Party's electoral fortunes after 1846. In Chapters 2 and 4, we shall examine the trigger for such a malfunction, namely, when one or both elements that make up the dual nature of the Conservative Party either endeavors to distance itself from or to exclude the other from the One Nation ethos of the party. However, the first Conservative to exploit the mythical term of One Nation in any explicit and systematic contemporary way was Stanley Baldwin when appealing for unity, as opposed to the sectional interests of Labour, in the intemperate political climate of the 1920s and 1930s. Baldwin in this period, as well as Chamberlain, advocated a course of action that utilized policies of the extended state to ameliorate the lot of the worker and to have as a goal:

> the sense that we stand for the union of those two nations of which Disraeli spoke two generations ago; union among our own people to make one nation of our own people at home which, if secured, nothing else matters in the world.[25]

For Williamson, Baldwin was a figure of the highest importance for the modern British Conservative Party as he was, in reality, "the first Conservative Prime Minister to preside over a full mass democracy," and he quotes Ramsay MacDonald's opinion that Baldwin had "turned 'Disraelianism' . . . from 'a sham . . . into an honest sentiment of pleasing odour.'"[26] Although, Williamson believed that Baldwin placed as much emphasis on the benefits of "independent sturdy individualism" as to policies of extended state intervention:

> At the *doctrinal* level it is indeed obvious that Baldwin deployed almost as much Gladstonianism as Disraelianism . . . Baldwin was in truth a skilful eclectic, who from the more promising and flexible elements in Victorian politics created in quite different conditions a highly effective Conservative position . . . .[27]

This then was the "ancestral mythology," which the One Nation group of MPs utilized in their first pamphlet in 1950 when they traced a lineage from Disraeli through to Winston Churchill of the Conservatives who displayed a concern with a One Nation approach to social problems.[28] However, just four years later in 1954, one member of the group was of the opinion that the "hereditary line" should reach back even further than Peel, let alone Disraeli, all the way to Lord Liverpool: the arch mediocrity himself, as found in *Coningsby*.[29] In a letter from Jack Simon to Angus Maude, Simon offers an extract from the House of Lords to advance the case for Liverpool being included in the group's 1954 booklet[30]:

> On 23rd November, 1819, in the House of Lords, Lord Liverpool said:
> "The legislature of no other country whatever has shown so vigilant and constant a solicitude for the welfare of the poorer classes; no other has so generally abstained from interference with the details and operations of trade; and it is almost equally demonstrable that the pre-eminent prosperity of our trading classes of every kind as been caused, or at least very quickly aided and promoted, by that judicious abstinence."[31]

To reiterate, this note to Maude neatly illustrates a crucial aspect of this book—
the underlying tension within the One Nation group, which reflects that found,
within the Conservative Party itself, on the amount of governmental intervention or judicious abstinence needed to address that solicitude for the welfare of
the poorer classes. In the next section, we see such "tension" embodied in the
actual membership of the One Nation group of MPs.

## The Myth Incarnate

The power of such a conceptual myth is matched by the mythical legacy of
the group of MPs who combined in 1950 and became known collectively as
One Nation. Indeed, as late as 1996, the group, while irritated at the quite puerile "definitions" of One Nation Conservatism from political enemies and ill-
intentioned friends alike, were cognizant of its "powerful brand-name attractions, which PR-conscious politicians want to grab."[32]But, such definitions
of One Nation Conservatism are, in reality, fuelled by the "ideological divergence" in the Conservative Party: mirrored within the membership of the
One Nation group itself. From its outset in 1950, the group's membership has
exhibited the full range of the Conservative ideological continuum. As we shall
see, the views of the free market, limited state Conservatives were espoused just
as much, or even more so, as the views of Conservatives adhering to *dirigiste*
policies of an extended state. Table 1.1 lists the membership of One Nation
from its inception in 1950 to 2006, and reveals this divergence in its ideological
makeup. A cursory glance finds limited state Conservatives like Angus Maude
and Enoch Powell in contrast to those who favor extended state solutions such
as Cuthbert Alport and Iain Macleod and later Keith Joseph in comparison
with Ian Gilmour, or David Heathcoat-Amory relative to Ken Clarke, respectively. Intuitively, one may think that such divergence could only constrain
debate, limit forthright views and lead to equivocation, but we shall also see that
although there may have been times when the "public face" of the "Nation" was so
curtailed, in the sense of publications, this was not the case in private where
group deliberations were to facilitate the candid debate so necessary for that
doctrinal refreshment in the Conservative Party.

The 1950 intake of Conservative MPs acquired and maintained a formidable reputation for ability and achievement. As early as 1954, the *Economist*, in
reference to this "class of 1950," added that: ". . . it is fair to say that the 1950
vintage (and notably its *premier cru* the 'One Nation' group) has made a unique
contribution to the revival of Conservatism after the 1945 disaster." And, as late
as 1976, this label was still in use to depict this exceptional cohort of MPs.[33] Just
one month after the 1950 General Election, we have evidence of an appeal from
this 1950 intake for some sort of recognition of their presence in Parliament,
as the Chief Whip Patrick Buchanan-Hepburn, in a reply to an internal memo

Table 1.1:  Members of the One Nation Group 1950–2006

| Year | | Year | | Year | |
|---|---|---|---|---|---|
| 1950* | Alport, Cuthbert (Cub) | 1976 | Brittan, Leon | 1992 | Ottaway, Richard |
| 1950* | Carr, Robert | 1976 | Butler, Adam | 1992 | Robinson, Mark |
| 1950* | Fort, Richard | 1976 | Clarke, Kenneth | 1992 | Shaw, Giles |
| 1950* | Heath, Edward | 1976 | Edwards, Nicholas | 1992 | Smith, Tim |
| 1950* | Longden, Gilbert | 1976 | Fowler, Norman | 1992 | Stewart, Ian |
| 1950* | Macleod, Iain | 1976 | Hurd, Douglas | 1992 | Taylor, Ian |
| 1950* | Maude, Angus | 1976 | Raison, Timothy | 1993 | Bowis, John |
| 1950* | Powell, Enoch | 1976 | Rees, Peter | 1993 | Coombs, Anthony |
| 1950* | Rodgers, John | 1976 | Walder, David | 1993 | Faber, David |
| 1951 | Vaughan-Morgan, John | 1984 | Benyon, William | 1993 | Hague, William |
| 1951 | Maudling, Reginald | 1984 | Blaker, Peter | 1993 | Jackson, Robert |
| 1952 | Ormsby-Gore, David | 1984 | Bulmer, Esmond | 1993 | Jopling, Michael |
| 1953 | Lambton, Viscount | 1984 | Carlisle, Kenneth | 1993 | Malone, Gerald |
| 1953 | Simon, Jocelyn (Jack) | 1984 | Cranbourne, Vicount | 1993 | Milligan, Stephen |
| 1956 | Balniel, Lord | 1984 | Forman, Nigel | 1993 | Paice, James |
| 1956 | Fletcher-Cooke, Charles | 1984 | Freeman, Roger | 1994 | Garnier, Edward |
| 1956 | Harrison, Brian | 1984 | Heathcoat-Amory, David | 1994 | Howarth, Alan |
| 1956 | Joseph, Keith | 1984 | Hirst, Michael | 1994 | Sainsbury, Timothy |
| 1957 | Ramsden, James | 1984 | Hordern, Peter | 1994 | Spring, Richard |
| 1957 | Rippon, Geoffrey | 1984 | Lyell, Nicholas | 1994 | Wells, Bowen |
| 1958 | Deedes, William (Bill) | 1984 | Needham, Richard | 1994 | Willetts, David |
| 1958 | Low, Toby | 1984 | Pollock, Alex | 1994 | Yeo, Tim |
| 1958 | Hill, John | 1984 | Pym, Francis | 1995 | Hendry, Charles |
| 1963 | Hobson, John | 1984 | Rathbone, Tim | 1995 | Hunt, David |
| 1964 | Channon, Paul | 1984 | Renton, Timothy | 1995 | Lait, Jacqui |
| 1964 | Chataway, Christopher | 1984 | Rhodes James, Robert | 1995 | Lloyd, Peter |
| 1964 | Gilmour, Ian | 1984 | Rhys-Williams, Brandon | 1995 | Trend, Michael |
| 1964 | Goodhart, Philip | 1984 | Rowe, Andrew | 1997 | Boswell, Timothy |
| 1964 | Longbottom, Charles | 1984 | Ryder, Richard | 1997 | Bottomley, Virginia |
| 1964 | Ridley, Nicholas | 1984 | Soames, Nicholas | 1997 | Dorrell, Stephen |
| 1964 | Royle, Anthony | 1984 | Spicer, Michael | 1997 | Goodlad, Alistair |
| 1964 | Worsley, Marcus | 1984 | Temple-Morris, Peter | 1997 | Hogg, Douglas |
| 1965 | Alison, Michael | 1984 | Walden, George | 1997 | Maples, John |
| 1965 | Howe, Geoffrey | 1984 | Watson, John | 1997 | Shephard, Gillian |
| 1966 | Howell, David | 1987 | Heseltine, Michael | 1997 | Green, Damian |

*(Continued)*

**Table 1.1:** *(Cont'd)*

| | | | | | |
|---|---|---|---|---|---|
| 1968 | Carlisle, Mark | 1992 | Ancram, Michael | 1998 | Letwin, Oliver |
| 1968 | Smith, John | 1992 | Arbuthnot, James | 1998 | Maude, Francis |
| 1969 | Biffen, John | 1992 | Bonsor, Nicholas | 1998 | Norman, Archie |
| 1970 | Macmillan, Maurice | 1992 | Burt, Alistair | 1998 | Spelman, Caroline |
| 1970 | Nott, John | 1992 | Critchley, Julian | 1998 | Tyrie, Andrew |
| 1970 | St. John Stevas, Norman | 1992 | Fishburn, Dudley | 1998 | Young, George |
| 1971 | Baker, Kenneth | 1992 | Hayhoe, Barney | 1998 | Simpson, Keith |
| 1971 | Kimball, Marcus | 1992 | Hughes, Robert | 1999 | Lidington, David |
| 1971 | Mills, Stratton | 1992 | Lee, John | 2002 | McLoughlin, Patrick |
| | | 1992 | Lester, Jim | 2002 | Baron, John |
| | | 1992 | King, Tom | 2003 | Cameron, David |
| | | 1992 | Mans, Keith | 2005 | Miller, Maria |
| | | 1992 | Mitchell, Andrew | 2005 | Robertson, Hugh |
| | | 1992 | Norris, Stephen | 2006 | Rifkind, Malcolm. |

*Original signatory to the 1950 One Nation pamphlet.

*Sources*: 1950–1971: Information gleaned from Gilbert Longden papers, London School of Economics and Political Science Library.

1971–1984: Information from the One Nation booklets: *One Nation At Work* (One Nation, 1976) and *Jobs Ahead* (Goodhart, 1984).

1992–2007: Information from the One Nation booklets: *One Nation 2000* (One Nation, 1992); *One Nation At the Heart of the Future* (One Nation, 1996) and *One Nation Again* (Tyrie, 2006) and the One Nation "attendance book for 1992–2004," with updates from Keith Simpson, MP. Of course, the booklets only identify members in that particular year of publication, which means in reality that such members could have joined in any year between 1971–1976, 1976–1984, and 1984–1992.

referred to just such a request:

> Thank you for your memorandum of the 6th of this month. I have had a talk with Craddock [GB Craddock, MP for Spelthorne] about a New Members Committee. I think it is a good idea and I am trying to find out how it was handled on the last occasion. I have told Craddock I will try and put something out with the whip to be issued next Thursday.[34]

However, the actual formation of the One Nation group in 1950 was partly fortuitous in that two of the three founding members, Cuthbert Alport and Angus Maude met by chance at a "brains trust" before entering Parliament in the new intake of Conservative MPs. Having met and dined together early in the Parliament of 1950–1951, they agreed on the idea of forming a group as both shared the opinion that the severe lack of detail in the front-bench speeches on social policy had to be addressed and such a group could help fill that particular lacuna. They, then, approached Gilbert Longden whom Alport knew from before the war from the candidate courses run at the "Ashridge Conservative College." Richard Fort, Robert Carr, and John Rodgers were recruited next. Rodgers then recruited Edward Heath, but later the other group members were to be disappointed to find that Heath's Balliol scholarship was an "organ scholarship" and (pun not intended) he played little, if any, part in the "intellectual discussion" of the group. These seven people then invited Iain Macleod to join them, and it was Macleod who proposed the inclusion of Enoch Powell in the group to form the original nine members of One Nation. At their first meeting at the Political and Economic Planning (PEP) offices at 16 Queen Anne's Gate, Macleod informed the group that he had been asked to write a pamphlet on the social services for the Conservative Political Centre (CPC), and it was agreed on Macleod's suggestion that this should become a joint production of the group and that, it would be published before the 1950 party conference as requested by the CPC.[35]

As Macleod was to be the original author of the CPC pamphlet, he was selected as an editor with Angus Maude, but it was Maude who, as the only journalist in the group, was responsible for "re-writing, editing and press preparation work" during the long summer recess of 1950.[36] Chapters were drafted by individual members, and the group would meet weekly to discuss their content before Maude eventually applied the polish to the final product. Indeed, it was from this process of meetings that the group agreed to continue dining weekly to become the most auspicious, well known, and abiding of the many Conservative dining groups since the war. Although chapters of the *One Nation* were drafted by certain individual members, there was collective responsibility for Maude's product, and this collective imprimatur of a pamphlet lasted for nearly 15 years before the policy regarding publication was changed to "a two-thirds majority in favor of publication, or if no-one objected to publication, then that pamphlet would bear the name of the One Nation Group."[37] For the 1950 pamphlet, Maude recounts that:

> The group failed for a long time to agree on a title for the pamphlet. In the end, not long before publication, Maude produced the title One Nation, agreed it on the telephone with Macleod and sent it to the printer. This name stuck to the group for good.[38]

An article in the *Daily Telegraph* of August 1950 reinforces this last minute sense of fate:

> Next month a group of Conservative MPs, all of them elected for the first time last February, will publish their views on social policy. Their pamphlet will take as its title—"the Strong and the Weak"—from a speech made last year by

Mr Eden. This book will not be official party policy, although Mr R. A. Butler has written a foreword. Nor will it be discussed at the annual party conference at Blackpool in October. But it may well colour some of the discussions on matters of domestic policy. There are nine MPs in the group, which met regularly last session under the chairmanship of Mr Iain Macleod (Enfield West). Mr Angus Maude (Ealing South), lately a senior member of the PEP, has done most of the editorial work. Members who have taken a prominent part in this production include Mr Macleod, Mr Cuthbert Alport (Colchester) and Mr Enoch Powell (Wolverhampton West).[39]

One can only muse on the longevity of such a group assuming the moniker of "the strong and the weak." It is also important to note that four years later when Hugh Massingham of the *Observer* similarly described Macleod as Chairman, he received a firm rebuttal from the group through Angus Maude, so that Massingham could "be in a position to correct [his] records for the future." After preliminary pleasantries, Maude stated:

But there are two points in your "Table Talk" note, which have caused a little distress, because they repeat a misconception, which the "Observer" has shown before. First, it really is a complete travesty of the facts to describe the One Nation group as a body of MPs who "gathered around Iain Macleod." In point of historical fact, Iain was either the fifth or the sixth recruit to the group, having been invited to join by those of us who were already meeting to discuss social policy . . . .This may seem unimportant, but I am sure you realise the extent to which the delicate sensibilities of politicians can be ruffled by misstatements of this kind; it would be extremely helpful if it were not repeated. Similarly, it is not now, and never has been, true to say that the majority of members of this group are either Anglo-Catholic or even "High Church."[40]

At a dinner on November 15, 1951 the group resolved that no member of the Government could remain as a member of the "Nation" as this would compromise the independence of the group. As Edward Heath had now become a Government Whip, it was decided that: "Mr Heath [be] informed accordingly."[41] It has been the convention ever since that a member will leave the "Nation" on accepting Governmental office and can re-attend only if that member returns to the backbenches or if the party itself loses office. While emphasizing the importance of conviviality and the assumption of friendship as important elements in the Nation's membership, Lord David Howell[42] also stressed that policy would raise its head in serious ways at dinner, in particular, when the party is out of office as Opposition is a much livelier affair when the ex-ministers are all back in attendance.[43] Of course, for a political party, Opposition is a period for deep reflection on its political future and on the possible policy options open to it, and with so much erstwhile but experienced Ministers returning to the One Nation ranks, a significant contribution to that political process is found in such a group as One Nation. And, moreover, bouts of "sever indigestion" there may well be in this political process, but such rumination is invaluable to any discussion on the party's ideological trajectory and thus, the provision of this "food for thought" is viewed as a crucial part of the mechanism for internal debate within the Conservative Party.

## Blue Moods and Blackballs

With such a notable list of distinguished Conservatives as that found in Table 1.1, it is hardly surprising to find that members did leave the group to begin their ascent on the greasy pole, some with more notable success than others. Thus, periodically, the One Nation group required a search for new blood and retrospectively, we can see from the table of members how successful such transfusions have been but indeed, intermittently, there were also times when members questioned not only the names of potential recruits but the position and viability of the group itself. In an invitation from Longden to Jack Simon, inviting him to join in March 1953, Longden adds that it:

is the rule that one blackball excludes, but I am to say that we were able to agree unanimously upon extending an invitation to join us to you and Tony Lambton. We dine together every Tuesday at 7.45. I am therefore writing to say that we should all be pleased and honoured to have you join us.[44]

Not all decisions were agreed with such unanimity, and blackball exclusions, although not numerous, cannot be classed as all that uncommon either.[45] Before leaving for a visit to the United States on January 23, 1956, Maude wrote to Longden with regards to a list of potential recruits with which they had prior discussion:

I would not be in too much of a hurry about new members, until we see how the 1955 boys make out. I would, I think, accept Balniel right away. Also, I am *most* anxious, if the Group can be persuaded, to get Gerald Nabarro in, and quickly. He would strengthen us and give us fresh ideas and great energy.[46]

Longden then wrote to the rest of the group:

We are writing as the two remaining founder-members of the One Nation Group . . . to ask your views on the future of the Group. You may recall that it was unanimously decided some meetings ago by all those present that, whatever the re-shuffle might bring, the One Nation Group would continue in being: but we want to be sure that this is the majority view . . . We feel that any impact we may have had on the fortunes of the party has been due to our two books; our election as officers of most of the Party Committees; our P.P.S.-Ships; and our corporate action on several critical occasions.[47]

The letter goes on to emphasize that the next few years will produce many more occasions for such influence and therefore the group should continue but only on the following conditions: they meet regularly once a week on Thursdays; agree on four new members from the 1955 intake; be intent on a new book by Autumn of 1957; and anyone not willing to give the necessary time and thought to their endeavors should resign from the group. It was also "proposed to hold a feast of the Passed Over on Thursday next, 26 January."[48] At this "feast," of those passed over for promotion to governmental office, there was "violent reaction to Maude's suggestions via Longden"[49] concerning the list of proposed new members, and we do know that the group could "not be persuaded" and that two of Maude's choices, Nabarro and Hinchingbrooke, were unsuccessful. Of course, by their very nature, minutes conceal more than they reveal but both men, along with Maude, had a committed involvement with the Suez group, which may have weighed against their candidature in the views of some attending the group's dinner that night.[50] But, with any backbench organization, the whips are to be found very much to the fore and one of the objectives of the group was to periodically use the whips to channel their collective views on issues to the party hierarchy. For example, in the mid 1960s, Willie Whitelaw dined with the group, the invitation emerging from a suggestion by Bill Deedes: "that the Nation might act during this Parliament as a cadre for an 'active backbenchers' committee, to tackle delegated legislation. This idea was well received and John Vaughan-Morgan will discuss the suggestion with the Chief Whip."[51] However, we should also take note of Lord Howell's view that the whips may well be informed of the One Nation discussions, but they "might or might not take the slightest notice of what we were saying."[52] And the whips will have their own "channels" in which "the dark arts" of parliamentary politics are practiced. With this in mind, we see that Edward Heath, as Chief Whip in 1956, was suspicious of the relationship between Maude and Nabarro. After John Morrison (chairman of the 1922 Committee) informed R. A. Butler (Leader of the House) that Maude was willing to serve on either the Nationalization or Agriculture policy committees, Edward Heath sent the rejoinder to Butler:

I return John Morrison's letter to you about Angus Maude. I do not suggest that he should be out on the Nationalised Industries Committee, where he would "gang up" with Nabarro and other undesirable elements. He might, however, be able to perform some useful services on the Committee on Agriculture when it is set up.[53]

It is instructive that the committee that Maude was not to "be out on" was "Nationalization"; we see in the following chapters that the debate within the party concerning the relationship of the individual to the state was just as keenly contested for the 1950s as for the 1960s, the 1970s, or even the 1980s. And, Maude and Nabarro were very much part of the "limited state wing" of the party who advocated less government intervention with greater emphasis placed upon individual endeavor. However, the end of 1956 gave rise to another event that was yet again viewed as "a critical date for the future of 'One Nation.'"[54] Maude had resigned because he believed that he could not do the indispensable job that Enoch Powell did for the group in keeping it politically active and influential, and he also had reservations over the group ever being able to take any useful action as their views differed so widely on a variety of subjects. This resulted in another bout of group introspection:

Angus's letter inevitably lead to a discussion on the future of the Group. A case was put for winding it up and contrariwise for continuing if at all possible because no other Group could so effectively think about many aspects of Tory policy provided we could agree to work harder. There was a wide range of subjects on the fundamentals of which we are all agreed apart from foreign affairs . . . John Vaughan Morgan pointed out the danger of our becoming dependent on one diligent member as we had been on Enoch, but we must have one or two members who can contribute as much as Enoch and Angus did collecting new ideas.[55]

Maude became so disillusioned with British Parliamentary politics that he applied for the Chiltern Hundreds in 1958 and, in effect, resigned his seat. In a rather trenchant article in the *Sunday Express* (January 12, 1958), he set out to justify this decision. While outlining his plans to move to Australia for a position as editor at the *Sydney Morning Herald*, he attacked the party machines for reducing the backbencher to the status of a contemptible lobby-walking robot and declared that we should face the fact that "the influence of a backbench MP is now almost nil." But this outburst was clearly a result of the "Suez crisis" and its aftermath as he offered his condolences to the five rebels he was leaving behind and did not see himself as a rat leaving a sinking ship, as the Country itself was being scuttled.[56] It was rather embarrassing for him then when just five years later, on behalf of the Conservative party, he began to contest Parliamentary elections again for a new seat. So, elevation to governmental office was not the sole reason for resignation from the group but in nearly all cases, those who left, for whatever reason, eventually returned to the "Nation" if they remained in the

House of Commons. Indeed, along with the usual pensive introspection, we find in 1970 that:

> Angus Maude restored by force to the Nation. Charles Fletcher-Cooke acting as strong-arm man. Decision to continue the Nation under existing rules, i.e. that Ministers and Peers are excluded from membership. Suggestion they be invited to dine more frequently than in the past . . . Long discussion on the purpose of the whole thing. Enoch "something to make one less lonely." John Rodgers still believing that it could actually do things.[57]

Such uncertainty over the continuance of the group again featured at the time of the party's "civil war" on the issue of Europe in the early 1990s,[58] but again the "Nation" showed its value in keeping the "conflicting voices" on board and the channels for debate and discussion open. David Willetts believes this to be one of its great functions, that a forum is provided where people with diverse and opposite views can come together and talk frankly and privately, so that "over the years it has definitely helped hold the party together . . . the best thing by far is free flowing civilised discussion over dinner with a dozen people who are at the heart of the Conservative party."[59] Thus, such introspection is no bad thing for a group examining the implications and consequences of future Conservative Party policy and the party's ideological trajectory because this is a perennial ideological question for the Conservative Party—*quo vademus?*

Another periodical issue that concerns the direction of the group, as well as the parliamentary party, is the conspicuous lack of women in its ranks. From Table 1.1 we see that it was 1995 before the first woman, Jacqui Lait, was elected to the group, and even now we find that currently there are only three women members, Lait, Caroline Spelman, and Maria Miller, as Virginia Bottomley and Gillian Shepherd have since departed for the Lords. The lack of women in the Parliamentary Conservative Party has long been of particular concern, but as early as 1968, the "Nation" was well aware of this paucity of women when offering a "supply side"[60] explanation as justification:

> A discussion took place on the poor quality of the women Members of the Tory Party in Parliament. It was unanimously agreed that the Party should be pressed to try and obtain the adoption in safe Tory seats, of more and better prospective female members of Parliament.[61]

Nearly 40 years later and the One Nation member David Cameron pressed the party to finally address this lack of Conservative women MPs. But his "A-list solution" was heavily criticized by other Tories in the media[62]; thus, it remains to be seen just how many women will enter Parliament through safe Tory seats at the next general election, which will add to that pool of "better prospective" female candidates for consideration by the "Nation." Whatever the future composition of the One Nation group, questions remain on how we measure and gauge its effectiveness and on the extent of its influence in the party: issues that are initially addressed in the next section.

## The Context of Influence

Most issues in British politics are contested, not the least of which is any analysis of the British Conservative Party; unsurprisingly, an examination of the extent of the influence of the One Nation group is of no exception. The list of distinguished Conservative names, as found in Table 1.1, do not by themselves demonstrate a causal connection between the One Nation group and a direct influence on party policy. Indeed, Seldon, speaking of the formative period of the group, accepts that the group "may have had some influence on opinion in the country in these early years, but it had virtually none on policy."[63] But, this opinion was based, to a considerable extent, on the interview with Robert Carr conducted in 1980, in which Carr added:

> . . . the One Nation Group proved themselves to be very valuable backbenchers . . . .So I think fairly quickly, whatever suspicions they [the whips] may have had about our, what might seem at times, over-radical ideas, was countered by the realisation that we were a very constructive, hardworking group on the floor of the House of Commons, who stuck by Party and Government when the going was tough. And of course most of us, in due course, did in fact become Ministers, and a number of us, ten or fifteen years later, very senior Ministers, in the Conservative Government.[64]

And Gamble stresses this particular role for the group: "as an educational forum for future leaders it was unique."[65] Julian Critchley, writing in 1961 as an MP but some time before becoming a member himself, commented:

> The Group has considerable influence both on the Government and on the Parliamentary Party. It contains many of the few really influential backbenchers of whom there are probably no more than twenty . . . [and] successive governments have leant heavily upon the Group for their new members.[66]

There is no doubt that this was an important aspect of the group's contribution to the party but the following chapters show that the influence of the "Nation" goes far beyond replenishment of ministerial payroll positions, crucial as this may be. We are aware that the question of influence was periodically part of the internal debate within the group itself, with Powell, in his more melancholic moments, believing it an answer to a feeling of forlorn seclusion. As we shall see, such sentiment was rather ironic, more tongue-in-cheek, from someone with such an impact on Conservative Party politics. Of course, the friendship and camaraderie, sustained by the conviviality of the weekly meetings and fortified with good food and wine, was an important part of maintaining the fellowship of the group. But, in the main, members like Rodgers believed that it "could actually do things"; evidenced by its longevity and its mythical place in the annals of Tory Party politics since the war. Indeed, Longden spoke of the group's corporate action employed on several critical occasions. One aspect of this was the persistent attempts to either fill the parliamentary committees with One Nation men, even having slates of candidates for the major positions, or by assisting those they had identified beforehand as being worthy of "Nation" support. Norton uses the One Nation group as an example of this relationship in the 1950s and states:

> The link between the attitude groups, at least those confined to a parliamentary membership, and the subject committees is an interesting one. Though they exist independently of one another, the attitude groups have variously sought to influence the subject committees.[67]

And this interesting relationship is seen at work in 1961.

The 1922 Committee:

> The Nation decided to support John Morrison again. We ought also to try and get some of our members on to the Executive, maybe Carr, Balniel, Longden or Chataway.

Finance:

> The Nation agreed that an approach should be made to Nigel Birch nearer the time, or if he was unwilling to stand, then we decided to support Maurice Macmillan who had intimated that he would accept nomination. It was considered possible that if neither of these two seemed likely to secure election we might throw our support to D'Avigdor-Goldsmid.[68]

Just two committees, "The 1922 and Finance" are listed, but the list itself covers the whole gamut of policy committees in the party, with a One Nation candidate put forward for most. And, although there is little chance here that any influence upon policy making will be demonstrated in such a way as to evoke a measurement resonant of the confidence levels in rigorous statistical analysis, nevertheless, we will see that there is an immanence of One Nation in the policy committees that were crucial for that "generational change" within the party; clearly, what we have is an immense and weighty contribution from the "Nation" to any rethinking of the party's policy trajectory. For example, in the late 1960s, Ted Heath had set up a research unit, headed by Ernest Marples, with significant involvement from David Howell. The thinking from the policy committees in this process would eventually lead to the neoliberal "Silent Revolution of 1970" but interestingly, in line with the "Marples exercise" we find in March 1967 that:

> Mr Edward Heath, leader of the Conservative Party, has asked Mr Angus Maude MP to take the chair of a group of academics and other experts to carry out an intensive study, examining economic and social trends into the 1980s, and identifying the changes needed to liberate the talents and energy of individuals in a technological age.[69]

We already noted that a decade earlier Heath had reservations about Maude's views and agency vis-à-vis the issue of nationalization and mindful of this previous circumspection, it is evident that someone's views had changed, and it will be obvious, from the evidence presented in this book, that it was not Maude who had a predilection for U-turns on policy.[70] We can also note at this juncture that the secretariat, which would service the above group and its "intensive study" —with "comparative technical analyses" —was to be chaired by the future One Nation member Michael Spicer. Thus, we will see throughout this work that One Nation names are prominent in this policy-making process, as the following quotes will clearly demonstrate; and thus, in the same month of March 1967, we find that the One Nation group reported:

> A discussion took place regarding another group, which has been formed to help Tony Barber to run his special operations against the [Labour] Government. This group is loosely organised and dines occasionally together. The Chairman is Angus Maude, the Secretary Sir Tatton Brinton, and the members as follows: Michael Allison, John Biffen, Mark Carlisle, Freddie Corfield, Bill Deedes, Sir John Eden, Miss Harvie Anderson, Peter Mills, Cranley Onslow, Nicholas Ridley, Norman St. John-Stevas.[71]

The Nation's most public "corporate action", states Gilbert Longden, was as political pamphleteers, and these pamphlets are analyzed in depth in Chapter 3, but we find that throughout 1967, the group was preparing a pamphlet on "denationalization" only to stall the process near completion.

> The Group has been writing a pamphlet on Denationalisation. This has not yet been completed. Three Members of the Group, Alison, Fletcher-Cooke, with Ridley as Chairman, are now on a Policy Committee set up by Edward Boyle to study the subject. The Nation are therefore going to hold up their pamphlet until some more background work has been done by the Policy Committee.[72]

A comparison of the names found in the above quotations, on the consideration of future policy, with the list of names from Table 1.1, leaves us in no doubt that the "Nation" played a significant role in this process of formulating policy, and we shall see that this was not an isolated year—far from it. It is hardly surprising really, to find such people who "collected ideas"—at times "over radical ideas" at that—involved in the necessary reconsideration of policy that is required for any future "adaptation to new challenges." In the following chapters, a case is made for the "influence" of One Nation, both as a "concept" that is fundamental to any understanding of the success of the British Conservative Party and as a group that not only influences policy initiatives but importantly, the "political climate," which, by extension, influences the party's doctrinal profile. In short, the "Nation" by individual and collective endeavors encouraged the party in its necessary refreshment at the "springs of doctrine." With this in mind, the next chapter examines *One Nation* in relation to "Conservative Party ideology" and illustrates how One Nation, as a conceptual construct, facilitated the ability of the party to successfully renew itself. But, the last words, in conclusion to this chapter, are those of Richard Ryder (Mrs Thatcher's private secretary before becoming an MP in 1983 and rising to Chief Whip in 1990). As a Cambridge undergraduate in 1971, he had heard Longden and Rodgers give a talk on One Nation, which he described as "most interesting and stimulating," and he went on to say: "The way in which the One Nation Groups' ideas have fashioned past and present Tory policy deserves greater attention. Seldom, if ever, can one section of the party have had so much influence on the Country's affairs."[73]

## Notes

1. However, although 92.7 percent voted in favor with only 7.3 percent against, there was only a 26.7 percent turnout, which meant in reality that only 24.6 percent of the total membership voted for Cameron's "aims and values."
2. Conservative Party, 2006a.
3. The use of the term "myth" in this book is not to be confused with any value judgment on what is true or false; whether such images are grounded in fact or fiction is quite secondary here to the impact of the "myth" on the political culture and behavior of the Conservative Party.
4. Kilmuir, 1964, p. 324.
5. Gamble, 1974, pp. 7–8.
6. Ibid.
7. White, 1950, p. v.
8. Ibid. p. 23.
9. Robert Walsha (2000, 2003) produced two excellent historical articles on the One Nation group and Robert Behrens delivered a conference paper on "One Nation Conservatives" to the Political Studies Association (PSA) in April 1988; see a copy in Alport papers: "Box 37," Albert Sloman Library, University of Essex, and there is a book chapter by me in 2005. The extant literature on the Conservative Party will generally feature, but mostly unsatisfactorily, some passing comment to the One Nation group of MPs.
10. Burke, 1986, pp. 194–195.
11. Southgate, 1977, p. 125.

12. For example, see Fielding, 2002, p. 15.
13. Kebbel, 1882, p. 524.
14. Ibid. p. 531.
15. Ibid.
16. Southgate, 1977, p. 123; Disraeli, 1980, p. 96.
17. Faber, 1987, p. 257.
18. However, the novel ends with what may be termed a "Cinderella turn" when Sybil is found to be of aristocratic blood, no doubt the source of her noble mien. Interestingly, in Disraeli's previous 1844 novel *Coningsby*, the symbolic union is one between the bourgeois mill owner and the aristocracy (see endnote 29).
19. Smith, 1967, p. 323.
20. O'Sullivan, 1976, p. 100.
21. Ibid. p. 101.
22. Butler, 1914, p. 26.
23. For example, see Blake, 1966.
24. O'Gorman, 1986, pp. 129–131.
25. Baldwin, 1926, p. 82.
26. Williamson, 1993, pp. 181, 203.
27. Ibid. p. 208.
28. Macleod and Maude, 1950, see note 14 in Chapter 3 for a full list of One Nation publications.
29. Disraeli, 1967, p. 59. We should note that Blake believed this soubriquet for Liverpool to be largely unjustified, for him it "colors" to this day the picture most people have of that able, hardworking, conscientious Prime Minister, 1966, p. 196. Indeed, Gash, 1977, assigned a notable role for Liverpool in the origins of the Conservative Party, in that Liverpool, as a disciple of Adam Smith and a great admirer of Edmund Burke, perpetuated the Pittite tradition in his long administration.
30. This pamphlet was *Change is Our Ally*; Powell and Maude, 1954.
31. Conservative Party Archive (CPA): CCO 150/4/2/1, Bodleian Library Oxford: "Letter from Jack Simon to Angus Maude 9 April 1954."
32. One Nation Group, 1996, p. 7.
33. "Class of 1950," *Economist*, December 25, 1954, p. 1059 and see also David Wood, "Last of the Conservative class of 1950," *The Times*, November 22, 1976.
34. CPA: CCO4/3/29 Bodleian Library Oxford.
35. See, for example, Alport papers: "The Red Notebook: 'Our Nation'" by Cuthbert Alport , undated in Box 44: Notes for a memoir, etc., Albert Sloman Library, University of Essex. See also Longden papers: Longden Box List: Temporary File Number 31, One Nation, 1950–1990, document entitled: "The Origin of the One Nation" by Angus Maude, March 1970, London School of Economics and Political Science Library.
36. Longden papers: Temporary File Number 31, "The Origin of the One Nation."
37. Rodgers Papers: U2332 OP27/6, Centre for Kentish Studies, Kent, "Memo from Charles Longbottom to group, 19 November 1964."
38. Longden papers: Temporary File Number 31, "The Origin of the One Nation."
39. Alport papers: Box 8, "Newspaper cutting from *Daily Telegraph*, 25 August 1950."

40. CPA: CCO150/4/2/1: "Letter from Angus Maude to Hugh Massingham, 31 May 1954, in reply to article in the *Observer*, 23 May 1954." However, by 1996, Alport believed that Macleod suggested the name and that he, Macleod, was one of the first members to join the group; see "Forming One Nation," *The Spectator*, March 30, 1996, pp. 15–16. But Alport in his "Red Notebook" file, op cit., for his future memoirs written in the 1980s (see p. 18 of the "Red Notebook" file) clearly accepts Gilbert Longden as the first recruit and states: "It was Angus Maude who suggested the title 'One Nation' for our book which had an immediate and remarkable success" (see p. 3 of file). The reason for such a revisionist account that places undue emphasis upon Macleod is addressed in Chapter 4.

41. Alport papers: Box 37, One Nation Minutes, November 15, 1951.

42. Lord David Howell was chairman of the group in the 1990s; the practice of having a formal position of chairman and secretary was only adopted in the 1960s; until then the form was to "rotate" the chairman at each dinner, a point Angus Maude stressed in his letter to the *Observer*, see note 41.

43. Interview with Lord David Howell at the House of Lords, June 23, 2004.

44. Longden papers: Temporary File Number 31, "Letter from Gilbert Longden to Jack Simon, 31 March 1953."

45. Indeed, Robert Walsha, lists blackballs for Sir Edward Boyle, Aubrey Jones, Gerald Nabarro, Lord Hinchingbrooke, Anthony Kershaw, Terence Higgins, Cecil Parkinson, Jock Bruce-Gardyne, and John Gummer. See Walsha, 2003, p.77.

46. In the full list of possible candidates, Maude would simply not countenance, Hugh Fraser, Alan Green, Hughes-Hallet, Denis Keegan, Ernest Marples, David Price, or Paul Williams. He had no strong views either way on Fletcher-Cooke, Brian Harrison, John Hay, Anthony Kershaw, or Rees-Davis. He put a tick next to the names of Balniel, Hinchingbrooke, and Gerald Nabarro, with Longden later ticking the names of Balniel, Fletcher-Cooke, and Brian Harrison as the successful candidates. See Longden papers: Temporary File Number 31, "Letter from Angus Maude to Gilbert Longden, 14 January 1956."

47. Longden papers: Temporary File Number 31, "Letter from Longden to the One Nation group, 17 January 1956."

48. Ibid.

49. Alport papers: Box 37, One Nation Minutes, January 26, 1956.

50. Fort, Lambton, Longden, Ormsby-Gore, Rodgers, and Simon attended the dinner.

51. Rodgers papers: OP27/8: One Nation Minutes, April 27, 1966, see also May 4 and 11, 1966.

52. Interview with Lord David Howell at the House of Lords, June 23, 2004.

53. "RAB" Butler Papers, Trinity College Cambridge: E5/2 Personal Letters 1954–1956, "Memo from Edward Heath to Lord Privy Seal, 3 August 1956."

54. Longden papers: Temporary File Number 3, "Letter from Richard Fort to Gilbert Longden, 12 December 1956."

55. Ibid. Unfortunately, the wider foreign affairs aspect of Tory policy is rather underplayed in this study; apart that is from how the issue of Europe impacts upon the party in Chapter 7. A decision was taken that in the main, and due to issues of space, domestic policy would be the route through which to undertake an analysis of how the party renews itself and refreshes itself at the springs of doctrine. However, as pointed out in Fort's letter, imperial, commonwealth, and foreign affairs created

acute differences for the group as well as for the party, and this remains an important aspect of Tory policy that requires further in-depth study.

56. Longden papers: Temporary File Number 3, "Newspaper cuttings."
57. Rodgers papers: OP27/8, One Nation Minutes, July 8, 1970.
58. Interview with Robert Jackson, at the House of Commons, June 23, 2004.
59. Interview with David Willetts, at the House of Commons, June 28, 2004.
60. See Norris and Lovenduski (1995) for a comprehensive study of such "demand and supply" issues in the selection of Prospective Parliamentary Candidates.
61. Rodgers papers: OP27/8, One Nation Minutes, January 24, 1968.
62. For example, see the *Daily Telegraph*, May 30, 2006, the A-list being described as London's chi-chi set of pseuds and posers.
63. Seldon, 1981, p. 58.
64. Lord Robert Carr interviewed by Anthony Seldon, July 15 and 18, 1980, as part of the British Oral Archive of Political and Administrative History (BOAPAH), British Library of Political and Economic Science.
65. Gamble, 1974, p. 258.
66. Critchley, 1961, p. 273.
67. Norton, 1994, p. 118.
68. Longden papers: Temporary file Number 31, "Memo from Paul Channon, M.P. 8th September 1961 to One Nation Group."
69. CPA: CCO20/1/15, Papers, Ernest Marples, "Memo of 16 March 1967."
70. Indeed, we should note also that Heath had sacked Maude from the Shadow Cabinet just two years earlier, for an excoriating article he had written in *The Spectator*, January 14, 1965, on the state of the Conservative Party. See Butler and King (1966), p. 20.
71. Rodgers papers: OP27/8, One Nation Minutes, March 22, 1967.
72. Rodgers papers: OP27/8, One Nation Minutes, May 10, 1967.
73. Longden papers: Temporary File Number 3, "Letter from Richard Ryder to Gilbert Longden, March 12th 1971."

# CHAPTER TWO

# Ethos and Doctrine in the Conservative Party

In an influential study of the Labour Party in 1979, Drucker utilized a "two-dimensional" approach of "doctrine and ethos" to examine its ideology.[1] By doctrine, he effectively meant the policy program of the Labour Party. His second dimension, ethos, was an incorporation of sets of values that had sprung from the experiences of the British working class, and which had an effect on all the internal and external relationships of the Labour Party. Of course, this ethos sprang partly from Labour's relationship with the trade unions and when Drucker was writing his thesis, he confidently predicted a problem for the Conservative Party with any future claim to be "the party of the whole nation," as in his opinion the Conservatives would simply not be able to adjust to the new corporate relationship that the trade unions had established with Labour after the 1974 general elections. And, for Drucker, such a problem would be exacerbated by the "middle class ethos of the Conservative party."[2] But, Drucker was not only to misjudge completely the trade union issue in British politics but also the Conservatives' ability to exploit it as a party challenging egregious sectional interests on behalf of the whole nation. And, as we shall see, *contra* Drucker, the successful strategy of the Conservatives to eschew any notion of a middle class ethos allowed for such an eventuality. Although the Labour Party— pre-New Labour—may have gloried in a working class epithet, the Conservatives would simply not countenance any official association with "middle class" groups or any representation with such a label to go unchallenged. Indeed, even in a period, which saw the rise of middle class pressure groups, formed to challenge and speedily reverse what these groups considered to be the harmful consequences of socialist policies, the Conservative Party itself was extremely careful not to be identified with any one section of the community. Thus, although the Conservative Party was fully cognizant of the aims of such groups, such as the Middle Class Union or the Middle Class Alliance, it was extremely circumspect in its day-to-day dealings with them, with such circumspection emanating from what was considered to be the true ethos of the Conservative party, namely—*One Nation*.

For example, periodically, in correspondence with such middle class groups, and even when sympathetic to their plight, the party's replies would invariably be couched in terms of One Nation. In receipt of the Middle Class Union leaflets in 1950, Central Office replied:

The Conservative Party embraces all classes of the community, and while it does not wish to give undue emphasis to any particular class or section of society since it is against any form of class legislation, we feel it is true to say that without the support of the Conservative Party the cause of the middle classes must go by default.[3]

In 1955, Michael Fraser, when replying to a letter on behalf of the Chancellor RAB Butler, stated:

I agree with you that this subject is important and feel that the Government, too, are entirely conscious of the need in the national interest to sustain the middle classes in their vital role. Six years of Socialism undoubtedly weakened them and left many reasons why they should be disgruntled. . . . The Conservatives, on the other hand, as your letter recognises, do not preach class war. We believe in one nation and our policies must be framed accordingly.[4]

And, as late as the 1980s, Mrs Thatcher evoked this ethos of One Nation in defending herself against those who were seemingly accusing her of being the principal agent in the creation of societal divisions. In an interview with Hugo Young for the *Sunday Times* in February 1983, she declared:

But I am much, much more nearer to creating one nation than the Labour Party will ever be. Socialism is two nations. The rule of the privileged rulers and everyone else. It always gets to that. But what I am desperately trying to do is to create one nation by having everyone being a man of property or the opportunity to be a man of property. Oh, no, I'm a one nationer.[5]

Thus, however, much the desire of Drucker to create a contrast with an unrepresentative middle class Conservative Party; the party itself eschewed any notion of "class" or sectional interest. In this chapter, we see that the Conservative Party did this with an express wish to utilize an ethos, which it claimed incorporated sets of values that sprang from the tradition and experiences of the British people. In the case of the Conservative Party then, this "two-dimensional ideological approach" embodies a "One Nation ethos" as a normative canopy, which ceremonially shelters the party's necessary doctrinal debates and under which changes in direction, regarding its policy program, are portrayed as being in the interests of the nation as a whole. And it is claimed that the party, as the self-proclaimed guardian of "enduring values," is ideally suited to such a role in policy provision. However, there are Conservatives who would not accept this two-dimensional approach to Conservative Party politics; for them, the one dimension of ethos would  suffice to explain that the party is working in the national interest. In fact, such Conservatives eschew the idea of ideology in its entirety, referring to the party's "philosophical thought"; claiming that ideology, which begets vehement "fluctuations in policy," is divisive and deeply damaging for the national interest. And, *a fortiori* the institutions of the country and national unity would be damaged by such fluctuations. Thus, for such Conservatives "nothing is more divisive than ideology."[6] But any academic study must go beyond this type of Conservative rhetoric, to examine the doctrinal reality in Conservative Party politics.

## Conservative Ideology

As a party claiming an ability to represent the entire British nation, regardless of class or status, "ideology," with its negative connotations, is not a term to be gainfully employed by Conservatives in their political discourse. With its conceptual etymological roots found in the era of Napoleonic dictatorial repression and with Marx utilizing its pejorative meaning in emphasizing social class consciousness,[7] not surprisingly, ideology was to be resolutely avoided in favor of concepts with greater electoral appeal. Ideally, such concepts would resonate with this putative empathy of a party in tune with the values of the British people. Thus, Conservatives much preferred comforting homely terms, such as "tradition,"[8] not only to help express this One Nation mindset but to aid a process of depoliticization. Indeed, politics itself was treated in a fashion similar to "ideology." It was not by choice that Conservatives were engaged in this shabby realm: "[t]he man who puts politics first is not fit to be called a civilised being, let alone a Christian."[9] We see David Cameron employing a similar strategy in his goal to "eliminate the negative" by speaking of "the planet first, politics second"[10]; the objective being of course to attenuate the electoral antipathy towards the party by once again utilizing this perception of being above the political fray on behalf of the whole nation. The party that symbolizes the customs, values, and beliefs of the British people developed, as part of its internal political culture, a contemptuous view of the necessity to engage in such base activities as politics or ideology. An illustration of this paradoxical position can be found in an amusing anecdote concerning Enoch Powell's initial attempt to obtain a Parliamentary seat at the end of the 1940s. Reginald Maudling and Iain Macleod, who were together with him in the Secretariat of the Conservative Research Department, had prepared a talk that Powell could use in constituency selection panels but warned him: "don't for God's sake re-write it into perfect English." The "talk" advised him to begin with: "We are all Conservatives, so no doubt we have different views, so I will not dwell on the subject of politics."[11] And, as we shall see, there is more than an element of truth to be found in this friendly but jocose advice.

Thus, the Conservatives appeared to utilize the concept of ideology in a pejorative way, and in such a way as to identify and reproach their political enemies, ironically in a similar but inverted fashion to how Marx and Engels remonstrated with those they believed to be laboring under a false consciousness;

as how else could we not accept their "scientific" socialist prescriptions. A cursory glance through the public statements of Margaret Thatcher will see this being routinely used in her discourse, where ideology is modified as being either "soviet," communist," or "socialist" ideology. For example, in a speech in New York in 2000, when receiving an honorary degree she said:

> Starting with the French Revolution, and then greatly encouraged by the Bolshevik Revolution, modern times have been plagued by "–isms," that is by ideologies, in effect secular religions. Most of them were unrelievedly bad. . . . About one thing though, I would like to be clear: I don't regard Thatcherism as an "-ism" in any of these senses. And if I ever invented an ideology, that certainly wasn't my intention. . . . The principles in which I believe, and the policies which we tried to put into effect in the 1980s, did not constitute a system of the sort described by T. S. Eliot as being "so perfect that no one will need to be good."[12]

Significantly, T. S. Eliot had a role in the perpetuation of this desire to look flexible and "traditional," rather than ideologically rigid and dogmatic. For Eliot, this was the result of the party arriving "at its actual formation through a succession of metamorphoses and adaptations."[13] But, before examining this role, it is salutary at this juncture to initially address the fact that there are some who try to exploit the extent of such differences in views—as aired all those years ago in the Conservative Research Department—in an attempt to exclude from the "Conservative tradition" those they deem unfit to grace its inviolable sanctum. And, for a minority of Conservatives an accusation of "ideology" is the irrefutable proof that someone cannot be part of this Conservative tradition. For example, Gilmour, while refusing to countenance the possibility of a Conservative ideology, echoes Hugo Young's assertion that Thatcher once proclaimed: "We must have an ideology"[14] and then accuses Thatcher of inserting into Conservative policy an ideological fervor and a dogmatic tone that had previously been lacking in the party. However, Jonathan Aitken, attributed as the source for this proclamation, states that Young placed far too much emphasis upon such a remark, made late at night in Flood Street and in such a context that it was not characteristic of Mrs. Thatcher; as she merely emphasized that to oppose Labour effectively, the party needed a pattern of new ideas that offered a coherent Conservative view, and from this discussion, added Aitken, was born the Conservative philosophy group.[15] And, for Michael Freeden, Gilmour's rather crude emphasis of this position only demonstrates that such an outlook, found in some Conservative texts, which is triumphantly anti-intellectual and which is blind to the phenomenon of ideology per se, only hampers quality research into "Conservative ideology."[16] But, here we find that however much the party's ideology includes a desire to appear nondoctrinaire or nonideological; there is no escaping the reality that what we have is an ideological position.

Unsurprisingly then, ideology, as a conceptual construct, is a highly contested term but the essential characteristics of an ideology are not as varied or as wide in scope as we might imagine and the basic expectation here is that there will be both a descriptive and a prescriptive element. In this context, ideologies constitute a mesh of interconnected concepts, sets of principles, and values that provide a belief system about human nature and society, and importantly, about the political action to be taken concerning those beliefs.[17] Huntington asked a pertinent question of what was to be gained from arguing over definitions and, as most are arbitrary, how was it possible to demonstrate the superiority of one to another?[18] Thankfully, this is not the place to examine or gauge the possibility of such superiority, suffice it to note that whatever main-stream academic definition is chosen, undoubtedly we find the Conservative Party to be utilizing an ideology—indeed, its own ideology. Huntington's definition was "a system of ideas concerned with the distribution of political and social values and acquiesced in by a significant social group."[19] The Conservative Party then has its own system of ideas. However, much of the systemic bounda-ries and dimensions are considered to be far wider and extensive in scope than those of its opponents, due in no small measure to its unique history; namely, Eliot's succession of metamorphoses and adaptations. Thus, this system of ideas is crucial because "ideologies are a vital and energizing ingredient in the fashioning of group identities and policies."[20] Freeden's work in this area leads to the conclusion that:

> To allege that conservatives do not have an ideology is a particularly offensive insinuation, since it implies that they are incapable of thinking about politics in a way that can be analysed or understood by even the rawest of observers or scholars.[21]

Such a sophisticated analysis of ideology, as found in the work of Freeden, helps underpin a vital claim of this book that the secret weapon of the Conservative Party lies in the way it successfully renews itself. And, a One Nation ethos, as a core concept in the ideology of the Conservative Party, facilitates such a vital process. Freeden, in his work, rightly criticizes the unwarranted assumption that there is such a thing as concrete ideologies consisting of mutually exclu-sive systems of ideas; as the concept of ideology itself is the recognizable form of organizing clusters of other political concepts. Utilizing a morphologi-cal approach, he emphasizes the interaction of the concepts that construct an ideology: as core, adjacent, and related concepts can be swallowed up whole or even cannibalized in the process of this interaction. Thus, the building blocks of ideologies are these clusters of concepts. And importantly, the diachronic, that is the cultural and historical tradition inherent in these concepts, will no doubt have an impact upon the synchronic interpretation of their meaning. Crucially, in this process of interaction, concepts that were once core can become marginal and vice versa. Freeden uses an analogy of a common pool of furniture in a room to illustrate the changing configurations of these concepts. Different furnishers will organize items differently, for example, if on entering the room we see that tradition, order, and authority are elaborately presented while equality is hidden under the bed then, for Freeden, we are looking at a version of a Conservative room. Throughout this work, we shall see that One Nation as a core concept of prodigious elegance and longevity has a striking impact on the other core, adjacent, and peripheral units that pattern the Conservative room. Indeed, extending the analogy further One Nation is the ornamental lamp, responsible for lighting this room and casting its glow, with relative intensity, onto the other core and adjacent items in the room but of course lamps, for a variety of reasons, can become defective and this we explore later. Ideologies, in this analysis, become the bridging mechanisms between political thought and political action, the aim being to obtain binding decisions in the decision-making processes: thus, the importance of decontesting a range of potential political alternatives in such a process.[22] And it is this very process of obtaining binding decisions within the Conservative Party while being proficient in the art of rearranging its clusters of political concepts that has contributed to its success.

This ethos of One Nation then is found to be a conceptual construct itself, constructed from core elements in Conservative thought and which has the crucial ability to aid the necessary process of reconfiguring those core Conservative concepts in order to address, what David Cameron termed, "the new challenges faced by successive generations." The electoral success of the Conservative Party is undoubtedly a product of such flexibility in this reconfiguration process, as sticking rigidly to ideational ends[23] may well lead to disaster at the polls. Such sentiments and the potential for such an outcome were expressed in a 1965 Conservative Party pamphlet, which stressed the advantages of not binding supporters to dogmatic rules fixed for all time, so that the party could easily jettison doctrine deemed to be obsolete:

> Because it is a party that has evolved over the years and continues to develop, not one created at a stroke from some blueprint, it is not rigid in its outlook. It accepts certain basic principles. There is a Conservative outlook; but there is no fixed written Code of Conservatism. . . . A party that makes shibboleths like the nationalisation of the means of production, distribution and exchange an untouchable item of its policy has the continual embarrassment of having to try and implement something that is irrelevant to the times.[24]

Written three decades before the Labour Party finally realized the disadvantages in written codes; the Conservatives fully reveled in—what Freeden referred to as the most important facet of ideological morphology—the absence of absolute boundaries that separate the features of ideological systems. And, if political concepts in this morphology bear accumulated burdens from their past[25]; the history of the Conservative Party, as revealed in Eliot's evolving metamorphoses and adaptations, highlighted a political knack of transforming these putative burdens into opportunities. The ideology of the Conservative Party contributed to such a political aptitude and one may even say that the party epitomized this absence in absolute boundaries, due to the inherent dual nature of its ideology.[26] This "dual nature" of the party reflected the fact that it contained: "within itself, perfectly preserved and visible like the contents of archaeological strata, specimens from all its historical stages and all its acquisitions from the Liberals."[27] Maude, in this emphasis upon the party's paleontology, emphasized the historical deposits of political thought in the party, layers that ranged from *laissez-faire* competition to state collectivism, with a few by no means useless eccentrics as well. In his magisterial work, Greenleaf referred to this as "the twin inheritance."[28] We are aware, from the previous chapter, that the party was perennially embroiled in that fundamental discussion concerning the relationship of the state to the individual and which ranged over the whole field of political thought and experience; the corollary of which was the question concerning the optimum level of state intervention. And, whatever birth date we choose for the party: be it in the "Tory" administration of the Younger Pitt, in the case advanced for Lord Liverpool by some in the One Nation group, in the sentiments of the Tamworth manifesto of Sir Robert Peel, in the organization created by Disraeli in 1870, or indeed, in the "legal entity" established by the 1998 *Fresh Future* Reforms of William Hague; there is no gainsaying the omnipresence of this "dual identity." Indeed, the "founding father" of British Conservatism, who classed himself as a Whig, did not differ in any substantive way from the "classical liberal" views held by Adam Smith on the functions of government: "*Laissez-faire* and decentralisation are sovereign in Burke."[29]

Eccleshall's perceptive analysis of the ideology of the Conservative Party places a similar emphasis on the complexity and importance of this dual character. He states:

> There have been two conservative versions of this heroic tale of the enduring virtues of the people of this land of hope and glory. . . . Each version has enabled conservatives to profess membership of a "national" party because of its peculiar capacity to preserve or restore features of this great inheritance.[30]

Eccleshall rightly challenges those whose "prognosis of conservatism rests on a shaky analysis of how [the party's] ideology operated in the past" and also the impression given that the Thatcher era and the rise of the "New Right" had "precipitated a post-lapsarian plunge into intellectual muddle because the doctrine became contaminated by some 'neo.'"[31] He mainly has the philosopher John Gray, a New Right convert but then subsequent apostate, in his sights when advancing a thesis of caution against any "apocalyptic pronouncements on the obsolescence of conservatism."[32] For Gray, the New Right had hollowed out the traditional institutions and values of British society with unrelenting free market policies of that period. "Moreover, it has become evident that conservative thought, lacking the intellectual resources needed to cope with the dilemmas thrown up by conservative policies of the past decade or so, has in effect created the conditions for its own demise."[33] But, David Willetts, echoing the concern with shaky historical and economic analysis, thinks it a fallacy to view the state as somehow being the embodiment or protector of British societal values: "The tragedy of twentieth-century Britain has been the way in which the state has taken over and then drained the lifeblood from a series of institutions which stood between the individual and the government."[34] Interestingly, in an article written over 50 years ago, we find the analysis similarly bedeviled by such complex semantic terminology. This time "neoliberal" is the term used to describe the "new conservatism" of the postwar years. And, although sometimes characterized as "liberal conservatism" the author has more in mind the ideas of Continental Christian Democracy but readily admitted: "to be sure, all the lines of division are rather fluid."[35] Furthermore, the "neoliberal creed" referred to was set out in Rüstow's "Free Economy–Strong State"[36] and it is instructive that such a title can be used to describe the politics of both the postwar Conservative government and that of the Thatcher administrations.[37]

Thus, the Conservative Party does indeed have an ideology with an inherent "dual nature" where all the concomitant lines of division are rather fluid. Eccleshall correctly stresses these diverse strands and criticizes the weak historical analysis that "underestimates the capacity of conservatives for self-renewal."[38] But in what is an otherwise excellent article his own historical perspective is weak in the way he portrays One Nation as exclusively belonging to some paternalist, patrician wing of the party and not to the full range of such "diverse strands"; as importantly, One Nation is a core element in the facilitation of any such process of self-renewal. Freeden states that "despite protestations from both conservatives and their critics, conservatism displays a recognizable morphology like any ideological family. It is endowed with a number of core elements that allow for its distinct classification."[39] In the following section, such an endowment is examined, identifying the core elements that Conservatives themselves classify as distinct Conservative principles.

## Conservative Principles

Conservative politicians were quite prepared to make a virtue of this dual nature. Indeed RAB Butler identified it as "the expression of our Conservative spirit, two strands of thought in logical interdependence,"[40] and which for Butler explained the increase in influence of the "Conservative mind" in the 1950s. A very similar message regarding the question of this Conservative success was outlined by Prime Minister Anthony Eden at Leeds University in 1955:

> At a glance our Party's programme will provide an answer. For there you will find, side by side, and without any incongruity, an emphasis upon constructive plans for developing the most modern industrial processes and the most advanced technical skills, and an emphasis upon individual freedom and social harmony which have been part of our faith for centuries. In this reconciliation of the impersonal forces of change with human values and principles which do not date, we discover the historic role of our Party and the secret of its perennial vitality.[41]

One way of identifying these "principles that do not date" and that are crucial for this perennial vitality is to examine those texts that the party itself suggested as containing the "core elements" of its political thought. Remarkably, the suggestions emanating from the Conservative Research Department and from Lord Hailsham in the 1950s, concerning such core texts, are very similar to those recommended 20 years later by Chris Patten when in the Research Department himself. For example, for correspondence with the Canadian Progressive Conservatives in 1954, Michael Fraser, "without recommending to them more weighty tomes," suggested: David Clarke's *Conservative Faith in a Modern Age*; Nigel Birch's *The Conservative Party*, and R. J. White's *The Conservative Tradition*.[42] And, in a series of letters between Mr. Neil McNeil of the U.S. Republican party and Lord Hailsham, on how the Republicans could learn from the Conservative Party's success post-1945, in relation to their own disastrous performance at the Congressional elections of 1958, Hailsham sends an assortment of party literature, which included his own work, *The Case for Conservatism* and *Toryism and Tomorrow*; but later he added a critique of a Republican account of this Conservative success that was published in the *New York Herald Tribune* of November 11, 1958:

> We have not created a "middle class party." On the contrary we have aimed at a national party, but we have studied the needs of the middle class, which we thought were not catered for by the Labour Party.
>
> We also studied the working class and reached the conclusion that, contrary to Socialist doctrine, it was not controlled prices and "fair shares for all" (i.e. rationing, planning and controls), but high wages and plenty of goods and freedom to buy them that they were primarily concerned with.
>
> I think it is putting slightly the wrong emphasis to say that we were able to "use" people like T. S. Eliot. What happened was that we created an intellectual ambience around the Conservative party which made it possible to invite people of the intellectual eminence of T. S. Eliot, G. M. Young, Bertrand de Jouvenel, etc. etc. to lecture or write under our auspices.

My first letter made no reference to our Political Education Movement. I am glad the *"Herald Tribune"* corrects this error (for which I apologise). I hope you will study this if any of you come here; we are very proud of this.[43]

The putative coyness of being identified with any notion of "intellectualism" is clearly absent in this private exchange with the American Republicans but of immediate note is that 20 years later Chris Patten, at the Research Department, advises Keith Joseph on recommended texts that could be supplied as a "short reading list" in reply to such an enquiry. And Patten recommends Quinton Hogg's *The Case for Conservatism*, Lord Hugh Cecil's *Conservatism*, along with David Clarke's work on the Conservative Party and that of Angus Maude, Ian Gilmour, and Sam Brittan's work on political economy; although unsurprisingly with regard to the Brittan texts, he states: "I do not agree with everything in them" and adds: "I suppose that what this all shows is that sooner the case for Conservatism is updated the better."[44] In the actual reply to the enquiry, written by Keith Joseph, the work of Gilmour is omitted from the list.[45] But, importantly from this recommended work we can get a clear idea of what Conservatives themselves regarded as "Conservative Principles" and the longevity of such recommendations supplement this image of enduring values that can be applied to new challenges.

A fundamental aim of such texts is to promote that very image of the Party as One Nation; in such a way that the Party's name becomes either synonymous or interchangeable with the term "national" or indeed "Britishness." For example, we find that: "On Conservatism there are many books. But the only text book of Conservatism is the history of the British people, their institutions, their traditions, their accumulated wisdom, and their character."[46] And that: "Toryism, in other words, is only a special kind of way of being British."[47] Or, from the eighth and last statement of the aims of David Cameron's Conservative party: "We will represent all our country in all its diversity."[48] This long-standing fundamental aim to promote One Nation is underpinned by core tenets of a Conservative ideology that help buttress such an image and are part of its conceptual construct. These overarching tenets comprise a "tradition" within which is found a spiritual dimension to an evolving organic society that places great weight on the freedom of the individual but is cognizant of the need for authority and order. It is argued that through our Christian tradition, humanism, and inherited culture we have a strong moral code. A code that guides us in the rights and wrongs of political behavior, in the relation of rights to duties, but importantly, due to the "imperfectability of man," also manifests itself in a healthy skepticism of the grand narratives making claims for the eradication of society's "evils" through social engineering.[49] This danger, of such claims for "utopia" that would replace the Conservative emphasis upon historical experience, as found in an organic, evolving living society, is a recurring theme for the party. Thus, in 1957, Hailsham's "intellectual ambience" allows for an "Israeli scholar of world eminence," Dr. J. L. Talmon, to lecture and write under the auspices of the Conservative Party on this theme. Talmon paraphrases Burke, on the "British Constitution," to describe the Tory party as "an inheritance solely and exclusively belonging to the people of this country,"[50] before adding that:

> In other words, Politics is concerned with the careful manipulation of concrete data of experience . . . whereas Utopianism postulates a definite goal or pre-ordained finale to history, for the attainment of which you need to recast and remould all aspects of life and society in accordance with some very explicit principle.[51]

And the Conservative is not prepared to embark on such ideational ends or to posit some vision of how society should be organized.[52] That, of course, does not rule out stability and order in society and the crucial role for the "rule of law," which utilizes one of the Conservative core concepts, "authority." Indeed, Hailsham had "constitutional authority" as "the first article of a Conservative creed."[53] Scruton believes that the family is a useful analogy for understanding this role of authority in politics, in that it "exists only in so far as we exercise, understand, and submit to it" and that the power of the state is always necessary for the Conservative although such power is "clothed" in the constitution and thus will never appear "barbarous or oppressive."[54] But, he also believes that "no serious Conservative" could therefore advocate, in a logical philosophical way, the benefits of a "minimal state."[55] However, in the world of historical experience this would place many a Conservative, indeed if not the majority, in the "non-serious category." And, as Andrew Gamble has pointed out, although Scruton criticizes such emphasis upon individualism as endangering the Conservative enterprise, in that it would destroy the web of obligations that bind citizens not only to each other but importantly, to the state: "Nevertheless, Scruton reaches similar policy conclusions to the libertarians, on many issues, such as progressive taxation and public ownership."[56] Thus, notwithstanding this protection of "constitutional clothes," Hailsham looked for further assurance in individual liberty, if power was not to be misused and abused absolutely "it must be spread as widely as possible throughout the community."[57] Much emphasis is thus placed upon an "attachment to the moral free agency of the individual" as "Conservatism is not, and never has been, a 'High State Theory.'"[58] Indeed, Cecil echoed such sentiments nearly 40 years earlier in 1912:

> Morality is an individual matter, and this gives a primacy to the individual over the State. To adapt a well-known phrase to a new purpose: the individual is the sun and the State is the moon which shines with borrowed light.[59]

And the fundamental idea of "property" underpinning freedom is based on this free agency of the individual. "Nothing has more effective significance in

Conservatism than its bearing on questions of property"[60]; this was the view of Lord Hugh Cecil in 1912, and in 1924 we find that:

> Private property, in the Conservative view, is the basis of civilisation, for on it rests the character and the economic freedom of the individual citizen. To Conservatism, therefore, the way lies open to expound the greatest of all social truths—that the success and the stability of a civilisation depend upon the widest possible extension amongst its citizens of the private ownership of property.[61]

As noted above, we know that 60 years later Mrs. Thatcher was advocating this concept of property ownership, or the opportunity for such ownership, as the essence of One Nation Conservatism. And as a Conservative, Hailsham equated this diffusion of economic property—"as widely as possible throughout the community"—with political freedom, espousing the Anthony Eden mantra of "a property owning democracy."[62] Little wonder then that Bertrand de Jouvenel was one of the eminent intellectuals invited by Hailsham to help the Party in the 1950s. De Jouvenel was involved with Hayek, in the *Mont Pèlerin Society*, to robustly promote a defense of capitalism and the "minimal state"; as this was seen as being far more effective in alleviating poverty in the long run than any *dirigiste* interference by the state, and that from capitalism there accrued far more benefits for society and for the working class than was ever acknowledged by the left intelligentsia in their distorted historical view.[63] In this period, De Jouvenel was part of the intellectual challenge to socialism:

> If "more goods" are the goal to which society's efforts are to be addressed, why should "more goods" be a disreputable objective for the individual? Socialism suffers from ambiguity in its judgement of values: if the good of society lies in greater riches, why not the good of the individual? If society should press towards that good, why not the individual? If this appetite for riches is wrong in the individual, why not in society?[64]

This emphasis upon the individual then—both in moral and economic terms—has been a long-standing core element of Conservatism and it was an important part of the party's political armory in the fight against socialism postwar. But, in echoing the thoughts of the One Nation group in 1996, it is clear that "political enemies and ill intentioned friends alike"[65] have sought a contemporary manipulation and distortion of its use in an attempt to demonstrate that society has been sacrificed on a New Right altar of individualism; to which Mrs. Thatcher gave slavish obeisance. Such distortion is evident in the now notorious remark, but quoted grossly out of context, that: "There is no such thing as society." However, in reality Mrs. Thatcher was only expressing a view of society, as an abstract concept, that had been emphasized so many times in the past by other "serious Conservatives" but had not previously, for whatever reason, been appreciated as such. The effectiveness of this distortion is found in the extent to which the party, in the early part of Cameron's leadership, took every opportunity to declare that "there is such a thing as society, it's just not the same thing as the state."[66] But, in the actual interview with Douglas Keay, that ostensibly covered the issues of aids and education but ranged more widely, Mrs. Thatcher was merely stressing the Conservative core elements of individual responsibility and that of duties vis-à-vis rights when she said:

> I think we have gone through a period when too many children and people have been given to understand "I have a problem, it is the Government's job to cope with it!" or "I have a problem, I will go and get a grant to cope with it!" "I am homeless, the Government must house me!" and so they are casting their problems on society and who is society? There is no such thing! There are individual men and women and there are families and no government can do anything except through people and people look to themselves first. It is our duty to look after ourselves and then also to help look after our neighbour and life is a reciprocal business and people have got the entitlements too much in mind without the obligations, because there is no such thing as an entitlement unless someone has first met an obligation . . . There is no such thing as society. There is living tapestry of men and women and people and the beauty of that tapestry and the quality of our lives will depend upon how much each of us is prepared to take responsibility for ourselves and each of us prepared to turn round and help by our own efforts those who are unfortunate.[67]

And, we find similar sentiments in the "Conservative faith" of the late 1940s, when that was "a modern age":

> The Conservative conception of a living organic national unity based upon the variety of qualities and activities of all individuals in it, both as individuals and through the myriad groups and organisations to which they belong, gives Society no existence separate from, or superior to, the sum of its members.[68]

Thus, in the Thatcher years we find that there is merely a greater intensity to the glow of Lord Hugh Cecil's "individualist sun" and not the eclipse to Conservatism, that some would have us believe.[69] Moreover, we shall see in this book that these core Conservative tenets are reflected in the principles, which constitute the doctrinal policy of the party. Indeed, at a One Nation dinner at the Carlton Club in November 1966: "a discussion took place on Conservative Principles. Particular reference was made to the electoral appeal of 'individual responsibility' and 'competition.'"[70] And, any cursory glance at the core texts that promote the Conservative case demonstrates such a prepotency of concepts that attach themselves to the limited state view of governance, as opposed to those associated with an extended state approach, within the dual inheritance. Individual responsibility, competitive markets, enterprise, opportunity, a low tax economy, and incentives have greater prominence in these texts than any central role for government and "planning."[71] But, tension over the best way to advance opportunities for all in society—by free competitive markets or by judicious governmental direction to wealth creation—is as enduring in the party as those "principles which do not date" and such tension is found to be a perpetual phenomenon in any analysis of the party's history.

## Political Recrudescence

There is little wonder that this "dual nature" or "twin inheritance" would beget tension, and as a result conflict and tension are perpetually present in party debates over the composition of the policy platforms that will be presented to the electorate, with a goal of addressing those new challenges that are needed for each generation. As Critchley has pointed out:

> The true picture is very different; the Tories are a coalition in perpetual conflict, the direction of its progress the subject of continual debate, the standing and regard for its leadership a matter of daily measurement. We have been known not only to raise our voices but also to throw plates. . . . But we have never believed it necessary to love one another, in order to dislike the other side.[72]

Of course, it is the creative aspect of this conflict and tension that is emphasized in Conservative texts, it is the catalyst that aids that "generational change" when such change is needed. Thus, Willetts believes:

> This is how Conservatives should argue with each other—about the interpretation of their own tradition. It is essential if the Tory party is to carry on being true to itself, that it should permanently engage in a debate about its own history. Otherwise, it will indeed be unable to answer what Disraeli in Coningsby called "the awkward question" of "what will you conserve?"[73]

Such "strains and stresses," in the party, have been a part of its political culture since its inception. Indeed, Geoffrey Butler emphasized the "double nature" of the doctrine of Bolingbroke that "it was at once a destructive and constructive creed."[74] Destructive in that it taught the Tories that they must give up on hopeless ideals and lost causes and to construct an alternative ideal of unity in "one national or Country Party" that contained "precious ideas" in what may be termed "The Constitution." Thus, this ability for self-renewal is part of the party's "DNA"; it is a "reconstruction" that is "a life giving" and "revivifying marrow to Tory doctrine."[75] This *political recrudescence* is as old as the party itself.

Such a concept neatly encapsulates the incorporation of both the destructive and constructive aspects of Conservative doctrine. Recrudescence is the quality or state of things "breaking out afresh (usually regarded in terms of disease or indeed of calumny or malignity)" but in its contemporary "transferred sense" we find that it is "a revival or rediscovery of something regarded as good or valuable."[76] And, both these aspects of political recrudescence are present in Conservative Party politics but it is only when the party offers a settled policy platform, emanating from its doctrinal debates, that we find electoral success based on this ability to renew itself within an ethos of One Nation. Political recrudescence is therefore perpetually present in the groups and committees that make up the Conservative Parliamentary Party and their debate is a prerequisite of this ability for self-renewal or of "breaking out afresh." But, returning to the analogy of the ornamental lamp that is One Nation, in Freeden's furnished room, casting its glow, with relative intensity, upon the other core concepts or tenets that is the Conservative Party ideology, we do indeed find that at times such a lamp may well become defective.

It is because this internal party debate is couched in terms of One Nation that periodically the party's "organic living body" may suffer from the "diseased element" inherent within political recrudescence. When issues arise that are viewed as so pivotal that the very essence of Britain's place in the world is questioned, vis-à-vis the political economic path it must take, then debate can become feverish and unhealthy leading to a collective breakdown in our necessary renewal process. Quite simply, the dual nature has to work, at the very least in terms of a *modus vivendi* but when both components have a desire to either distance themselves, or to eject the other, from the One Nation canopy then the outcome is usually malign. When the mass electorate cannot discern just what the politics of the Conservative Nation are, then it is impossible to ensure that this politics of the nation will be coterminous with the politics of the state. And, this breakdown is clear in the Corn Laws debate, that of Tariff Reform, and over the issue of Europe; where protagonists on each side would appeal to a One Nation ethos in a strident unyielding defense of their own doctrinal position, with a consequent debilitating effect on the necessary renewal mechanism for electoral success. A very good example of such a debilitating period is found recently over the issue of Europe and whose "malign influence" would eventually give rise to a perception of "factionalism" within the party,[77] which encroached on the necessary party mechanisms that could have led to self-renewal. One has only to read the book, *Tory Wars*,[78] to understand the extent to which this "malign calumny" can have such a debilitating effect; even within the more ideologically cohesive "No Turning Back" group of Conservative MPs. Thus, what is necessary for the party's success is at the same time so potentially dangerous, particularly if the party forgets to dislike the other side more than its own. The One Nation group of MPs were well aware of this historical tradition of political recrudescence within the party. In the draft pamphlet on denationalization that we encountered in Chapter 1, that was not published due to the amount of One Nation members involved in the relevant policy committees, we find:

> We have fallen victims to a sort of fatalistic "progressivism." This mood is difficult to define. It springs partly from a weariness of the spirit in face of the great age and complexity of the problem and partly from false analogies drawn from the history of the Conservative Party. Peel, for example, opposed the Great Reform as hard as he could, but in 1834 accepted defeat and with it "the principle" of Parliamentary Reform. Disraeli fought bitterly against the repeal of the Corn Laws but in 1851 "accepted" the principle of Free Trade. In the 1940s, Churchill declared that he would "not preside over the liquidation of the British Empire," but his Government of 1951 and its immediate successors actually performed that task. If these great men could "come to terms with history," who are we to try "to put the clock back" in the apparently predestined movement towards state dirigisme in industry?
>
> It is the purpose of this pamphlet to shatter the mood, to show that there is nothing predestined about such a movement, that it can be reversed, and that if it is not reversed it will certainly continue. The days of the holding operation, of "thus far and no further," are over.[79]

Thus, tension and even conflict in the party can be creative and can also be conducive to that necessary need for refreshment at the springs of doctrine but, of course, only if that dislike for the other side leads to a "breaking out afresh" of "valuable and good" policy proposals and not if it manifests itself in some malign condition of introspective calumny.

Clearly the electoral history of the party for over 200 years is a history of the presence of political recrudescence in the Conservative party creed. And, in a 1976 Shadow Cabinet paper, from Keith Joseph and Angus Maude, on the "the next stage of Policy Work," we see that these One Nation members were well aware of the potential value of such tension and the benefits of exploiting it by seeking publicity; in this instance through that "Political Education Movement" (the Conservative Political Centre (CPC)) mentioned above by Hailsham:

> We obviously have no desire to dissuade other individuals or groups of members of the parliamentary party with particular interests from developing their own ideas for policy. In suitable cases these could be published by the CPC [Conservative Political Centre] with the usual disclaimer. So long as such ideas were not flagrantly at variance with party policy and of the requisite intellectual standard for the CPC, these activities do not probably need to be very closely co-ordinated. An element of controversy may not be a bad thing. Indeed the Liberal Party, the Labour Party and its associates like

the Fabian Society have probably derived something of their spurious reputation for intellectual vigour by publications of this sort.[80]

The dual nature of the party's ideology then can facilitate that essential aspect of being "permanently engaged in a debate about its own history" and in "the interpretation of their own tradition," which in turn can be conducive to a successful outcome of political recrudescence. Such contingency is rooted in the ideology of the Conservative Party, with this stress on experience over ideational ends epitomized in the Macmillan maxim of "events dear boy, events." Indeed, for Freeden, the morphology of Conservatism relegated the individualist—collectivist divide to contingent status and it is because of this that the party is erroneously labeled "opportunistic" but consistency lies in the morphology as a whole, as this allows for a constant process of doctrinal trial and error.[81] The *modus vivendi* of the party therefore, particularly in parliament, is resonant of Oakeshott's use of the Schopenhauer porcupine metaphor, which the Conservative philosopher used to explain civil association, but, which neatly describes the associative relationship that is the Conservative Parliamentary Party:

> There was once, so Schopenhauer tells us, a colony of porcupines. They were wont to huddle together on a cold winter's day and, thus wrapped in communal warmth, escape being frozen. But, plagued with the pricks of each other's quills, they drew apart. And every time the desire for warmth brought them together again, the same calamity overtook them. Thus, they remained, distracted between two misfortunes, able neither to tolerate nor to do without one another, until they discovered that when they stood at a certain distance from one another they could both delight in one another's individuality and enjoy one another's company. They did not attribute any metaphysical significance to this distance, nor did they imagine it to be an independent source of happiness, like finding a friend. They recognized it to be a relationship in terms not of substantive enjoyments but of contingent considerabilities that they must determine for themselves.[82]

This is why tradition, and the ability to interpret these "contingent considerabilities" within their own tradition, is such an important facet of the ideological approach of the Conservative Party. Oakeshott, stresses this aspect of tradition, in that its nature is "to tolerate and unite an internal variety, not insisting upon conformity to a single character, and because, further, it has the ability to change without losing its identity."[83] He spoke of this identity of tradition in Burkean terms, diffused between the past, present, and the future that nothing was ever completely lost to a tradition and that although we could recover something topical from its remotest moments nothing for long would remain unmodified. There is an inherent potential for change but all its parts will not change at the same time. Thus, what is to be learned is the "whole," the concrete, coherent manner of living in all its intricacies. "It is steady because, though it moves, it is never wholly in motion; and though it is tranquil, it is never wholly at rest."[84] T. S. Eliot similarly emphasized the "common principles" that could be elicited from the work of such diverse minds in Conservative thought and the importance of the "pre-political," "the stratum down to which any sound political thinking must push its roots, and from which it must derive its nourishment."[85] And, while stressing this complex relationship between the past and the present, the kernel of Eliot's argument was that this was a shared tradition, that Conservatives shared ideas, themes, and images that make up that tradition. Quite simply you could not have a tradition, without those who belonged to it, working within that tradition,[86] and this was represented as an individual artifact, "to belong to a tradition is also to make that tradition."[87] In the following chapters, we will encounter the One Nation members working within this tradition while aware of its political recrudescence and their part in making that tradition by their preparedness to refresh themselves at the springs of doctrine. Thus, we have a Conservative Party ideology, which utilizes the term ideology pejoratively but which "turns Marx the right way up" by emphasizing the error in accepting utopian grand narratives. "Unlike their opponents, the last thing Conservatives believe is that they have the monopoly of truth. They do not even claim the monopoly of Conservatism."[88]

## Notes

1. Drucker, 1979.
2. Ibid., see pp. 8–11 and 116–120.
3. Conservative Political Archive (CPA): CCO3/2/115, Middle Class Union, "Letter of 5 July 1950, from Miss Spencer of Conservative Central Office," Bodleian Library Oxford.
4. CPA: RAB Butler Papers, "RAB 19: oddments 1952–6, Letter of 26 January 1955, Conservative Research Director Michael Fraser to Sir John Prestige."
5. Margaret Thatcher: complete public statements 1945–1990. Database and Compilation, Oxford University Press, 1999, UDN: 83_057: Interview with Hugo Young February 22, 1983 and see also the interview, UDN: 87_158, with John Cole of the BBC on the May 11, 1987, where she again expresses very similar sentiments.
6. Gilmour, 1978, pp. 132–133.
7. See Nisbet, 1986.
8. Reflected in such famous texts as Butler, 1914; White, 1950.
9. Hogg, 1947, p. 11.
10. David Cameron, "The planet first, politics second," in *The Independent on Sunday*, September 3, 2006.
11. Powell Papers: Poll/3/1/6, "Other Political Subjects: Miscellaneous Files, 1946–1949," Churchill College Cambridge.
12. Margaret Thatcher: complete public statements 1945–1990: UDN: 00_001, "Speech in New York, 27 March 2000," Oxford University Press, op. cit.

13. Eliot, 1955, p. 14.

14. See Gilmour, 1992, p. 8. Indeed, Young, 1990, p. 406, references Jonathan Aitken for this remark, ostensibly recounted from a Conservative philosophy group but we should note that no such sentiment is to be found in all of her "complete public statements."

15. Interview with Jonathan Aitken, December 20, 2007 and see Aitken, 2006, pp. 130–131.

16. Freeden, 1990, p. 15.

17. For example, see Vincent, 1995.

18. Huntington, 1957, p. 455.

19. Ibid., p. 454.

20. Freeden, 2001, p. 1.

21. Freeden, 1998, pp. 317–318.

22. Ibid., pp. 4–88 *passim* and p. 551.

23. Ibid., p. 79.

24. Block, 1965, p. 5.

25. Freeden, 1998, pp. 87 and 98.

26. See Gash, 1977, pp. 76 and 83: "Conservatism had therefore from the start a dual nature . . . the two sides of a single coin. . . . The division was between two schools of thought, both claiming to be Conservative, over the nature of Conservative principles, the definition of Conservative interests, and the most intelligent way to apply those principles and safeguard those interests."

27. Maude, 1963, p. 319.

28. Greenleaf, 1983a; 1983b.

29. Nisbet, 1986, p. 37.

30. Eccleshall, 2001, p. 73.

31. Ibid., pp. 67 and 69.

32. Ibid., p. 67.

33. Grey, 1997, p. 64.

34. Willetts, 1997a, p. 91.

35. Friedrich, 1955, p. 509.

36. Ibid., p. 512.

37. See Gamble, 1989.

38. Eccleshall, 2001, p. 67.

39. Freeden, 1998, p. 318.

40. CPA: RAB Butler Papers, 'RAB 19: oddments 1952–1956, Draft Christmas message to Young Conservatives, December 13, 1955.'

41. CPA: RAB Butler Papers, "RAB 19: oddments 1952–56, Prime Minister's message to Leeds University Conservative Association, 28 November, 1955".

42. CPA: CCO4/6/88, "Memo from Michael Fraser to Lady Maxwell Fyfe regarding letter from Progressive Conservative Association, 23 June 1954."

43. CPA: CCO4/8/102, "series of letters between Lord Hailsham and Neil McNeil of the US Republican party, 1958–1959." Quote from "Hailsham's letter to McNeil 11 February 1959" ibid.

44. Chris Patten attempted such an update in 1983, in his book *The Tory Case*, and interestingly the work of Samuel Brittan is not utilized in this book at all, nor that of his old boss Keith Joseph, as no doubt, for Patten as for Gilmour, these views emanated

from "those who are more representative of the Liberal than the Tory strain in modern Conservatism, like Sir Keith Joseph" (p. 5). But the One Nation conceptual myth is present in the assertion that the Conservative Party was not simply against things. "Its history demonstrates this clearly, just as it shows that whereas the Labour Party (in Ernest Bevin's words) grew out of the bowels of the trade union movement, the Conservative Party grew out of the character and traditions of the country which it has governed for longer than any of its political opponents" (p. 2).

45. CPA: Keith Joseph Papers, KJ/8/1, "General Correspondence: Letter from Chris Patten to Keith Joseph, 4 November 1975 and Letter from Joseph to the original enquirer, a young lady from the YWCA, 6 November  1975," Bodleian Library Oxford.
46. Clarke, 1947, p. 7.
47. Hailsham, 1957, p. 9.
48. Conservative Party, 2006b, p. 11.
49. See, for example, Birch, 1949, pp. 31–32.
50. Talmon, 1957, p. 7.
51. Ibid., p. 8.
52. Huntington, 1957, p. 457.
53. Hogg, 1947, p. 47.
54. Scruton, 2001, pp. 22–24.
55. Ibid., p. 23.
56. Gamble, 1996, p. 122.
57. Hogg, 1947, p. 62.
58. White, 1950, pp. 4–5.
59. Cecil, 1912, p. 164.
60. Ibid, p. 118.
61. Skelton, 1924, p. 9. I am indebted to my colleague and friend, Professor Geoffrey Fry, for bringing this work to my attention. As early as 1924 Skelton realized that the Conservative Party could simply not be a "caretaker" but had to be "an architect"; it had to be proactive in challenging the socialist "omnipotent State and the kept citizen" where we would have "responsibility checked, initiative crippled, character in cold storage, and wealth squandered," see ibid., p. 7.
62. Hogg, 1947, p. 63.
63. For example, see De Jouvenel, 1954; Hayek, 1954.
64. De Jouvenel, 1951, p. 12.
65. One Nation Group, 1996, p. 7.
66. Conservative Party, 2006a, p. 5: Although, this was dropped from the updated edition of August, 2006b.
67. Margaret Thatcher: complete public statements 1945–1990. Database and Compilation, Oxford University Press, 1999, UDN: 87_384: Mrs. Thatcher's interview with Douglas Keay, *Woman's Own*, October 31, 1987, and see the statement requested by *The Sunday Times*, July 10, 1988.
68. Clarke, 1947, p. 20. And see, Brittan's, 1992 book *There Is No Such Thing as Society*, where he defends this as one of the best things that Thatcher ever said because of the error in elevating such concepts into collective beings. Thus, the need to emphasize that nation and state consist of individuals. Indeed, RAB Butler similarly made the point in April 1961 that: "the State must always remember that it is dealing with

individuals and not with a collective abstraction," in an article, 'The Role of the State in a Conservative Society', for the Cambridge University Conservative Association magazine. See CPA: RAB Butler Papers, "RAB 20: oddments, 1957–61."

69. For example, see Gilmour, 1992.
70. Rodgers papers: OP27/8, One Nation Minutes, November 2, 1966, Centre for Kentish Studies, Kent.
71. See, for example: Hogg, 1947, 1959; Raison, 1964 and Willetts, 1997b.
72. Critchley, 1973, pp. 401–402.
73. Willetts, 1992, p. 4.
74. Butler, 1914, pp. 23–29.
75. Ibid., p. 27.
76. See Oxford English Dictionary on line, http://dictionary.oed.com.
77. This idea is explored in greater depth in Chapter 5 and see, for example, Norton, 1998.
78. Walters, 2001.
79. Rodgers papers: OP27/9. This draft was sent to all One Nation members for comment, by Charles Fletcher-Cooke on March 30, 1967, "and also to Tony Barber who saw a copy of the original draft and who is, of course, taking great interest in such activities."
80. CPA: Keith Joseph Papers, KJ/26/4: Policy Groups, "The Next Stage of Policy Work," point 11, in paper dated October 21, 1976.
81. Freeden, 1996, pp. 349, 382–383.
82. Oakeshott, 1991, pp. 460–461.
83. Ibid., p. 227.
84. Ibid., pp. 61–62.
85. Eliot, 1955, p. 22.
86. See Eliot, 1964, pp. 47–59.
87. Scruton, 2001, p. 33.
88. Hogg, 1947, p. 13.

# CHAPTER THREE

# The Thracian Boxer and Ideological Movement

In this chapter, we find that the complex and problematic debate concerning the dual nature of Conservative Party ideology, as outlined in Chapters 1 and 2, is mirrored in the controversy of when the party followed either a limited state or extended state approach to policy formulation. E. H. H. Green has the history of the party in the twentieth century "steeped in ideological dispute," and he correctly challenges the illusion of a "postwar settlement"; as one has to grasp that "the Conservative party never fully accepted that anything had been settled."[1] From the evidence of the previous two chapters, we are aware that the history of the party was steeped in such ideological disputes for far longer than one century, and we shall see in this chapter, through an examination of the published work of the One Nation group, that there was, in fact, no acceptance of anything being fully settled regarding party policy in the postwar period. Indeed, in the final part of this chapter, we can estimate the extent of this ideological dispute by utilizing a spatial analytical approach to examine the "content" of these One Nation publications while, at the same time, comparing them to the manifestos published by the party between 1950 and 1997. This "content analysis," as a methodological approach, allows us to plot the differences in "distance" over time, on our extended state-limited state dimension, which, in effect, allows for an estimation of the degree and direction of such ideological movement in both the One Nation and official party policy documents. After all, this "spatial context is assumed by almost everyone when they talk about politics."[2] But, as we shall see, there is no similar assumed agreement to be found concerning the positioning of the Conservative Party on this spatial dimension, or concerning the timeframe for such a positioning.

Nigel Harris's account has the party following a competitive, limited state approach at the end of the nineteenth century but changing sometime in the interwar period to become more corporatist and interventionist by the 1930s, with this approach continuing up to 1948. However, he argues that "between 1948 and the late 1950s, the party became increasingly influenced by a recreation of certain elements of economic Liberalism," but in the late 1950s, "the party swung back to a selection of some of the ideas it had abandoned in 1948."[3] David Willetts offers a similar outline and time frame, while using the terminology of "dry" and "wet," so popular in the last quarter of the twentieth century, to describe periods of limited and extended state Conservatism respectively. He roughly outlines the swings between dry and wet periods as – "dry dominance, 1948–58, wet, 1958–65, dry during 1965–71, and wet for 1971–5"[4]; with, of course, a commensurate rise in the desiccate index for the advent of Mrs Thatcher in 1975. However, the more orthodox approach classifies the postwar period as a "collectivist age,"[5] and an example of such an account is found in the work of Charmley, where he believes that the libertarian strand in Conservatism is only visible with a microscope and hindsight and that, any such line of thought before the 1970s was therefore marginal at best[6]. But, in this chapter, we find that there is no need for a microscope to view the existence of a limited state tradition; so prominent is such a tradition in the writings of the One Nation group in this postwar period.

If we can discern Conservatives settling on a consensus at all, in relation to this spatial context, it would appear to be in the agreement that the 1930s marked a watershed in the level of state intervention. Willetts viewed the interwar years as a period when the party drifted towards economic interventionism and corporatism; a world in which planners thought they could "control the economy like technicians sitting in front of an array of dials at a power station."[7] And, for Harris, the attempt in 1938 to nationalize mining royalties was a clear indication to how far the government was prepared to go in this direction.[8] Gilmour approaches this issue from an alternative party political tradition than Willetts but concludes similarly that the interwar years were interventionist. He eulogizes the corporatist tendencies of the Conservative Party in this period, and he quotes Baldwin's view that the party had to "face left" in order to deal with Labour in the 1920s, before delineating a lengthy list of institutions and businesses that were "rationalized" or more appropriately, nationalized.

> Thus, not only before the Labour party had created one single corporation, but before it had even decided that it favoured such corporations, the Conservative party had started setting them up and the Liberal party had pronounced in their favour.[9]

And:

> Certainly the hallmarks of Conservative economic policy in the thirties were cheap money, protection, rationalisation of industry, control of prices and output, subsidies and agricultural marketing boards rather than competition, free trade and *laissez faire*, which Chamberlain regarded as "an obsolete and worn out system."[10]

E. H. H. Green thought these years—the "hungry thirties"—colored the judgment of postwar Conservative leaders, in that the 1945 election defeat was perceived as punishment for them, and as such they had an impact on postwar policy, particularly in relation to that of unemployment.[11] But, the One Nation group were in no doubt that if blame were to be apportioned, then it lay more with the erroneous path followed in the interwar period and with the "almost pathetic belief in the cartel of the 1920s and 1930s." In a series of group memos in 1953, regarding the "themes" to be included in a second One Nation pamphlet, we find sentiments that anticipated those views we found in Chapter 1 on "fatalistic progressivism"—with regard to the need for greater efforts on denationalization in the late 1960s. John Rodgers was of the view that compulsion from the centre must be rejected, along with the imposition of a national wages policy, coupled with central planning of investment and that the fallacy of the Man in Whitehall knows best be exposed.[12] But, the most cogent memo was written by Enoch Powell, on March 18, 1953, and the lengthy extract from it below clearly shows the level of resentment within One Nation over the issue of "planning" at this time; and, of course, it underpins the claim for perpetual tension and the existence of political recrudescence within the Conservative tradition, even in this putative period of a postwar settlement.

> Theme: Great political reactions are nearly always delayed reactions. The Labour party in its first thirty years was busied with remedying abuses of the industrial revolution, the greatest of which already lay fifty years in the past. Similarly, the era of nationalisation 1945/51 was a delayed reaction from the conditions of the 1920s and 1930s. Political parties are often like the Thracian boxer in Demosthenes, always putting their hands where the last blow fell instead of warding off the next. No parties are so prone to this error as "progressive" ones. . . . In 1945 it was the height of eccentricity to question the planning assumption. The Conservative Party's "Industrial Charter" (1947) reeks with it: we were to be distinguished from our opponents by strategic planning instead of tactical planning, by Government (Treasury) planning instead of nationalised planning. The generation of politicians who came into the Conservative Party after the war delighted to enlarge on our Nineteenth Century record of opposition to Liberal laissez faire. Toryism, it appeared, had always meant state control. Carried to power by the emergence and supremacy of such ideas, the Labour Party effected, as it were at a stroke, all that was formulated of its policy of nationalisation . . . the official Conservative Opposition were estopped by their declarations of the past fifteen years or so. They had in one form or another recommended the cartelisation of coal and steel, the abolition of competition in transport and power, the planned use of the land. Now they were getting what they said they wanted, even if the method sometimes seemed a little rough.[13]

Rather, it was planning and controls that were obsolescent in the minds of the One Nation group, and such views were not just for private consumption either, as will be clear in an examination of the One Nation views that were in the public domain in this period.

## The Pamphlets: "Let the Dog See the Rabbit"

In Chapter 1, we encountered Gilbert Longden chivvying the One Nation group along, stressing his desire that it continue because of the impact its corporate action had had on several critical occasions. The Group's most public "corporate action" was through the publication of their pamphlets. In all, there were just nine of these published by the Conservative Political Centre (CPC), from the first in 1950 to the last one in 2006,[14] and it is important to remember that "no one chapter" was to be identified with any "one individual" in the group. "All [were] collective compromises—though no principles had to be jettisoned in arriving at them."[15] The first and most famous of course was *One Nation*, the eponymous booklet responsible for the rekindling of such ancestral mythology. For Longden, no principles may have been jettisoned, but it is evident from its inception that the group were all too well aware of the tension in balancing the need for policies to elevate the condition of the people while mindful of Disraeli's caveat that such policy cannot violate "those principles of economic truth upon which the prosperity of States depends." This is important as in the next chapter we shall see that the image of One Nation, both in "mythical" and group terms, was portrayed exclusively as belonging to just one tradition of the Conservative Party, the one at ease with state interventionism and the promotion of such policies by an extended state to redress the condition of the people. In fact, the first chapter of the 1950 booklet is entitled "the conflict of ideas" and does in part appear to bask in the praise of the *Manchester Guardian* for the party's progressive approach to social policy as evidenced in the 1950 manifesto: "The Conservatives have never in their history produced so enlightened a statement on social policy— from full employment to education and the socials services."[16] And chapter two of the booklet is a veritable delineation of those Tories who had "intervened" to ameliorate the condition of the workers (with the emphasis placed upon Disraeli's "all is sanitation" policy) through different eras towards support for the social service state of the early twentieth century and then to the acceptance by the party of the welfare state in the middle of that century. Indeed, in early 1951, at their second dinner, the group agreed that the object in meeting RAB Butler that evening should be to emphasize that nothing in One Nation was affected by the prospect of rearmament and to stress the danger of "certain elements in the party urging necessity to slash housing and other social services."[17]

But, we should note that the other traditional elements inherent in the dual nature of Conservative policy—on private wealth, on individual responsibility and initiative—were emphasized also; along with the promotion of a competitive market system as the best possible way of producing the necessary resources needed for the elevation of the condition of the people. The booklet is careful to incorporate Disraeli's warning on "economic truth." The obverse component found in the "conflict of ideas" was very much the "fundamental disagreement between Conservatives and Socialists on the questions of social policy":

> Socialists believe that the State should provide an average standard. We believe that it should provide a minimum standard, above which people should be free to rise as far as their industry, their thrift, their ability or genius may take them. . . . Socialists believe that private charity has little place in a public service. We do not agree. We believe, in Mr Eden's words, in the "strong helping the weak," rather than in the weakening of the strong . . . . Our economic position does not, and will not for many years, allow us . . . to implement in full the social legislation that has been passed since 1944. Therefore, Conservative policy insists on administrative efficiency in the social services, and on the clear recognition of priorities.[18]

Such prioritizing between the social services led the group to identify education as second in importance only to housing as these two social services would determine the health, prosperity, and morale of the British people. The 1944 Butler Education Act was praised very highly as another Conservative achievement in social policy; indeed, the group actually viewed education as a bulwark of defense against communism in the ongoing cold war.[19] In chapter five of the One Nation booklet, housing is viewed as crucial in respect to many aspects of national life, and social collectivist explanations are utilized in identifying bad housing with the rise in broken homes, retarded education, and the increasing numbers in borstals and approved schools. But the chapter then becomes a eulogy to private enterprise and the need to remove the state and the local authorities from the backs of the private builders. The building industry was to be given an open field with full competition between purchasers and in price of materials, which would stimulate the necessary successful investment and enterprise. "Government assistance is not only unnecessary, but positively harmful." The solution was in incentives for the private builder: "Our task is to bring back the mass-production element into the house-building industry, which can be done only by enabling it largely to work on its own authority for a prospective demand—by 'letting the dog see the rabbit.'"[20] Interestingly, Alport, writing in the early 1980s, identified the speech by Duncan Sandys, Shadow Minister responsible for the building industry in 1950, as part of the yawning gap in expertise in Conservative policy, which led directly to the creation of the One Nation group. Although, he states in retrospect: "it was not a bad speech and would certainly have appealed to the 'market forces private enterprise, laissez-faire' Conservative Party of the present day."[21] The evidence presented in the *One Nation* pamphlet suggests that such sentiments would have appealed to such Conservatives then as now.

In terms of influence, Angus Maude claims that the 1950 booklet was "indirectly responsible (with the fillip of Harmar Nicholls' démarche at the Party Conference) for the famous '300,000 Houses' policy; apart from its influence on Tory policy for the other social services."[22] It is important to note, then as now, that *One Nation* was viewed as an influential pamphlet, and a review of it was broadcast at the time in many languages on the BBC's European Service: General News Talk by E. W. Ashcroft.[23] And, we should also take note of the section on "rights and duties" in chapter three of the *One Nation* booklet, as what we have here is an anticipation of Mrs Thatcher's ideas on no entitlements without obligations, in relation to that existential question concerning "society." In this influential pamphlet then, we find the Conservative view that the nation is endangered as soon as *rights* are regarded as more important than, or a prior condition to, *duties*. If the state is to have a role at all, it can only be as a result of the "existence of aggregations of wealth at the disposal of individuals"; and if we are to have "fair shares for all," then it "is certainly the death of human society."[24] So, this famous *One Nation* document espoused Conservative free enterprise ideas as much, or as more, as the acceptance of safety nets for the unfortunate in society. Indeed, in conclusion to the 1950 pamphlet, the group offers the caveat that:

> It [the state] must not so tax industry that it cannot replace its own capital, with the result that its prices become uncompetitive in world markets. It must not burden the individual so that he loses his initiative and enterprise, or is driven to emigrate . . . [The] long-term aim is to encourage, through the financial system, those qualities in which Conservatives particularly believe—energy, initiative, thrift, and individual responsibility.[25]

If a case can be made for free market Conservatism being extant in the 1950 *One Nation* publication, then we may describe it as positively thriving by the time of the publication of *Change Is Our Ally* in 1954.[26] In the concluding chapter of this 1954 pamphlet, entitled "Opinion and Change," the group adumbrates their position that during "the last 40 years," but, in particular, throughout the 1930s when Conservative policy of "rationalization" was in many respects similar to that of Labour's *nationalization* policy, political thought and practice had swung away from laissez-faire to the opposite extreme of centralized planning and control. If greater wealth was to be achieved, then the pendulum had to swing back towards a more competitive system.[27] Contemporary comments on the pamphlet illustrate just how much this document was viewed as a return to the principles of free market economics and criticism of past practice by both the political parties. "Their book is a riot of idol smashing. They lay violent hands on all party idols—not only Socialist idols like nationalization but Tory idols like tariffs and farmers—and they pitch the lot in to the dustbin."[28] And Ian Mikardo, in *Tribune* of May 28, 1954, facetiously talks of Mr Maude's and Mr Powell's pregnancy and the infant produced by it:

> a booklet called Change Is Our Ally, edited by the two of them, but bearing the sign-manual of no fewer than ten Tory MPs who call themselves the "One Nation Group". It shows us exactly what a fundamental counter-revolution

the Tories will carry out in the life of this country if the Labour party and the electorate are silly enough to let them get away with it.[29]

This criticism of the Conservative policy of the 1930s as *dirigiste* rationalization and the idea of a radical counterrevolution is reminiscent of the neoliberals' critique in the 1970s on the failure of the party to address the "ratchet of socialism." Indeed, such parallels with Conservative Party doctrinal debates of the 1970s are clear in the correspondence between RAB Butler and Angus Maude, where we find a similar tension concerning the trajectory of doctrine for the 1950s. The *Daily Telegraph* in 1954 had noticed the "one small but significant point of difference." RAB Butler had failed to supply a forward in 1954 as he had done for *One Nation* in 1950, but the *Telegraph* ascribed this to the fact that he was now Chancellor of the Exchequer without the freedom of maneuver as found in Opposition. Although the paper did point out that: "It is also true that 'Change Is Our Ally' has—certainly in respect of one Conservative Minister— a very much sharper cutting edge."[30] The galley proofs of the pamphlet had been sent to Butler with the request for him to write a forward. But on May 1, 1954, Michael Fraser of the Conservative Research Department sent a memo to Butler intimating that he and David Dear had looked at the booklet, and he was now going to get James Douglas to have a look at it in detail. Fraser takes issue with the pamphlet's assertion that interwar rationalization was simply nationalization writ small. Fraser then offers two reasons why Butler should not be connected with the ideas presented in the booklet. The first is that as Chancellor he should not be associated with any controversial publications touching on economic and industrial policy. But, of greater import is the second reason outlined by Fraser:

because the first part of this document, which is an historical analysis of the inter war years, the war economy and the socialist period, contains much criticism of the policies of the pre-war and wartime Governments of which you yourself were a member.[31]

Fraser then offers the advice that Butler uses only the first argument in replying to Mr Maude. This, Butler does on May 3, 1954 and Maude replies on May 13, 1954 intimating that he fully understands the reasons for this. On May 20, 1954 Maude sends the finished booklet to Butler: "with the compliments of the authors," but Butler scrolls across it in red ink: "Fundamentally insincere." But on May 21, 1954, he then thanks Maude "for so kindly letting me have a copy of 'Change Is Our Ally.'"[32] Again, such correspondence of the early 1950s informs us of the existence of a greater doctrinal tension in the Party than is commonly thought, and if nothing else, it throws into sharp relief the ostensible picture of unquestioning loyalty. The *Financial Times*, May 21, 1954, observed that such views, as found in the pamphlet, represented "a considerable change in Conservative thinking, a change, which had already been observable in policy, but of which this is the first coherent and thorough statement." One other published comment is of note here. In the *Glasgow Herald*, July 12, 1954, we find a Prospective Unionist Candidate who describes the pamphlet as "the most important [Conservative] report of them all" produced in the past year. The author is fulsome in his praise for the pamphlet although he does suggest that there will be Conservatives "who will resist many of the specific proposals as outright Liberal heresies." The author was Ralph Harris, soon to be the co-founder of the Institute of Economic Affairs (IEA) in 1957.[33] It is quite clear then that E. H. H. Green is right to stress that there is no validity in the assertion that 1975, with the onset of Thatcher, marked something new in the ideological nature of the Conservative Party; as "aspects of 'Thatcherism' had existed *avant la letter*."[34]

## Forecast Is for Dry to Wet, Then Dry Again

The *Responsible Society*, published in 1959 as the Conservative Political Centre's 200th publication, adopted a less strident but similar line to that taken in the 1954 pamphlet. In fact, *The Times*, March 24, 1959, interpreted it thus: "The writers see the past eight years of Conservative Government as a period during which some progress has been made in halting and indeed reversing the trend towards State domination and giving the individual back some share of initiative." At a special CPC dinner to launch the publication, Gilbert Longden as the oldest surviving member, summarized the Group's views of the 1950s as condemning indiscriminate State largesse in 1950 and encouraging economic change to a freer economy in 1954; as a prerequisite to enabling any expansion of the social services, and for 1959, a "movement away from State domination, and towards a greater share of individual initiative, as one of the 'most beneficial results of Tory rule.'"[35] This interpretation chimes with David Willett's view of the 1950s, that it was in this period that the party promoted judicious abstinence of state activity as opposed to the adoption of policies associated with an extended state.[36] Although the pamphlet stressed the beneficial effects of this abstinence, particularly since 1955, the authors argued that this trend towards reversing state domination was not widely perceived or appreciated as such and thought it the object of the One Nation group to "underline the significance of the trend."[37] The pamphlet emphasized the dismantling of the last of the wartime controls and regulations but misquoted Shakespeare's Macbeth in stressing the point that a Socialist Government would have reintroduced them if given half a chance, and that it would now be far more difficult in the future, with the removal of the wartime emergency legislation under *The Emergency Laws (Repeal) Bill*. "We should have 'scotched the snake not killed it—she'll turn and be herself.' Under a Socialist Government she would have turned very quickly."[38] Emphasis was also placed on the benefits of lower taxation as "freer taxation policies will bring more opportunity and strength to the individual men and women who create the national wealth."[39] However, with this in mind, the correspondence between Bill Deedes (editor/collator of the chapters) and Peter Goldman (director of the CPC) regarding this pamphlet, illustrates for us the ideological tensions and compromises within the group. For example, Deedes declares himself almost defeated by Keith Joseph's style and blames this on the influence of "All Souls," and then declares: "I think the last Tory Objective 'To reduce taxation more' more or less superfluous, but you shall judge. It is not quite what we want; but he exhausted himself producing it and it is impossible to re-write. I apologise."[40]

Only one pamphlet was published in the 1960s, *One Europe*, and this will be addressed in Chapter 7, while the many drafts and ideas for pamphlets in this period will be referred to in subsequent chapters, but it may well be that Bill Deedes's remarks signaled a future change in the ideological direction of the group, as the group's short pamphlet, in the year after Mrs Thatcher became leader, espoused those interventionist policies so redolent of the more active state of the thirties and forties. Ironically, Margaret Thatcher supplied a forward for this pamphlet welcoming the work of the One Nation Group of MPs. This 1976 booklet, on relations in the workplace, was replete with notions of corporatist arrangements for *One Nation at Work*. The state would compel the establishment of employee councils in works employing over 500 employees[41] and the solutions offered echoed not only codetermination as found in Germany but the compulsive legislation of the Heath Government's Acts of 1972, 1973, and 1974, which forced consultation on employers.[42] Participation, between employees and management, would start from below, on the shop floor, and employees' interests would be "recognised more fully by giving them rights, which are comparable to those of shareholders."[43] Little wonder then, that such views would be contrasted with the trajectory of actual party policy throughout the late seventies and eighties. In 1984, Philip Goodhart, while reflecting the concern felt in the group for the level of unemployment in society, pointed out that:

[I]ndividual members of the One Nation Group have advanced a number of widely different arguments as to how the economy should be managed. This pamphlet does not seek to choose between these individual arguments, but it puts forward a number of ideas for coping with the impact of unemployment, which we believe are wholly consistent with the Government's economic strategy.[44]

The tradition of collective compromise without the jettisoning of ideological principles does appear to be alive and well in this 1984 booklet, as he echoes the Thatcher message that unemployment could only be defeated through the adoption of a competitive market and that the example of what befell the French Socialists across the Channel was evidence for this. However, in contradistinction to such a view, what we have is a whole array of policies and strategies for government intervention towards job creation, such as work sharing, job splitting, encouraging early retirement, and that government would only have to spend just short of £1billion to achieve such aims.[45] In reality, these proposals, as outlined in 1984, fall rather short of the ideal of a competitive market. But, the One Nation group returned to a limited state perspective in the arguments put forward in the pamphlets of the 1990s as "economic rectitude is the enabler, not the enemy, of social welfare."[46] David Howell drafted the 1992 *One Nation 2000* pamphlet and *One Nation: At the Heart of the Future*, in 1996. In 1992, the emphasis was placed on the unchanged goal of the group "to create a Britain in which growing prosperity of the fortunate is reflected in the better welfare of the disadvantaged; in which the benefits of enterprise are to the benefit of all . . . ."[47] In contrast to the views of 1976, the 1996 pamphlet ruled out any notion of corporatism and, in particular, any adoption of the German model where "ever higher taxes combine with rising unemployment."[48] It was claimed that the Conservative neoliberal reforms of the 1980s were now paying off and that Britain was being transformed into a low tax, high wage society— "at once competitive, adaptable and ideally positioned to take advantage of the new world trading conditions as the centre of economic power moves to Asia."[49] What we have then is movement along an extended state/limited state ideological dimension, and this is confirmed below in what is a systematic analysis of these "wet and dry" periods: quantitatively mapping such policy movement, over time, in our One Nation documents, while comparing them to the policy preferences found in both Conservative Party manifestos and campaign guides of similar periods.

## Mapping Conservative Policy Preferences

To reiterate, there is a more systematic method of analysis open to us that will help us to confirm or refute the above impressionistic interpretation of the ideological movement in the One Nation group. This method is quantitative textual analysis, and it is a powerful tool that will allow us to map the policy preferences of the One Nation group and to highlight any interesting changes in the direction of such preferences, particularly when they are compared to those found in the "official" publications of the party at each general election. A necessary first step in undertaking such an analysis was to familiarize oneself with the methodological approach of the Manifesto Research Group (MRG), now based at Wissenschaftzentrum, Berlin (WZB).[50] The MRG developed a common coding scheme for the analysis of party manifestos, which covered an extensive listing of politically relevant policy areas (see appendix Table A3.2 for a full list); and each sentence of the manifesto was coded under one, and only one, of these categories. The resultant numerical distribution of sentences was then taken as a percentage of the total number of sentences to standardize for the varying lengths of the manifestos.[51] Of course, in this study, it is the data from the Conservative manifestos between 1950 and 1997 that are of singular interest, and their total numbers of quasi-sentences are listed in Table A3.1 of the chapter appendix, along with those of the One Nation documents between 1950 and 1996 and the party's Campaign Guides published for each election since 1950. The One Nation documents and Campaign Guides were coded in line with the MRG coding frame, and this allows for a comparison over time between the data from our One Nation pamphlets and the data from the party's publications.[52] Fortunately, this methodology offers us versatility in studying political change, either broadly or discretely, "permitting the use both of the telescope and microscope."[53] From the extensive list of relevant policy areas, the MRG constructed a combination of particular indicators to develop a left–right scale that has been consistently and successfully utilized in the analysis of party manifestos because this is indeed the spatial context that is assumed by almost everyone when they think about politics.

> Previous research across a number of countries has identified a number of policy strands and emphases as classically "left-wing" and another set as characteristically "right-wing." By adding all the percentages of sentences in "left" categories and subtracting the total from the sum of percentages in "right" categories, we can create a unified scale going from +100% (all sentences in a manifesto are "right-wing") to –100% (all sentences in a manifesto are "left wing").[54]

The creation of this scale from the list of categories in Table A3.2 is also found in the chapter appendix, in Table A3.3. In Figure 3.1, we can examine the ideological movement of the Conservative Party, in relation to these left–right scores, in the party manifestos, Campaign Guides and, of course, in our One Nation documents.

It is immediately apparent, from Figure 3.1, that the above impressionistic interpretation of the ideological movement of the One Nation group is confirmed by this textual analysis. The *One Nation* pamphlet itself has a score of +26, which is replicated in the 1959 *Responsible Society* document, and indeed the 1954 *Change Is Our Ally* pamphlet is even further to the right than the others produced by the group in the 1950s. The One Nation pamphlets of the 1990s are similarly right wing on this scale, with the 1996 pamphlet further to the right than that of 1992. Confirmation is also found here that, in the initial period of Mrs Thatcher's leadership of the party, the One Nation group adopted policy preferences diametrically opposed to those views of the neoliberals; the limited state strand that was to become the "accepted" Conservative tradition of the time. Thus, in 1976, the One Nation's "public corporate action" is as left of centre as the 1996 pamphlet is right wing. However, the 1984 pamphlet, written by Philip Goodhart, is less so; and this is just before we discern an assimilation of policy preferences, in the late 1980s and 1990s, in a rightwards trajectory, for

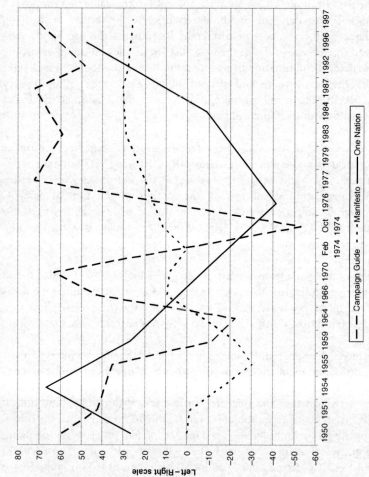

Figure 3.1: Ideological Movement in the Conservative Party, on a Left–Right scale, 1950–1997

*Source:* Budge, I., Klingemann, H.D, Volkens, A., Bara, J. and Tannenbaum, E., *Mapping Policy Preferences,* *CD Rom*, 2001, data adapted from the SPSS file— PPP,por—for the Conservative party manifestos, this was included along with the data from the One Nation pamphlets and Campaign Guides to create a "One Nation merged data" file.

all the manifestos, the Campaign Guides and the One Nation pamphlets of the period.

Unfortunately, the evidence from Figure 3.1 will not unequivocally resolve for us the debate regarding those periods when the party adopted either a "leftist" or "rightist" position in policy preferences. This seems destined to remain as an acutely contested issue in British politics. The party manifestos are, in fact, relatively left of centre in the 1950s, which would seem to underpin the claim that this was indeed an age of collectivism. It is 1966 before we see a move to the right in policy preferences in these Conservative Party manifestos, and apart from a slight blip in February 1974, a right-wing position is consistently adopted thereafter. But, manifestos are unique policy documents; these are the glossy texts with which the parties present themselves to the public at each election, and more importantly, with this in mind, they are a crucial part of the control and manipulation process that the major parties feel the need to engage in with the printed and electronic media. Because of this symbiotic relationship with the media and the knowledge that these election policy programs will be filtered through such media outlets, the manifestos are usually presented as balanced and moderate documents. The example of the 1979 manifesto is usually referred to in this context, as the small section on the issue of nationalization was less than a true indication of what was to become a radical program of industrial privatization. Thus, it makes perfect sense to have these manifestos written in a style, which is at once disarming and palliative rather than controversially red in tooth and claw. Indeed, the MRG refer to this "moderation" in their analyses of British postwar manifestos in relation to the relative leanings of the left–right score. "This is generally in the range −40 to +30, reflecting the general ideological moderation of British parties."[55]

It was because of this that the Campaign Guides were introduced into the equation, as these "blue bibles," although in the public domain, are written much more for the prospective parliamentary candidates and local constituency parties than for public consumption per se. In manifestos, parties have a tendency to "talk past each other," the claim being that such documents do not engage in a confrontational style and do not attack outright the other parties' stance on policies.[56] But, this is indeed the style of the Campaign Guides, where opposition parties' policies are subject to overt criticism and are usually debunked only in slightly less proportion to the praise heaped upon Conservative "solutions." Again, this style makes perfect sense for the prospective candidates and local parties who need to have such knowledge and arguments at their disposal, as they are so necessary for the defense and attack strategies to be employed in any head-to-head hustings-type debates. And when we examine the ideological movement in left–right scores, from these "blue bibles," what we find is that the Campaign Guides' ideological trajectory mirrors that of One Nation much more than those left–right scores found for the manifestos in the graph. The housing sections of the Guides were chosen for analysis here as this was the issue that was "first in importance" for the One Nation group and, which they addressed in their eponymous pamphlet. And, interestingly, although the Campaign Guides of the 1950s echo those "right-wing" policy preferences found in our One Nation pamphlets, they would appear also to underpin David Willetts's views on the changes in ideological direction of the party, as the Guides move left for the Macmillan period and left again for the "post U-turn" period of Edward Heath, before taking a consistently right-wing approach after 1977.[57] The extent of "this right wing score" in policy preferences, found in the manifestos throughout the 1980s, is referred to by Ian Budge as "the extreme Thatcherite positions."[58] However, the evidence presented in Figure 3.1 suggests that such "extremism" was clearly evident in the party of the 1950s, as well as in that of the 1980s: particularly within the One Nation group in the postwar period.

Of course, for a party that eschews the very notion of ideology, a question arises over the efficacy of such a scale of "left–right" as found in Figure 3.1, as its appropriateness may well be challenged for any analysis of Conservative policy preferences and more so for the tracking of ideological movement within the party. Indeed, the One Nation group did not recognize any efficacy to such a dimension in 1996. "One Nation thinking has little to do with being 'left' or 'right' or at this ideological pole or that one."[59] Although the group did declare in 1992 that: "We seek neither to pull the party to the left or the right, but only to point more clearly the broad and solid way forward, which we are confident our leaders are already treading."[60] But, fortunately there are specific policy positions within the MRG categories that have a greater bearing on an examination of the dual nature of the Conservative Party, particularly in the context of economic policy and in our extended/limited state dimension. The combinations of categories that compose these specific policy positions are set out in Table A3.4 in the chapter appendix, and ideally we have new categories that cover a limited state position, on the extent of preferences for a "market economy" and an extended state position, on the number of quasi-sentences in support of "planning in the economy": with a concomitant examination on the level of support in our documents for a new category of "welfare." The numbers of quasi-sentences in each document, for these three policy positions, are set out in Figures 3.2 to 3.4.

When a specific focus is applied to the policy categories, it is clear, by viewing the data in Figures 3.2 and 3.3, that the Conservative Party did have more of a predilection for policies that promoted free enterprise and a market economy than for the creation of wealth through a planned economy. However, the manifesto data does show that in the elections of 1955, 1959, then in 1970, and February 1974, and somewhat surprisingly in the defeat of Major in 1997, that the party was prepared to endorse policies to regulate capitalism and

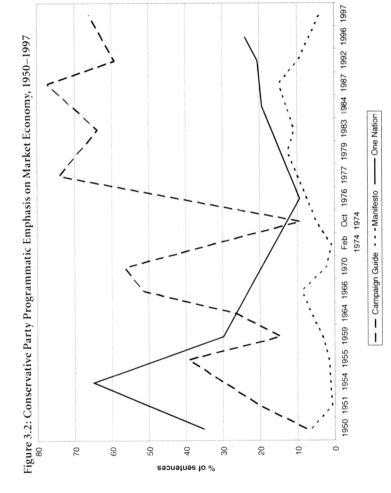

Figure 3.2: Conservative Party Programmatic Emphasis on Market Economy, 1950–1997

*Source:* One Nation merged data file.

Figure 3.3: Conservative Party Programmatic Emphasis on Planned Economy, 1950–1997

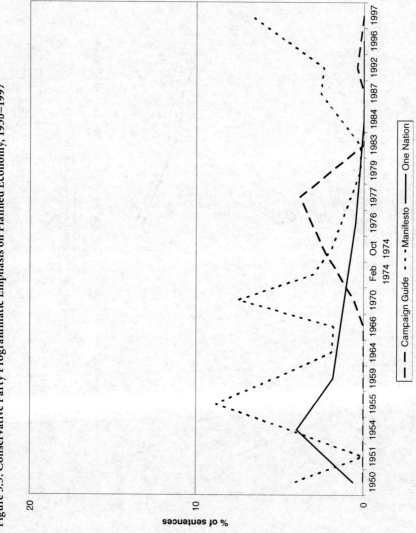

*Source:* One Nation merged data file.

control the economy through economic planning: notably to a greater extent than the emphases usually placed upon a market economy and free enterprise found in other years. And, again surprisingly, in the election of 1970—when the received wisdom had Mr Heath's policies culminating in the silent revolution of "Selsdon Man" who was so keen to promote an invigorated market economy— what we actually find is more emphases on "planning" in this manifesto than references to an enterprise economy. Although, in the 1970 Campaign Guide, the views of Selsdon Man are very much to the fore in relation to a competitive market approach for "his housing." However, the minutes of the One Nation group in this period once again highlight the fact that the ideological lines of division are fluid within the party and that, there is a concomitant level of tension over such policy preferences. For example, with regards to prices and incomes policies, being used as levers for controlling the economy, the One Nation group is decidedly opposed. In 1966, when discussing prices and incomes, there "was general agreement that the Party should oppose the Government's policy, with the exception of Charles Fletcher-Cooke."[61] And one year later, we find that there was a general feeling among the group to oppose the next phase of prices and incomes that were announced by the Government, as such a policy would bring greater distortion and anomalies to an economy already adversely affected by the Labour Government's interventions to date, and thus, there "was an overwhelming majority against granting the Government any further powers, with only Ian Gilmour in favour."[62]

Thus, the views of the One Nation members reflect this image of political recrudescence in the party with a manifest tension amongst members over the doctrinal path to be followed. Indeed, in the same year of 1967, we find Enoch Powell calling for de-control of exchange rates:

A proposal was put forward by Enoch Powell that the Tory Party should now support a policy of a floating pound and he considered that devaluation would probably be a great success. The Government had devalued by an unnecessarily large amount, making the pound $2.40 instead of $2.80, and in his opinion this would show weakness as a result in six months time. In view of the fact that the Government had undervalued the pound, he maintained that the pound would be very strong in twelve months from now. Rippon agreed and said that we must consider this a real possibility. The Group agreed that the idea of a floating exchange rate was very attractive and should be carefully considered by the Party. Apparently Reggie Maudling was in favour, but Ted Heath was not very keen. In Enoch's opinion this was because Ted Heath never approved of anything Enoch put forward, on principle.[63]

Such debate and discussion undermines Sam Brittan's charge of docility in the party, particularly in the claim that: "there was, for example, the ukase imposed by Mr Heath, in July 1967, against any discussion of devaluation or floating rates by Conservative backbenchers, which was accepted in docile fashion."[64] And, John Ramsden has 1965 as a year when the party came close to "committing itself to the introduction of a wealth tax"[65] but, by December 1967, the One Nation group minutes suggest that although Iain Macleod may have favored such an impost, there was not much support for it in One Nation as: "it was thought wise that we should express to Ted Heath our firm disapproval of any move of the Conservative Party to support the tax."[66] Such debate underpins David Willett's claim, found in Chapter 1, of One Nation being a forum for diverse views but we should be mindful that such diversity is crucial for policy renewal and for the party to refresh itself at the springs of doctrine in the first place. And, a diversity of views is what we find again when the policy of "welfare" is considered in Figure 3.4.

When we consider the data for the combined category of welfare in Figure 3.4, we see again that the Campaign Guides concur with Willett's version of the party's changes in ideological direction, with the Macmillan/Home era and then that of the post-1972 Heath period displaying the greater propensity for emphases on "welfare." With its concern with a Tory approach to the social services, it is reassuring to find that the 1950 *One Nation* pamphlet does indeed have the greatest emphases placed on welfare of any of the other One Nation group publications, although, *The Responsible Society* of 1959, is not that far off in contrast to the others. However, we should not forget the evidence of Figure 3.2 and its emphasis upon "market solutions" because this was mainly the view of both the party and the One Nation group. Indeed, Richard Fort believed, as early as 1951, that "enterprise and laissez faire with profit inducement can no longer do harm, can only do good."[67] Moreover, we should note that the One Nation group was also well aware of the "destructive" element in the Tory approach to politics that Bolingbroke identified all those years ago and was highlighted in the previous chapter; in short, the party should never be constrained in the construction of alternative ideals that can be floated past the electorate.

It was agreed unanimously that the Leader's speeches should include "Destruction". . . One provocative thought once a month could have great impact throughout the country. For example, "Some people must be asking whether we should be pressing for some change in the methods of financing the National Health Service." This could be slightly expanded and then it could be left to the press to pick up the hint and go to town on it.[68]

Timothy Raison, writing in 1964, acknowledged that the doctrine of One Nation was not easy to uphold or promote, especially with policies that increased health service charges, but he stressed that some unpopular policies can be good

Figure 3.4: Conservative Party Programmatic Emphasis on Welfare, 1950–1997

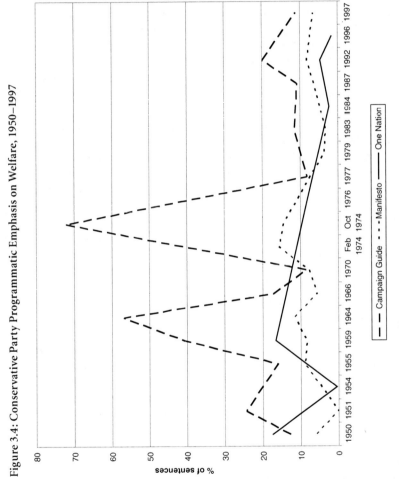

*Source*: One Nation merged data file.

for the nation as a whole, and thus, it was sometimes "necessary to risk unpopularity and dissension for the sake of long term benefits."[69] Of greater import is the fact that Raison was aware of how such conflict and tension on policy preferences could be conducive to a process of party "renewal." Even in periods when the party looked exhausted, it was always, in Raison's view, capable of renewal, and in periods of electoral success it could even provide a check on its own executive, from within itself, when the opposition seemed terminally weak. Suffocating mediocrity was not for the Tory Party, and he recognized that "some forms of aggression can be constructive," and thus, "there must be room in society for the individual, and even for the clash of different individuals and bodies."[70] And, the party had the ability to benefit from such a "clash" because the party was well equipped "to draw out of its varied components the attitude and policies, which are required to meet a particular mood and situation in the country at any given moment."[71]

In conclusion then, the textual analysis confirmed the inherent dual nature of Conservative Party policy preferences over time and that for much of that time, a microscope was not required in order to view the prominence of the limited state approach to policy in the preferences of the One Nation group. Ironically, the "clash" of individuals and bodies, from the varied components of the party in the mid 1970s, which led subsequently to *Thatcherism* was also the only time when the published work of the One Nation group deviated in any significant way from that limited state approach. However, in the 1990s, the One Nation group returned to the ideological path it had followed previously in the 1950s. For example, in the 1996 pamphlet, the "essence of One Nation Conservatism" was outlined in conceptual as well as traditional terms—very simply, the family was the building block, which binds society together and social cohesion could never be imposed from above.

> From this, and not from the State, comes the responsibility, the civic commitment and the common pride and purpose which gives a nation binding strength . . . .It explains why attempts either to link One Nation to some trendy interventionist vision, or, *per contra*, to brand One Nation Tories as a bunch of wets who want a federal Europe, are so contemptible.[72]

The important role played by Lord David Howell in the formation of Conservative policy over three decades enhances this critique of "skilled propaganda from ill-intentioned friends"; and we examine the basis for such a critique in the following chapter.

## Appendix to Chapter Three

### Table A3.1: Documents Used in Coding (Number of Quasi-sentences in Parentheses)

| Manifestos | One Nation Pamphlets | Campaign Guides (housing sections) |
|---|---|---|
| 1950 (365) | 1950 (806) | 1950 (174) |
| 1951 (138) | 1954 (804) | 1951 (160) |
| 1955 (789) | 1959 (490) | 1955 (199) |
| 1959 (333) | 1976 (194) | 1959 (210) |
| 1964 (460) | 1984 (441) | 1964 (199) |
| 1966 (448) | 1992 (322) | 1966 (209) |
| 1970 (436) | 1996 (185) | 1970 (168) |
| 1974F (1038) | | 1974 (206) |
| 1974O (367) | | 1977 (182) |
| 1979 (409) | | 1983 (185) |
| 1983 (774) | | 1987 (258) |
| 1987 (1047) | | 1992 (247) |
| 1992 (1686) | | 1997 (206) |
| 1997 (1084) | | |

*Source*: Budge, I., Klingemann, H. D., Volkens, A., Bara, J., and Tannenbaum, E., *Mapping Policy Preferences, CD Rom*, 2001, data adapted from the SPSS file—PPP.por—for the Conservative Party manifestos, this was included along with the data from the One Nation pamphlets and Campaign Guides to create a "One Nation merged data" file.

### Table A3.2: The Saliency Coding of Election Manifestos 1950–1997

| | | | |
|---|---|---|---|
| 101 | Foreign special relationships: positive | 410 | Productivity |
| 102 | Foreign special relationships: negative | 411 | Technology and infrastructure |
| 103 | Decolonization | 412 | Controlled economy |
| 104 | Military: positive | 413 | Nationalization |
| 105 | Military: negative | 414 | Economic orthodoxy |
| 106 | Peace | 415 | Marxist analysis |
| 107 | Internationalism: positive | 416 | Anti-growth economy |
| 108 | European Community: positive | 501 | Environmental protection |
| 109 | Internationalism: negative | 502 | Arts, sports, leisure, media |

*(Continued)*

**Table A3.2: (Cont'd)**

| | | | |
|---|---|---|---|
| 110 | European Community: negative | 503 | Social justice |
| 201 | Freedom and domestic human rights | 504 | Social services expansion |
| 202 | Democracy | 505 | Social services limitation |
| 203 | Constitutionalism: positive | 506 | Education expansion |
| 204 | Constitutionalism: negative | 507 | Education: limitation |
| 301 | Decentralization | 601 | National way of life: positive |
| 302 | Centralization | 602 | National way of life: negative |
| 303 | Government efficiency | 603 | Traditional morality: positive |
| 304 | Government corruption | 604 | Traditional morality: negative |
| 305 | Government effectiveness and authority | 605 | Law and order |
| 401 | Free enterprise | 606 | National effort and social harmony |
| 402 | Incentives | 607 | Multiculturalism: positive |
| 403 | Regulation of capitalism | 608 | Multiculturalism: negative |
| 404 | Economic planning | 701 | Labour groups: positive |
| 405 | Corporatism | 702 | Labour groups: negative |
| 406 | Protectionism: positive | 703 | Agriculture |
| 407 | Protectionism: negative | 705 | Minority groups |
| 408 | Economic goals | 706 | Non-economic demographic groups |
| 409 | Keynesian demand management | | |

*Source*: Budge, I. et al., *Mapping Policy Preferences*, 2001, pp. 80–81.

**Table A3.3: Scoring a Left–Right Scale**

| Right emphases (sum of percentages for) | **minus** | Left emphases (sum of percentages for) |
|---|---|---|
| Military: positive (104) | | Decolonization (103) |
| Freedom, human rights (201) | | Military: negative (105) |
| Constitutionalism: positive (203) | | Peace (106) |
| Effective authority (305) | | Internationalism: positive (107) |
| Free enterprise (401) | | Democracy (202) |
| Economic incentives (402) | | Regulate capitalism (403) |
| Protectionism: negative (407) | | Economic planning (404) |
| Economic orthodoxy (414) | | Protectionism: positive (406) |
| Social services limitation (505) | | Controlled economy (412) |
| National way of life: positive (601) | | Nationalization (413) |
| Traditional morality: positive (603) | | Social services: expansion (504) |
| Law and order (605) | | Education: expansion (506) |
| Social harmony (606) | | Labour groups: positive (701) |

*Source*: Budge, I. et al., *Mapping Policy Preferences*, 2001, p. 22.

Table A 3.4: Combination of Full Policy—Coding
Categories into Relevant Groupings

| New Category | | Old Category |
| --- | --- | --- |
| Market Economy | 401 | Free Enterprise |
| | 414 | Economic orthodoxy |
| Planned Economy | 403 | Regulate capitalism |
| | 404 | Economic planning |
| | 412 | Controlled economy |
| Welfare | 503 | Social Justice |
| | 504 | Social services expansion |

*Source*: Adapted from Bara, J. and Budge, I. "Party Policy
and Ideology: Still New Labour? " In Norris, P. (ed.) *Britain
Votes 2001*, Oxford University Press, 2001, p. 42 and see also
Budge, I. et al., *Mapping Policy Preferences*, 2001, p. 242.

## Notes

1. Green, 2002, p. 14 and 218.
2. Budge, 1987, p. 26.
3. Harris, 1973, p. 19.
4. Willetts, 1992, p. 48.
5. Beer, 1976.
6. Charmley, 1998, pp. 118–125.
7. Willetts, 1992, p. 185.
8. Harris, 1973, p. 49.
9. Gilmour, 1969, pp. 44 and 52.
10. Gilmour and Garnett, 1998, p. 5.
11. Green, 2002, p. 236.
12. See Rodgers papers: OP27/3, 1953, Centre for Kentish Studies, Kent.
13. Ibid.
14. One Nation Publications: Macleod, Iain and Angus Maude (eds) *One Nation: a Tory Approach to Social Problems*, London, Conservative Political Centre, 1950. Powell, Enoch and Angus Maude (eds) *Change Is Our Ally*, London, Conservative Political Centre, 1954. Balniel, Lord, Robert Carr, William Deedes, Charles Fletcher-Cooke, Richard Fort, Brian Harrison, Sir Keith Joseph, Gilbert Longden, Sir Toby Low, James Ramsden, and Geoffrey Rippon, *The Responsible Society*, London, Conservative Political Centre, 1959. Ridley, Nicholas (ed) *One Europe*, London: Conservative Political Centre, 1965. Butler, Adam, Kenneth Baker, Leon Brittan, Philip Goodhart and Michael Alison, (eds) *One Nation At Work: By The One Nation Group Of MPs*, London, Conservative Political Centre, 1976. Goodhart, Sir Philip. *Jobs Ahead*, London, Conservative Political Centre, 1984. One Nation, *One Nation 2000*, London, Conservative Political Centre, 1992. One Nation, *One Nation: At The Heart Of The Future*, London, Conservative Political Centre, 1996. Tyrie, Andrew, *One Nation Again*, Surrey: 4 Print, 2006: although this particular pamphlet was

produced after the content analysis for this chapter had been carried out, it is addressed in Chapter 8.

15. Longden papers: Longden Box List: Temporary File Number 31, "Longden in a letter to an old acquaintance on the success of One Nation, 5 February 1951," London School of Economics and Political Science Library. The 1984 pamphlet, *Jobs Ahead*, by Philip Goodhart was single authored but again this was given the Group's imprimatur.

16. Macleod and Maude, 1950, p. 9.

17. Alport papers: Box 37, One Nation Minutes, February 5, 1951, Albert Sloman Library, University of Essex.

18. Macleod and Maude, 1950, p. 9.

19. Ibid, p. 39. But, we find at a dinner on January 29, 1953— with Alport, Carr, Fort, Longden, Maude, Ormsby-Gore, Powell, and Ted Heath as a "guest," all in attendance— that: "The Education Act, 1944, was deplored": Alport papers: Box 37, One Nation Minutes, January 29, 1953. This private lack of reverential loyalty could be a feature of One Nation dinners especially when directed at Ministers of the day.

20. Macleod and Maude, 1950, pp. 27–38.

21. Alport papers: "The Red Notebook, p. 2: 'Our Nation'" by Cuthbert Alport, undated in Box 44: Notes for a memoir, etc.

22. Harmar Nicholls was MP for Peterborough, 1950 to October 1974, see Biffen, 1961, p. 262, for an account of this historical decision of Conference and see Howard, 1988, p. 172, for Butler's elitist critique of such bottom up participation in the party.

23. Longden papers: Temporary File Number 31, "transcript of talk on *One Nation*."

24. Macleod and Maude, 1950, pp. 18 and 93.

25. Macleod and Maude, 1950, pp. 90 and 93.

26. This was the booklet that was the cause of the memos of March 1953 and was to be entitled: "The Thracian Boxer." But, after much discussion and suggestions as diverse as "Change or Decay," "We Beg to Move," "Change is Constant," the group settled on "Change Is Our Ally," which was edited by Powell and Maude, 1954. See Alport papers: Box 37, One Nation Minutes, March 26, 1953 and April 12,1954.

27. Powell and Maude, 1954, pp. 96–97.

28. *Daily Mirror*, May 21, 1954.

29. Conservative Party Archive (CPA): CCO 150/4/2/1, "Newspaper cutting of Tribune," 28. May (1954), Bodleian Library, Oxford.

30. *Daily Telegraph*, May 21, 1954.

31. "RAB" Butler Papers, Trinity College Cambridge, RAB H54:32 and 33, "Memo from Mr Fraser to Mr Butler, 1 May 1954." Thus, rather surprisingly, 35 years later while reviewing "Thatcherism," James Douglas offers a contraposition that the One Nation group: "had been genuinely convinced of the need for policies along the lines developed during the closing years of the Coalition Government." See Chapter 5 and Douglas, 1989, p. 420.

32. "RAB" Butler Papers: RAB H54:35, 36 and 37.

33. The role the One Nation members played in what Crockett, 1995, calls the economic counter revolution, is addressed in Chapter 5.

34. Green, 2002, p. 14.

35. Longden papers: Temporary File Number 31, "C.P.C.: 23 March 1959." Moreover, Longden was later to associate the *One Nation* work with an anticipation of

THE THRACIAN BOXER AND IDEOLOGICAL MOVEMENT 69

Thatcherism. "I hope that I have distilled the thoughts of some Tory backbenchers 35 years ago; and I maintain that they have more affinity with 'Thatcherism' than with the views of the 'wets' of today," in *Crossbow*, Autumn 1985, pp. 22–24.

36. See note 4. And, cf., the chapters by Harriet Jones, 1996 and Rodney Lowe, 1996 on Conservative social policy, 1945–1957 and 1957–1964, respectively.
37. One Nation Group, 1959, p. 6.
38. Ibid., p. 11. The actual words are: "We have scotched the snake not killed it; She'll close and be herself" (Macbeth, Act 3, scene ii).
39. One Nation Group, 1959, p. 24.
40. See CPA: CCO 150/4/2/6; in particular the letter of January 19, 1959.
41. One Nation Group, 1976, p. 17.
42. Ibid., pp. 14–16.
43. Ibid., p. 13.
44. Goodhart, 1984, p. 5.
45. Ibid., pp. 23, 28, and 31.
46. One Nation Group, 1992, p. 9.
47. Ibid., p. 5.
48. One Nation Group, 1996, p. 13.
49. Ibid., p. 14.
50. Ian Budge and David Robertson had initially directed this ECPR group before its comparative manifesto collection was taken over by the WZB; see Budge, 2001, pp. 210–223.
51. See Bara and Budge, 2001, p. 28; Budge et al., 2001: for a comprehensive description of these procedures.
52. I owe a debt of gratitude to Joe Organ, then a research student at Leeds University, who coded all the One Nation pamphlets and the housing sections of the Campaign Guides. I would also like to thank Andrea Volkens, of the Wissenschaftzentrum, Berlin, for her generous help and her advice, which helped tremendously towards an understanding of the MRG coding procedures.
53. Budge et al., 2001, p. 2.
54. Bara and Budge, 2001, p. 29.
55. Ibid.
56. See Budge, 1987, p. 25.
57. This Guide was produced in 1977 with an expectation of the imminent collapse of the Callaghan government, which, of course, lasted in coalition to 1979.
58. Budge, 1999, p. 7.
59. One Nation Group, 1996, p. 8.
60. One Nation Group, 1992, p. 3.
61. Rodgers papers: OP27/8: One Nation Minutes, February 2, 1966.
62. Rodgers papers: OP27/8: One Nation Minutes, March 22, 1967.
63. Rodgers papers: OP27/8: One Nation Minutes, November 29, 1967; and on November 27, 1968, there was general agreement that the pound should float. "Enoch much cross questioned. Apparently it would solve all our problems over night."
64. Brittan, 1968, p. 125.
65. Ramsden, 1987, p. 62.
66. Rodgers papers: OP27/8: One Nation Minutes, December 6, 1967.
67. Alport papers: Box 37, One Nation Minutes, July 23, 1951.

68.  Rodgers papers: OP27/8: One Nation Minutes, July 12, 1967.
69.  Raison, 1964, p. 40.
70.  Ibid., p. 140.
71.  Ibid., p. 28.
72.  One Nation Group, 1996, p. 8.

# CHAPTER FOUR

# Skilled Propaganda from Ill-Intentioned "Friends"

Not since a radical minority in the Russian Social Democratic Party assigned to themselves the "majority" label—Bolshevik—have we had such a successful hegemonic exploitation of a term as that found in the willful distortion of One Nation by sections of the political commentariat, ably assisted of course by some Conservatives on both the left and the right of the party. Notwithstanding the evidence to the contrary as outlined in the previous chapter, and as delineated in the content analysis of the One Nation group's published work, the received wisdom is to portray One Nation in terms of an extended state approach to wealth creation in sharp contrast to the policies pursued by neoliberal Conservative Ministers in the Thatcher era; many of whom, ironically, had belonged to the One Nation group.

> A curious coded language came to be used by Conservative critics including some inside the Cabinet. If a minister talked about One Nation and praised Disraeli, it was a safe assumption that he was attacking Mrs Thatcher and Sir Geoffrey Howe.[1]

Thus, from the late 1970s, with the help of what at best can only be described as lazy journalism, contemporary commentators utilized One Nation as a coded term to denote opposition to Thatcherism.[2] By 1996, the One Nation group thought it necessary to expose the fallacy in such "coded criticism" and by extension the idea that the previous 17 years of Conservative Party policy was somehow not part of the Conservative tradition.

> It has been claimed that the ideals and traditions of One Nation Conservatism no longer lie in the mainstream of Tory Party thinking. The pages which follow totally refute, contradict and destroy this notion. They show that the One Nation view of society—resting on individual rights and duties and on moral obligations of family life—remains, as it has done all along, the founding concept on which modern Toryism rests. Skilled propaganda from critics and ill intentioned "friends" has sought to portray a different picture of today's Conservative Party—a parodied cameo of grasping individuals hell-bent on

selfish gain. But at no time has the Tory emphasis on duty towards others, on family values or on civic responsibility changed.[3]

Especially ridiculous, for the One Nation group, was the claim by New Labour to the title of One Nation. The group was in no doubt that "PR-conscious politicians want to grab" the mantle of One Nation because of its "powerful brand name attractions" but for the One Nation group itself the mantle stopped short of advocating "state-driven, we know best," policy packages.[4] However, with a "bias against understanding" so prevalent in the contemporary mass media,[5] and the fact that the media could exploit such an eloquent term to describe the internal opposition to Thatcher's policies, the scene was set for those controversial and provocative headlines that "sell news." Not only could the age old complex and problematic debate within the party over the efficacy of state intervention be simplified but as a bonus a compelling concept could be applied to show putative government insensitivity on unemployment and lack of sympathy with the plight of the poor. As we shall see, such willful distortion and hegemonic exploitation of the One Nation term was to become particularly evident in the critique by Ian Gilmour. Of course, the extended state tradition was, and is, a constituent part of the "dual nature" of Conservative Party ideology, which has a long and distinguished history of contributing to that necessary process of "party renewal." But such crude and sometimes personal attacks by "ill-intentioned friends," that implied a lack of concern from Conservative colleagues over the welfare of the whole nation, was to merely discredit the extended state position within the party for some considerable period of time. Much of this debate on the efficacy of state intervention was carried out in the letter columns of the newspapers and there is no doubt that the media accepted and promoted with alacrity an exaggerated and distorted dichotomy of "One Nation and Thatcherism."[6]

A flavor of such exchanges in the debate can be found in the pages of *The Times* in the early years of Thatcher's premiership and usually around the time of the Conservative Party conference. What we find is an augmentation of an already developing but erroneous theme that the One Nation tradition is exclusive to an extended state and economically interventionist approach to governance and thus diametrically opposed to the policies pursued by the Thatcher government, with the concomitant leitmotiv that only "extended state" Conservatives are concerned with the less fortunate in society. For example, Cub Alport believed that the leadership of the party had fallen below the ideals of his generation and that the spirit of One Nation within the party was created in order to "capture and hold the middle ground" and "to wean" the party away from the "hard-faced business men who had done well out of the second world war."[7] However, a close perusal of all the One Nation documents, let alone that of 1950, will show that such a concept as the "middle ground" is not mentioned nor indeed is the notion of "hard-faced business men," which was associated more with the era of Baldwin and a previous war. Ian Gilmour, who had been sacked from the Government by Mrs Thatcher, thought it wrong that her policies should consciously impact inimically upon the least well off in society and that the Thatcher fight against inflation was a "blot on the Tory Tradition"; as there was no compassion shown for the unemployed.[8] In the same issue, Ted Heath insinuated that the group that was now leading the party were less caring and less compassionate than him.

Interestingly, with regard to such views, Gilbert Longden received a letter from the editor of *The Times*, dated the October 11, 1982, which stated: "As you will see from the attached proof, the Editor had hoped to print your recent letter in the correspondence columns. Unfortunately this has not after all been possible, but your comments have been read with interest."[9] This was to be just one of many instances where Longden endeavored to challenge, through the press, the increasingly orthodox view that One Nation represented some "statist" position in the party and that Thatcherism in some way deviated from the One Nation approach. In the letter that was not published we find:

> To take the NHS as an example ought we to insist that every man, woman and child must make do with what the state can provide?, or should we encourage (not of course compel) people to pay by insurance for their own medical care and thus leave more resources with which to achieve the ideal of making the public services as good as anything one can buy outside it? I repudiate the accusation that those who prefer the second way are less "caring" or "compassionate" and I often wonder how many Conservatives today have actually read *One Nation*, which seems recently to have become the bible of the "wets."[10]

In the reply to the editor, on October 16, 1982, Longden regretted that *The Times* did not feel able to publish his letter but pointed out that: "the view of the Welfare State as expressed in 'One Nation' is admirably summed up in Sir John Hoskyns's letter in your issue today" and he further mused on how "another of the authors of 'One Nation' seems to have made another of his U-turns."[11] Hoskyns, who had recently headed the number ten policy unit, had commented:

> As ever those who question any aspect of the welfare state are assumed to be less concerned about human suffering than those who defend it. No one is proposing that the state disowns responsibility for those who genuinely cannot help themselves. The question is whether the state should provide large amounts of goods and services "free" for almost the entire population. This is only partly a matter of economics. It is also, and perhaps more importantly, about the effect on attitudes and behaviour of transferring responsibilities to the state, from people who could perfectly well discharge those responsibilities for themselves.[12]

And, as early as 1975 Keith Joseph defended the Conservative neoliberal position against the charge that it lacked concern for those who were relatively disadvantaged in society, while espousing the belief that free competitive markets actually advanced opportunities for all. After receiving a letter from a Sheffield lady, which included the entreaty—"my plea is do not drift too far to the right and so pass out of sight of thousands like myself, ordinary working class people who vote Conservative" —he replied:

> Your letter so kindly meant was thoughtful. But can you not accept that we only suggest what we suggest because we are convinced that present policies and, to some extent, passed policies are bad for ordinary people, for ordinary working class people, however they vote. The sort of policies we want adopted—policies that encourage talent and enterprise and thrift, all within the law and subject to competition where applicable, are those that have made our neighbouring countries more prosperous with better social services and less poverty than here.[13]

Of course, this criticism from Keith Joseph that not only highlighted the egregious nature of Labour's "present policies" but the "passed policies" of Conservative administrations as well was to become an integral part of a developing critique, which would soon have as its eponymous title, Thatcherism. In the period between the two general elections of 1974, Joseph delivered a series of provocative *mea culpa* speeches that effectively denounced previous Conservative Party policy. He believed that such policy, with which many Conservatives like himself must take responsibility, had debilitated economic life and society for over 30 years; through the socialistic fashions that *every* postwar government had followed, which had led to a "present nightmare" where governments thought it impractical to reverse the accumulating detritus of socialism. Indeed, in 1975 he made the now famous announcement of his "conversion" to Conservatism, as he had not previously understood the essential aspects of its nature.[14] Notwithstanding this claim for conversion,[15] we will see that there is far more consistency to Joseph's views, throughout the postwar years, than such a claim would imply. No doubt such a claim was made more with an eye to newspaper column inches and to the utilization of the powerful theme of "change" in electoral appeals.[16] But, crucially, the unintended consequence of such a strategy was the acquiescence in the left's successful hegemonic exploitation of the One Nation term. Mrs Thatcher may well have stressed her "one nationer" status, with particular comparison to the claims of the Labour party,[17] but in their eagerness to appear radical and to distance themselves from a putative but spurious consensus period a number of the Thatcherites were to be just as culpable, as those on the left of the party, for the long term damage to that ideological canopy so essential for self- renewal—the ethos that is *One Nation*.

It can be argued that the neoliberal rhetoric by Joseph in the 1970s had parallels with the One Nation group's 1954 critique of Butler's and the party's interwar "quasi-nationalization" and in that sense was again a manifestation of political recrudescence within the ranks of the party. But here the malign element of political recrudescence could not be clearer, with a small minority on the left of the party aiming to marginalize, or even to eradicate, the free market tradition in the party (which the One Nation group itself had dated all the way back to Lord Liverpool); while, astonishingly, for short-term gain some of the advocates of the free market tradition willingly acquiesced in this delegitimization project. Thus, while mindful of the role of certain Conservative neoliberals in distancing themselves from the One Nation ethos, this chapter challenges a certain portrayal of One Nation as a group exclusively on the left of the party as there is a need for an effective exposure of what has erroneously become the received wisdom. To demonstrate just how distorted and pervasive such a view has become, this "selective account" is analyzed below, along with the tendency of some extended state Conservatives to enthusiastically promote the formal coalition of parties in the British body politic. But, first we examine the process whereby those on the left of the party have shown a tendency to construct a form of discourse hegemony when it comes to the use of the One Nation term.

## A Great Moving Left Show

A common theme running through the press reports, with regards to the publication of the One Nation pamphlet and the formation of the group in early October 1950, is the pivotal role of Iain Macleod. For example, *The Times*, October 5, 1950, referred to the work of the group "under the chairmanship of Mr Iain Macleod" and *The Observer*, of October 8, 1950, went much further in declaring:

> The group of newly elected Conservative MPs who have produced a pamphlet called One Nation are the first sign in the present Parliament of a ginger group within the party. Under the careful leadership of Iain Macleod they are scrupulously avoiding any suggestion of rebellion or even lack of discipline. It was while working in the Conservative Central Office as head of the home affairs department that Macleod absorbed from R.A. Butler this strong interest in improving the social services which is the main theme of One Nation. With this wide knowledge of internal Conservative politics Macleod feels certain that it would be suicidal to attempt the sort of shock tactics which brought such notoriety to the Keep Left Group.

In Chapter 1, we encountered the irritation of the members of the group concerning this "complete travesty of the facts" that described One Nation as a group "gathered around" Macleod. And, what is never in doubt, in any discussion of the particular talents of Iain Macleod, is his capacity for self-publicity combined with a peerless ambition among the 1950 intake of Conservative MPs. "Macleod proved himself the most effective political salesman and, to the chagrin of some other members, rather stole the show at the launch [of the 1950 One Nation pamphlet] being widely—and wrongly—described in the press as the group's chairman."[18]. Of particular interest here, is Macleod's relationship with James Margach, the political correspondent of the *Sunday Times*, with whom he was periodically a close political confidant.[19] In November 1959, Margach, under the by-line "a student of politics," penned a quite politically preposterous article on the ideological character of the One Nation group but which was, nevertheless, seminal in developing such an erroneous view of One Nation. In this article he uses the One Nation group and its presence within an officer corps appointed to command the various backbench committees, to imply that the rank and file of the parliamentary party would be "centrist" and not "lurch ominously to the right" after the 1959 election. He refers to the "Macleod–Heath" group, as bizarrely they now become solely "the founding fathers of the One Nation group" and that the group was formed by them "deliberately to correct the dangers of Right-wing reaction." The pamphlets, *Change Is Our Ally* and *The Responsible Society*, are mentioned only in passing so as not to detract from the "spin" that: "Mr Macleod and his colleagues undoubtedly helped the Tory Party to come to terms with the social revolution of the post war world and to develop a progressive approach to health, education, housing and other social services."[20] Margach failed not only in a diligent reading of the One Nation pamphlets but appears to be willfully unaware of Gilbert Longden's comments—made at the launch of *The Responsible Society* in March 1959 as outlined in the previous chapter—and indeed of the report in his sister paper, *The Times* March 24, 1959, which emphasized that the group advocated policy that was "halting and indeed reversing the trend towards state domination." Of course, one may immediately think of Enoch Powell and the problem here with "fit" for his views but Margach was obviously in no mood to allow reality to interfere in such a political yarn:

> So far so good. But here the cynic would enter a *caveat*. Is Enoch Powell a progressive, a Tory Fabian or a reformist? Though in social policies he has often been further Left than most other Tories, since he resigned from the Macmillan Government with the Thorneycroft-Birch-Powell Treasury team two years ago he has been regarded as the watchdog of the Right in protecting the purity of Tory financial thinking. . . . But the truth is that Mr Powell is not so far Right as many people imagine; his social contributions to One Nation writing could withstand the most stringent tests of Butskellism.[21]

It is just so difficult to comprehend how anyone could interpret *Change is Our Ally* in Butskellite terms. However, Margach manages to turn reality on its head and he ends his article with the implicit message that the 70-odd new Conservative MPs from the 1959 cohort have been strongly influenced by the One Nation approach to politics and that their instinct will be to "back the man with an established reputation for pioneering new ideas," no doubt that man being

Mr Iain Macleod. Three years later and Macleod was offering a similar left of centre interpretation of One Nation which praised Macmillan's *dirigiste* regional policies for Wales and Scotland, in particular the steel strip mills located, by the government, at Llanwern and Ravenscraig respectively; along with £75 million in aid for job creation. Indeed, in this four page leaflet produced in 1962, which he entitled *One Nation*, Iain Macleod linked the approach of the One Nation group closely to the work of Lord Hailsham and the Tory Reform Group (TRG), to RAB Butler, and to the work over the years of the Prime Minister, Harold Macmillan.[22] But, by now we should be well aware of the misgivings the group had with some of the policy prescriptions associated with RAB Butler; one may even venture to stress the "contingent considerabilities" in their relationship. And, even though a minute in 1951 indicates that the group did dine with the members of the "Tory Reform [Committee]," there was never any formal connection let alone a conflation of views.[23] Importantly, in the following chapter, we shall see that the lines of division in the views of the membership of such groups are as fluid as the ideology of the party itself and that over the years there was always cross membership of One Nation with other dining groups on both the left and the right of the party; and even today there are joint membership of the "Nation" with such groups on the left as "Nick's Diner," as with the "No Turning Back Group" on the right of the party.

But, it was to be the dining groups and the extra parliamentary groups on the left of the party that were to continue with this fabrication of prioritizing Macleod's role in the group and with it the tendency for discourse hegemony regarding the One Nation term. "Pressure For Economic and Social Toryism" (PEST) was formed in 1963 by university undergraduates and London journalists and was supported by such Tory luminaries as Edward Boyle and of course, Iain Macleod. It urged the Tory Party "to lead a 'One Nation' Britain into an outward-looking Euro–Atlantic partnership and to follow policies at home which will induce economic efficiency and ensure social freedom."[24] On September 20, 1975 the TRG was formed by the merger of PEST with two smaller regionally based groups, the MACLEOD Group based in the north-west and the Social Tory Action Group (STAG) based in the south, and in the TRG New Year message of 1976, Bill Shearman stated:

> The Party must continue to represent all sections of the community, must pledge itself to end class conflict and govern again on the basis of Disraeli's One Nation . . . The way forward to a genuine renaissance of ideas lies in the traditional Tory concern for the social conditions of the people and a society based on fairness, where exploitation by one group by another is curtailed by State intervention.[25]

The TRG's president was Nicholas Scott of "Nick's diner" fame but more importantly the vice president was Robert Carr and another guest speaker of note at its inaugural meeting was Ian Gilmour. Carr and Gilmour were close friends of Macleod, and Gilmour became a political acolyte of Macleod in the 1960s. In November 1962, Macleod persuaded Gilmour, then owner and editor of *The Spectator*, to stand for parliament in the by-election in Central Norfolk.[26] Indeed, in Shepherd's book on Macleod, the similarity in their views is uncanny, to the extent that Macleod's views and actual words are often uttered through Gilmour. Although Gilmour's views on income policies were out of step with the rest of the One Nation group in 1967,[27] and that the party's policy on this issue for the 1970 election echoed the sentiments of a 1968 conference motion which declared that "attempts to control prices and incomes by statute are at complete variance with the basic Conservative principle of free enterprise"[28]; we find, as the 1970 election drew near, that Macleod tells Gilmour "that there would have to be an incomes policy of some sort."[29] But, we should note David Howell's comments regarding his attempt to "introduce Macleod to markets," in the period running up to the silent revolution of 1970, as Macleod was "very willing to go along with it," in fact declaring: "I don't understand what you young chaps are saying but I am willing to learn."[30] Indeed, while criticizing the stridency of Mrs Thatcher's approach and that of other neoliberals like Norman Tebbit, Howell portrayed Gilmour as the paternalist rich aristocrat who wanted to give the workers bread and who was right out on the other wing of the party; and that such strident approaches from both sides were making it "harder and harder to create a feeling of unity as people started to get cross with one another."[31] However, Macleod did not live to see such a claim on incomes policy vindicated in the post 1972 U-turns of Edward Heath or to see his predisposition for indicative planning and state intervention taken up by Gilmour and promoted with an ever increasing level of vigor and zeal in direct proportion to the electoral success of Thatcher and the free market supply side policy prescription, which prevailed after 1975. Indeed, in the very year that the One Nation group expressed their incredulity at New Labour's "especially ridiculous" claim to be One Nation, Gilmour believed: "that both Tony Blair's New Labour and the Liberal Democrats also show signs of being closer to One Nation Toryism than does Major's government."[32] And also in 1996, before crossing the floor to join the Labour party, Peter Temple-Morris repeats such self-deception by emphasizing the prominence of Macleod and Heath in the 1950s group.[33] In fact, Heath had to resign from the group in 1951 and Macleod in 1952, both being ineligible to attend as members of the government until the loss of office in 1964. But, in this edition of the TRG's journal, *Reformer*, we see this travesty of the actual history of the group along with the selective utilization of the One Nation term:

> The party's left, or One Nation, wing has too often been modest in its pronouncements and gentlemanly in it political activity [w]hile the right wing have been comprised of wholly enthusiastic zealots, with all the commitment that implies . . . We welcome Peter Temple-Morris's article in this magazine—and his recent high profile . . . If it is true that half the cabinet,

and a significant proportion of the parliamentary party, adhere to Macleod's oft articulated values of One Nation, then it is time they stopped being so shy about saying so . . .[34]

Such a willfully obtuse neglect of the party's adherence to Maude's, Powell's, and Joseph's oft articulated values of One Nation became the entrenched position for the left throughout the 1980s and for most of the 1990s before more thoughtful Conservatives from the Party's left wing, such as Alistair Burt and Damian Green, could once again contribute seriously to that creative tension so necessary for self-renewal. In a TRG Macmillan lecture in 2000, Green stressed that Mrs Thatcher's policy prescriptions were a force for good and those people, inside and outside of the party, who opposed free markets, free trade, individual responsibility, and limited government for the 1980s and 1990s were quite simply wrong. And while these policy prescriptions were relevant for those times Green also emphasized that the lesson to be drawn was that "the underlying principles that lie behind One Nation Conservatism need to be re-invented in every generation to make them relevant." Indeed, with regard to both traditions within Conservative ideology, Green speaks of the need for a "creative synthesis" for future policy prescription, and we return to this in a concluding chapter when the future of the party, under Cameron, is examined.[35] However, this willful distortion of the history of the One Nation group and of the Conservative Party per se, as outlined in these hegemonic claims from some on the left of the party, is examined in the next section through a detailed look at the work of such "enthusiastic zealots" as Ian Gilmour, with Cub Alport in suitably retrospective supportive mode.

## Retrospective Procrustean Polemics

Gilmour once observed that in ideological wars truth is the first causality due to "a rewriting of the history of the very recent past, if not the present"[36]; and that this was a conspicuous feature of the Thatcher years. Admittedly so, but here we find Gilmour et al. in an enthusiastic and wholehearted participation in such an exercise. Their retrospective accounts of the history of the One Nation group and of the party postwar become "Procrustean polemics," which merely push, pull, stretch, and compress material to "fit" a particular interpretation of One Nation. Writing in 1980, Alport corroborated Maude's account of the formation of the group, with Gilbert Longden named as the first recruit, and that:

> We had no chairman, but for the purposes of the pamphlet Iain Macleod was the collator, Angus Maude, the editor and, in due course Enoch Powell acted as secretary. It was Angus Maude who suggested the title One Nation for our book which had an immediate and remarkable success.[37]

However, in an article written for the *Spectator* in March 1996 history is now apparently rewritten so as to fit with the left's privileging of Iain Macleod's role. "One of the first of our colleagues whom we invited to join was Iain Macleod. It was he who suggested that we should call ourselves One Nation . . . ."[38] He then goes on to suggest that the political attitude of the group could be discerned in a decision to invite Nye Bevan to dine with them at Lord Lambton's House.[39] Of course, what he conveniently fails to disclose is the fact that he was not present when this was discussed; having resigned in December 1953 due to personal reasons and not being invited back until December 12, 1954. In fact, what Alport refers to here is a minute of November 23, 1954: "Agreed subject to opinion of absent members, to invite Aneurin Bevan to dine with the Group *chez* Lord Lambton," but somehow he managed to miss the minute of a fortnight later which read: "Resolved that Aneurin Bevan be NOT invited."[40] In isolation such comments could be dismissed as superficial waffle thus having a greater propensity for memory lapse but their cumulative weight leads to the conclusion that what we really have is a systematic rewriting of the recent history of the party to color the present perception of One Nation. And, we will see that such retrospective distortion is epitomized in the polemic, *Whatever Happened to the Tories*[41]

Immediately, in this text, we find that Macleod is given the leading role in the group and it is he who suggests the title of One Nation and rather surprisingly only the *One Nation* pamphlet exists in the book, others like *Change is Our Ally* in 1954 or the *Responsible Society* of 1959 are conveniently airbrushed from Conservative Party history in order to maintain the thesis. And neither is Gilbert Longden acknowledged in this work, and yet he was one of the three founding members of One Nation. But, this may be due to his retrospective article in 1985 which stressed the affinity of One Nation with Thatcherism and which was published in *Crossbow* after being rejected by Bill Deedes at the *Daily Telegraph*.[42] Indeed, Gilmour's own earlier views appear to receive the same treatment, in that they are ignored in order to maintain a level of consistency in the critique of the limited state approach and it would appear that there is nothing at all from the right of the party that can be considered "traditionally Conservative." For instance, Keith Joseph's view on "the socialistic fashions," as practiced by both the major parties since the war, is rubbished because this "socialist 'ratchet effect' of the fifties, sixties and seventies [was] an invention of the New Right."[43] However, compare this with Gilmour's opinion in 1977, when he shared the view that council house sales were an excellent way to reverse "the concentration of power in the state" and that the aim of Conservative policy should be to sell very large numbers, on the easiest possible terms, so that a decisive downward twist could thereby be given to the "ratchet effect" of socialism.[44] Moreover, we know that the One Nation group, as early as 1954, was criticizing the quasi-nationalization inherent within pre- and postwar Conservative policy and just ten months before Gilmour became the principal shareholder and editor of the *Spectator*, the journal itself, in a leader, was in accord with such an interpretation.

The journal welcomed the explicit criticism of state intervention in the *Change is Our Ally* booklet and the significant contribution of the group towards a necessary intellectual basis for party policy, before concluding:

> This argument is bound to become louder and shriller in the face of the One Nation group's contention that the dismantling process [of controls and regulations in industry] has not gone far enough. Nor are the Tory intellectuals likely to escape opposition within the ranks of their own party, for there are still plenty of Tories who cling to the doctrine of "Me Too." That doctrine, of painless Socialism applied by Tories, was most fully stated in *The Right Road for Britain*, a curious document which appeared in the most dangerous of all political colours, Sky-Blue-Pink.[45]

And, similar to Joseph's use of the "ratchet of socialism," this "Me Too Doctrine" was described by Viscount Hinchingbrooke as the "stairway to socialism." Hinchingbrooke, by then, was complaining that the "rather dismal Mr Butskell"—who had been buried some time ago but whose ghostly spirit was a major constraint on the equal opportunity for all to rise to whatever level of wealth their ability could command—was the "product of both political parties. His blood was composed of the red corpuscles of socialist doctrinaire prejudice and the white corpuscles of Conservative doctrinaire pusillanimity."[46] Indeed, Hinchingbrooke is a very good example of the fluidity of thought in the Conservative Party and which is left undeveloped in the *Whatever Happened to the Tories* text so as to prosecute the claim that only extended state, economic interventionist Conservatives are "true" Conservatives. For example, approbation is given to Hinchingbrooke for his work in the Tory Reform Committee of the 1940s but as he is on the right of the party by the 1950s he is criticized as part of the Suez "blue blood and thunder brigade" of backbenchers; to which Enoch Powell and Angus Maude also belonged.[47] And, rather than explain the "dual nature" of Conservative Party ideology and with it the mechanisms for renewal that can facilitate such ideological movement within the party, the approach is more the delineation of periods when individuals either act in a Conservative One Nation fashion—that is as enthusiastic dispensers of public money—or being beyond the pale as "prophets of Thatcherism." The Thorneycroft-Birch-Powell Treasury team resignation from the Macmillan government, over the level of public expenditure, is a good example of this approach[48]; where it is claimed that Thorneycroft is led astray by Birch and Powell, "who in their different ways are both rather mad," as it was difficult to discern any great issue of principle over such a "fairly small sum" as £50 million more in expenditure.[49]

This delegitimization of the limited state tradition within the party, in such a procrustean polemic, is extremely difficult to maintain; thus the search for consistency by praising a Conservative *prelapsarian* period in which individuals are not defiled by New Right ideology. In this context, Nigel Birch before 1958 is "far from being a prophet of Thatcherism," evidenced by his "fine little book in 1949," which surprisingly it is claimed Enoch Powell failed to mention in a biography of Birch.[50] Of course, we know that the One Nation group was willing to support Birch's election to the finance committee in 1961,[51] just three years after his treasury resignation, and in 1954 Birch is fulsome in his praise for the *Change is Our Ally* booklet, intimating that he agreed with almost all that was said by One Nation in this publication, before going on to say:

> Lots of us did try when the Socialists were in power to put across some of these ideas, both in the House and on the platform. But the tide of nonsense was running so high that we did not get very far. The tide is now on the ebb and I can't help feeling it may be right to try again.[52]

And, from this "fine little 1949 book," entitled *The Conservative Party*, we find that any consistency in views belong with Birch, and indeed it is surprising that Powell did not mention his views, as Birch quotes Bertrand de Jouvenel in stressing that the Conservative Party need not be pessimistic concerning "our standard of life and the scope for individual choice and decision." Birch then states in the conclusion to the book:

> We have seen in the Liberals an inability to deal with the dangers that face us and in the Socialists an absence of the will and faith that are needed. The Conservatives remain. . . . They know that the answer to slavery is not a milder form of slavery but freedom. They know that if Britain is to regain her position in world trade, if she is to compete with America, she will need to have American standards of efficiency and that these are not likely to be attained by wholesale collectivism but by a revived, reinvigorated and up-to-date capitalism.[53]

Thus, this wonderful little book by Birch in 1949 merely refutes the airbrushing exercise that attempts to exclude the free market and limited state views from the Conservative Party tradition. Gilmour was sacked by Thatcher in September 1981 and on October 15, 1981 the Party's chairman, Cecil Parkinson, pointed out to him that: "I think it is too easy to exaggerate the scale of the 'great divide.' I personally do not believe that there is such a huge gap."[54] But, if such a gaping lacuna did indeed exist between the dual elements of the Conservative Party ideology, which now seemed unbridgeable as a consequence of the malign element of political recrudescence, then Gilmour had been a major, if not the principal, contributor to the extent of that divide; however much he strived to brand others as the deleterious zealots. Interestingly, on the previous evening of October 14, 1981 Gilmour had drafted notes for a speech, which asserted that:

> Every politician has convictions and every politician seeks to build a consensus of some sort. Otherwise, at least in a democracy, his convictions will be

irrelevant to everybody but himself, since they will never be translated into action. The only controversial point is how wide the consensus should be. Plainly, a Tory politician will hope to build as wide a consensus as possible.[55]

In the next section, the predilection for consensus and coalition formation among the left of the party is examined but ironically, on the evidence presented in the *Whatever Happened to the Tories* book, plainly the consensus was not wide enough to accommodate those Conservatives from the New Right. However much we accept such a book as a polemic and address it as such there is nevertheless a rather reprehensible suggestion that merits our excoriation and condemnation, which is the claim that support for the appeasement of Hitler was only to be found on the right of the party.[56] Astonishingly, in this context, the role of one of the arch appeasers, RAB Butler, is conspicuous by its absence. In fact, Butler, as late as the summer of 1939, wanted to "influence the Poles" as Herr "Goering was still working for peace."[57] And, there is the strong impression that Butler's appeasement actually bordered on the treasonable when he informed a neutral Swedish Minister in July 1940 that "no diehards would be allowed to stand in the way of a compromise peace with Germany if one was felt desirable."[58] For some in the party this attack on "diehards" has been a particular feature of their "concessionary conservatism."

## Concessionary Conservatism

In March 2006, Ken Clarke urged the Liberal Democrats to join with the Conservatives to form a coalition if after the next election there was no outright majority in the House of Commons. He believed that Sir Menzies Campbell had championed his "radical roots" during the Liberal Democrat leadership contest of that year and that in essence Sir Menzies was "an old Tory." Clarke went on to claim: "He is someone Conservatives can do business with . . . I am glad to say the fates could condemn the Conservatives and the Liberals to form a coalition."[59] In this section then an analysis is undertaken of the apparent correlation between some extended state Conservatives with an aim "to build as wide a consensus as possible"; in short, the predilection of some Conservatives to participate in what Disraeli alluded to in *Coningsby* as: "concessionary Conservatism."[60] However, it will be shown that traditionally the Conservative Party has been anything but "glad" about the need to form a coalition, however much they have actually participated in them throughout their long history. Indeed, Austen Chamberlain was to lose the leadership of the party over just such an issue.[61] Moreover, such "concessionary Conservatism" as reflected in the desire to form a coalition has been considered a form of weakness even by those who would not shrink from greater governmental intervention,[62] and that a convincing explanation of Britain's postwar decline sprang from this desire to bring such harmony to society.[63] Thus, we will see that it is erroneous to equate One Nation with the concessionary politics of coalition governance or with the idea of "me too socialism" that some "right out on the other wing" of the Conservative Party believe is encapsulated within the very idea of coalition politics.

Indeed, in Birch's fine little book of 1949 he dates the antipathy in the party towards such a "fate" back to the last quarter of the eighteenth century. "The experiment ended with the loss of the American colonies and the unprincipled coalition between Fox and North. From these days may be dated the Conservative dislike of coalitions."[64] And, in the budget speech of 1852, Disraeli voiced the now famous condemnatory remarks about not submitting to the degradation of others with regards to coalition: "The combination may be successful. A Coalition has before this been successful. But Coalitions though successful have always found this, that their triumph has been brief. This too I know, that England does not love Coalitions."[65] By its very nature a coalition means a considerable extension to the concessionary politics that is normally found *within* British parties, and in his novel *Coningsby*, Disraeli was quite scathing about what he perceived to be the concessions that Peel had submitted the party to:

> The duke talks to me of Conservative principles; but he does not inform me what they are. I observe indeed a party in the State whose rule it is to consent to no change, until it is clamourously called for, and then instantly to yield; but those are concessionary, not Conservative principles.[66]

England may not love coalitions but some on the left of the Conservative Party have flirted enthusiastically with the idea: Ken Clarke being just the most recent example in a long line of extended state Conservatives who have not only followed Macleod in the goal to appropriate the One Nation term but who have advocated an extension of this concessionary approach to governance *between* the parties. Just ten months before the Conservative victory at the election of 1951, Iain Macleod was writing to Gilbert Longden, in strictest confidence, about the One Nation group giving consideration to the idea of a coalition. The early 1950s were years of anxiety concerning the threat from communism and the potential for concomitant hostilities on a global scale. Thus, Macleod, in his letter, noted that there was a good deal of talk at that moment concerning the possibility of a coalition and of the high level of public support for it and, moreover, that the newspapers were reporting that backbenchers were having conversations about such an arrangement. Macleod intended to bring the matter up for discussion at a One Nation dinner and sounded out Longden on the potential views of the others. He added:

> As it happens I believe that amongst the Socialists is Paget of Northampton, who spoke to me some time ago asking me what my views would be about a Coalition on the general basis that the Socialists kept the Social Services and Economic posts and that we took over the Defence, Imperial and Foreign.

Apart from press comment there are a great number of other inferences that point to there being something in this although I do not want to put them all in a letter. . . . It may be, of course, that we cannot reach agreement, but this, above everything else, is the precisely the sort of subject on which the voice of a group is of importance where the individual opinions count for little or nothing.[67]

Longden replied a few days later and was unequivocally against pointing out that it was a grievous business if MPs now act as delegates because the people in the street are moved by a weariness and distrust of party politics.

I think you have done the Group a Service in having thus drawn its collective attention to the Whisperings of the advocates of Coalition. . . . But we are not delegates, but leaders of our respective flocks along paths which we think it is in the Country's best interests that they should travel. In that capacity, I am motivated by the fast-held belief that there is nothing about Socialism, except perhaps the intentions of its sincere adherents, that is not UTTERLY BAD for our Country and for every one of its inhabitants. I should myself therefore be against Coalition now on the grounds: (a) that you will not cast out the Devil by allying yourself with Beelzebub; (b) that it would give added publicity to the Communists and fellow-travellers—the Bevans, Foots, Dribergs, horresco referens!—who would become the official opposition; (c) that the initiative (if any) must come from the Government and that therefore presumably Attlee would remain Prime Minister, and a Socialist would retain the Exchequer.[68]

When the subject was debated at the One Nation dinner on January 23, 1951, with Iain Macleod present, there was now a collective "shudder to relate" the implications of this coalition idea: "Agreed (Alport dissenting) that any proposals for coalition be attacked and denounced."[69] We see that Alport certainly did not think the concept "too horrible for words" but he was one of the foremost and consistent advocates of coalition politics within the party. When reviewing a prospective publication while at the Conservative Political Centre in 1949—which *inter alia* called for the Conservative Party to transmogrify into the "Middle party"—Alport expressed the view that although a great many people seek the middle way in politics there needs to be a spontaneous coming together of people from different parties, following a realignment at the Parliamentary level, to give practical expression to such a hope.[70] But, by the late 1960s, Alport was clearly impatient with the idea of spontaneity and with the help of Max Beloff, Gladstone Professor of Government at All Souls Oxford, he actively involved himself in the cause of coalition. Beloff wrote to Alport in early January 1968 detailing progress to date, with the sentiment that "coalition was not just desirable but inevitable." However, Alport replied that when he had broached the subject in the House of Lords, Frank Longford and

Toby Aldington (Toby Low, formally of the One Nation group) had "soundly berated him" and that the "newspapers took no notice."[71] On becoming a life peer in 1961 Alport had left the Commons to take up a position as High Commissioner in Rhodesia and Nyasaland and he later returned to Rhodesia as an emissary of Harold Wilson in 1967 but similar to how Tony Blair would later utilize Tories, like Clarke and Heseltine over Europe, it was to mightily displease many within the ranks of the Conservative Party.[72]

Of course, in the crisis of governance between the 1974 elections, Ted Heath had offered the Liberals places in a coalition Cabinet. But, after being snubbed by Jeremy Thorpe he still maintained the rhetoric of coalition politics, speaking of a government of national unity with which he planned to develop the National Economic Development Council (NEDDY) into a televised forum that would publicly propose the necessary course of action. And the One Nation MP Maurice Macmillan had supported a call for a government of national unity five months earlier.[73] This was a time when many Conservatives gave serious consideration to a coalition, Longden himself had talked of one but believed that it was not enough that this cooperation between the "coalition of moderates" be merely antisocialist, he believed they must agree on a positive program, which would "stabilize our money, restore self-confidence and ethical and moral standards."[74] In this climate Alport took the opportunity to publish a "Draft Manifesto for a National Government" in the *Spectator* on September 14, 1974 but before doing so he had roundly criticized Ted Heath and the failings of his government in March 1974.

> Although I have been one of your persistent critics in the Conservative party and realise that advice from such a quarter may not be very agreeable, I am not sure that the advice you have been receiving recently has been either very wise or objective. My advice to you now is to resign from the leadership of the Conservative party and to offer, as you would do, to serve the Nation and the Party in any other capacity which seemed to be right. . . . I would like, as you know, to see a grand coalition . . . the Conservative party must get itself into a position of being seen to be a spearhead of national unity and being able to attract back to it the support it lost to Liberals and Labour.[75]

In 1977 Alport wrote a similar letter to Peter Thorneycroft, the Party chairman, complaining about Thatcher's leadership and her criticism of the Labour party because to "identify the whole party with Marxism does nothing except weaken the position of the Social Democrats with whom the Tory Party has, since Randolph Churchill's time, had an affinity." Thorneycroft replied that he was misguided and that he should pop in to Central Office to watch a video of Thatcher's distinguished performance on *Panorama*, which "anyone who would claim to call himself or herself a Conservative would, I feel, find themselves in much agreement."[76] In 1984, Lord Denham deemed it necessary to withdraw the party whip from Alport in the House of Lords because of his constant criticism of Government policy and his outspoken attacks on Mrs Thatcher.[77] There then followed a number of letters of support for Alport from some back-benchers on the left of the party. For example, Tim Yeo commented that he entirely shared Alport's concern about the future of the Conservative Party and he hoped "we shall continue to hear your voice clearly speaking out before too much irreparable damage is done." Hugh Dykes was "in shock" and offered sympathy and Ian Gilmour thought that "the spectacle of government panic is indeed encouraging" and he expressed "solidarity" for the joint struggle in 1985.[78] Thus, although Alport and Gilmour strived to represent themselves as the embodi-ment of the One Nation ideal; in reality, the perception of them from within the party, apart from a few malcontents on the Conservative backbenches, was more one of isolated mavericks than the elder statesmen of "true Conservatism."

From 1969 Gilmour had also increasingly moved towards the specific endorsement of coalition politics with those Social Democrats that Thatcher had later dared to criticize; from questioning a party system that divided par-ties into Montagus and Capulets, he went on to make the claim that there was much in British Social Democracy which is admirable and which Conservatives can accept and that being partners in a coalition would transcend the narrow interests of the Conservative Party.[79] From the 1980s Gilmour would emphasize that such a predilection for coalition politics and for state interventionism was the essence of the Tory tradition. In 1981 he said:

> Much of what I say this evening will doubtless be attacked as "wet." What is today characterised as "wet" is quite simply the main Tory tradition. Disraeli, Baldwin, Churchill, Eden, Macmillan, Butler were all wets to a man. I believe that my remarks tonight will fall fair and square within the Tory tradition.[80]

However, just under ten years earlier Gilmour had mocked the "mere ances-tor worship" in the very idea of such an "apostolic succession" of Conservative doctrine, particularly through Baldwin, Churchill, Eden, and Macmillan, as "Conservative leaders have not believed the same things themselves for any great length of time, let alone held the same views as their successors and predecessors."[81] But, the success of the left's hegemonic project, which fettered One Nation to just one element of the dual nature of Conservative Party ideology, has been self-evident, particularly by its use in the contemporary mass media and even in much of the academic press. But, such "success" and the crude approach inherent within such procrustean polemics had come at a price. Not only had it contributed to a marginalization of the extended state tradition within the party, for over 30 years, but as a consequence of such cumulative attacks in conjunction with a certain level of neoliberal acquiescent contrivance, there has been exten-sive damage done to the One Nation ethos itself and thus to the mechanisms for doctrinal self-renewal in the party. However, an emphasis must be placed upon the reality that this correlation of the One Nation idea with "moderate politics," as reflected in the desire for coalition, is as spurious as the concomitant claim for One Nation being solely or uniquely of the extended state approach to wealth creation. Indeed, there is an alternative view that the semi-socialism attributed to Baldwin—by many Conservatives, including his own cousin Rudyard Kipling— was due to the existence of the coalition after 1931.[82] And crucially, we see in the view of one Conservative "'wet'"[83] that the "strongly antisocialist" sentiment of the 1950 One Nation booklet—of which Maude and Powell did the lion's share of the work, though Macleod attracted the limelight—was owed, in no small measure, to the fact that the authors had not served in the coalition government and thus had no underlying sense that Conservatism was about how to carry out a graceful withdrawal with minimum losses.[84] Thus, there is a clear distinction to be made between the positive contribution from such so-called "wets" as Timothy Raison and the facile exaggeration of a great divide from those "right out on the other wing of the party." If such a gaping lacuna existed in the dual nature of the Conservative Party ideology then "party self-renewal" would not be possible, but in the subsequent chapters we see that this is indeed not the case.

## Notes

1. Blake, 1985, p. 346.
2. For example, see Cole, 1996, pp. 209 and 251. On page 209, he equates One Nation with Ian Gilmour and "the wets" and on page 251 he identifies Pym as One Nation and makes an explicit contrast with him and John Nott who was more "Thatcherite than Thatcher" but of course John Nott was a member of One Nation for well over a decade before Francis Pym.
3. One Nation Group, 1996, p. 5.
4. Ibid., p. 7.
5. For example, see the articles by John Birt and Peter Jay, in *The Times*: "Television Journalism: The child of an unhappy marriage between newspapers and film" and "The radical changes needed to remedy TV's bias against understanding," September 30, 1975 and October 1, 1975 respectively.
6. Indeed, Radio Four's *Today* presenter, John Humphreys, refers to this tendency as the "basic law of journalism: First simplify, then exaggerate"; *The Spectator*, November 11, 2006, p. 9.
7. *The Times*, November 13, 1981.
8. *The Times*, October 7, 1982.
9. Longden papers, Longden Box List, Temporary File Number 6, "Letters exchanged between Gilbert Longden and *The Times* between 11 October and 16 October 1982," London School of Economics and Political Science.
10. Ibid.
11. Ibid.
12. *The Times* letters page, October 16, 1982.

13. Conservative Party Archive (CPA): Keith Joseph papers, KJ/8/1, "Letter from Elizabeth Birks, 10 October 1975 and reply 20 October 1975," Bodleian Library Oxford.

14. Butler and Kavanagh, 1980, p. 64, quote Joseph's 1975, p. 4, document when they point out that: "One of Sir Keith's more remarkable statements was that, although he had been a member of the Conservative Party for years, 'it was only in April 1974 that I was converted to Conservatism. I had thought that I was a Conservative but I now see that I was not one at all.'"

15. What Lord David Howell called the "repentance syndrome," interview House of Lords, June 23, 2004.

16. Indeed, Raison, 1990, p. 83: gives a "useful reminder that the Joseph who emerged in 1974 was not a wholly new being."

17. See Chapter 2, Endnote 5.

18. Shepherd, 1994, p. 63. And see p. 58 on the level of his ambition and interestingly on p. 56 we find his attraction to Roman Catholicism; which may well give meaning to Maude's concomitant disclaimer, found in Chapter 1 of this book, that the majority of members were never "Anglo-Catholic or even High-Church."

19. Ibid., p. 7.

20. 'Whose Bright Eyes Rain Influence: by a student of politics', *The Sunday Times*, November 22, 1959.

21. Ibid.

22. Longden papers: Temporary File Number 31, "Macleod, One Nation pp. 1–2," and see Harvester Archives of the British Conservative Party, 1962/107. Here Macleod means the Tory Reform Committee rather than the Tory Reform Group formed in 1975.

23. Alport papers: Box 37, One Nation Minutes, June 28, 1951, Albert Sloman Library, Essex. Indeed, a similar erroneous extrapolation could be made for an association with Lord Hinchingbrooke [Victor Montagu], who was Chairman of the Tory Reform Committee in 1943 (and was present with Hailsham at this dinner) and who was later to move to the "right" eventually becoming an active member of the Monday Club, see more in Chapter 5 and Seyd, 1972, pp. 464–487.

24. See CPA: CCO 3/6/138 and CCO 3/7/43.

25. CPA: CCO 3/7/52; Norton, and Aughey, 1981, p. 236.

26. Shepherd, 1994, p. 288, and see pp. 83 and 160.

27. See note 62 in Chapter Three where in 1967 Gilmour is the only one of the One Nation group to favor further intervention on this measure.

28. Gamble, 1974, p. 134.

29. Shepherd, 1994, p. 464.

30. Interview with Lord David Howell, House of Lords, June 23, 2004.

31. Ibid.

32. This was an article for the *Prospect* magazine entitled: 'Evaporating Wets', February 1996, p. 11.

33. Temple-Morris, 1996, p. 9.

34. Tory Reform Group's journal, *The Reformer*, Spring 1996, p. 3.

35. See the Macmillan lecture, March 3, 2000, on the Tory Reform Website: http://www. trg.org.uk/ and the concept of "creative synthesis" was employed in a telephone interview with the author, November 13, 2006.

36. Gilmour, 1992, p. 2.
37. See Alport papers: 'The Red Notebook: "Our Nation'" by Cuthbert Alport, undated in Box 44: Notes for a memoir, etc. This appears to be notes for a proposed autobiography but reference to "thirty years ago" in the text suggests a date of around 1980.
38. Alport, 1996, p. 15.
39. Ibid., p. 16.
40. Alport papers: Box 37, One Nation Minutes, November 23, 1954 and December 7, 1954.
41. Gilmour, and Garnett, 1998.
42. Longden, 1985, pp. 22–24. And see Longden papers, Temporary File Number 31, "Letter from Bill Deedes to Longden, 28 July 1985, in which he informs Longden that the *Telegraph* could not publish it as "frankly, they would [features people] find it very difficult to mill into the sort of piece we would carry.'"
43. Gilmour, and Garnett, 1998, p. 53.
44. Gilmour, 1977, p. 149.
45. Leader column entitled: "Tory Intellectuals," *The Spectator*, June 4, 1954, p. 672.
46. See *The Times* June 30, 1959 and Norton, and Aughey, 1981, p. 80.
47. Gilmour and Garnett, 1998, pp. 18 and 95.
48. Ibid., pp. 135–143.
49. Ibid., pp. 140–141. But, as early as the eighteenth century William Pitt drew attention to such specious reasoning: "He attacked the idea that the £200,000 that would be saved was too insignificant a sum to bother with. 'This was surely the most singular and unaccountable species of reasoning that was ever attempted in any assembly'", quoted in Hague, 2004, p. 65. And, see Cosgrave, 1990, p. 159; where Powell rejects the idea of one percent of national expenditure as a triviality.
50. Gilmour and Garnett, 1998, p. 142.
51. See note 69 in Chapter 1.
52. CPA: CCO150/4/21, "Letter from Nigel Birch to Angus Maude, 15 June 1954." Indeed, in a similar letter of praise, "to the authors of Change is our Ally," on the 19 May 1954, Cuthbert Alport, states: "It will I am sure be regarded as a most valuable contribution to the intellectual life of the party. . . . It is not easy to repeat a success. I believe however that "Change is our Ally" will have just as big an effect upon political thought as did One Nation, see ibid.
53. Birch, 1949, pp. 48–49.
54. In CPA: CCO20/1/25/Ian Gilmour papers.
55. Ibid.
56. Gilmour and Garnett, 1998, pp. 7–13.
57. Howard, 1998, pp. 85 and 101.
58. Roberts, 1995, p. 173.
59. *Daily Telegraph*, March 16, 2006.
60. Disraeli, 1967, p. 122.
61. McKenzie, 1955, p. 109.
62. Pym, 1985, p. 97.
63. Annan, 1990, p. 347.
64. Birch, 1949, p. 10.
65. Blake, 1966, p. 345.
66. Disraeli, 1967, p. 122.

67. Longden papers: Temporary File Number 9, "Letter from Iain Macleod to Gilbert Longden, 5 January 1951."

68. Longden papers: Temporary File Number 9, "Reply from Longden to Macleod, 9 January 1951."

69. Alport papers: Box 37, One Nation Minutes, January 23, 1951.

70. See CPA: CCO3/2/115, "Middle Class Union."

71. Alport papers: Box 29; see "letters between Beloff and Alport, 8 January and 9 January 1968."

72. Indeed, in Rodgers papers, OP27/8, One Nation Minutes, July 12, 1967, we have the sentiment that: "clearly he was sent out by Wilson as a gimmick," Centre for Kentish Studies, Kent. And, it would appear that Alport was excluded from a Conservative public meeting in the Red Lion pub, in his old constituency of Colchester in 1967, as from correspondence we know that Ted Heath regretted to hear that Alport had been kept out and could not get in to see him. See Alport papers, Box 29, 'letter from Heath to Alport, November 6, 1967.

73. See *The Times*, October 4, 1974 and June 29, 1974.

74. *The Times*, July 27, 1974. Although the idea of doing a deal with the Liberals was anathema to John Nott, see Nott, 2002, p. 163.

75. Alport papers, Box 42, "Letter from Alport to Heath, 5 March 1974," not surprisingly Heath curtly dismissed his criticism in a reply of March 11, 1974, ibid. And see *The Times*, January 28, 1975 also.

76. Alport papers, Box 42, "Letter from Alport to Thorneycroft, 7 July 1977" and the "reply 7 July 1977."

77. "Peer loses Tory whip," *The Times*, December 19, 1984.

78. Alport papers, Box 31, 'Letters: Yeo to Alport, December 19, 1984; Dykes to Alport, December 19, 1984, and Gilmour to Alport December 30, 1984.

79. See Gilmour, 1969, p. 54; Gilmour, 1978, pp. 172 and 226.

80. In CPA: CCO20/1/25/Ian Gilmour papers.

81. Gilmour, 1969, p. 84.

82. Barnes, 1994, p. 340.

83. For example see Norton, 1990, p. 54; where Norton categorizes Timothy Raison as a "wet."

84. Raison, 1990, pp. 26–27.

# CHAPTER FIVE

## Factions, Tendencies and "Bondstones"?

The One Nation group is but one of a number of groups that occupy ideological space in the British Conservative Party. There is much variation to these groups in terms of organizational structure, operational dynamics and even in their raison d'être, but more often than not they exist to promote a particular ideological position within the Conservative tradition: confirming the doctrinal nature to such intraparty competition and the potential for destructive or constructive outcomes that is the nature of political recrudescence. In Britain, one of the most well-known and seminal examinations of this "semi-visible"[1] world of competing "internal policy parties" was undertaken by Richard Rose.[2] Indeed, cognizant of the claim in the previous chapter, for "me too socialism," we should note that Rose made the point that such internal divisions, as reflected in the competition between the internal policy parties within the "electoral parties" themselves, served to reduce the ideological distance between those electoral parties.[3] But, questions surrounding the very structure of these internal policy parties and the extent to which such structural properties impact upon those internal divisions, particularly within the Conservative Party, have been a hotly contested issue in the study of British political parties. In short, inextricably linked to the myth of loyalty being the secret weapon of Conservative Party politics has been a concomitant characterization of the party as relatively harmonious and united due to the lack of "faction" within its parliamentary ranks.

Of course, *faction* is a value-laden political term and as such has normative implications associated with it.[4] And it has been to the considerable electoral benefit of the Conservative Party to have a form of electoral imprimatur given to its claims for unity in contrast to a schismatic Labour Party "riven" by dissension: thanks in no small part to the putative presence of "factions" within it. Moreover, underpinning such claims for Conservative Party unity was a belief that its "internal variety" or internal differences were insubstantial and transitory: particularly, in comparison with the inveterate sectional divisions that were commonly held to be the state of the parliamentary Labour Party. Thus, in 1949, while clearly utilizing a One Nation ethos and in praise of Burke's societal trinity of the living, the dead and those yet to be born, Birch could state:

This conception of fundamental national unity in time, the conception that our ultimate identity of interest, our common experiences, the dangers we have faced and must face again together are of infinitely more importance than the differences that divide us, is the exact opposite of the Marxist conception of the class war. Mr Bevan's savage boast, "We are going to see the right people squeal for a change," or Mr Shinwell's belief that anyone who does not pay the political levy does not matter a tinker's curse, are sound Marxism, but anathema to a Conservative, who could never rejoice in the sufferings of any class or body of citizens any more than he could rejoice if he crushed his own thumb with a hammer. This does not mean that the existence of injustice or the obligation to remedy injustice is denied but that our ultimate unity is fundamental and perpetual while our differences are temporary and removable.[5]

And this impression of transient differences reinforcing an image of unity found resonance in the academic literature, which examined the parliamentary behavior of the political parties postwar. For example, in an analysis of Backbench opinion in the parliaments of both the 1945 to 1955 and the 1955 to 1959 periods, the claim is made that the Conservative Party can more ably present a united front because within it was a collection of evanescent pressure groups or ad hoc groups whose members joined together to contend for one specific objective and then dispersed as soon as the issue had been resolved or rendered nugatory by the passage of time.[6] In contrast, it was believed that internal Labour Party groups had more of a continuity of doctrine as well as duration that conditioned their reaction to any particular event and around which opposition to the leadership was facilitated. Undoubtedly, such orthodoxy of informed opinion led to the construction of the factions and tendencies typologies that were meant to explain in part the contrast in parliamentary behavior of both Conservative and Labour MPs. In this context, the idea of a "faction" is defined as a group based on parliamentary representatives who, on a broad range of policies, seek to further their objectives through a self consciously organized body within the electoral party itself and importantly, that such groups have the inherent elements of persisting through time while displaying a measure of discipline and cohesion, so that such qualities create the expectation that members will consistently take the same side in quarrels within the electoral party.[7] Conversely, a "tendency" lacked such coherence and discipline as it was often not self consciously organized and its adherents displayed a stable set of attitudes that were held together by a more or less coherent political philosophy but importantly, without an expectation that its members would continue to follow the same tendency for any length of time.[8] In short, and again to its considerable electoral advantage, the received wisdom was one of viewing the Conservative Party as a party of tendencies and not one of fissiparous factions.

Party organizational theory set this dichotomous approach in a wider explanatory context: these factions and tendencies being merely symptoms of the historical development of the parties' organizational structures. For Panebianco,[9] both the Conservative and Labour Parties' formative genetic phase and subsequent institutionalization phase resulted in the Conservative Party being a "Governmental party," whereas Labour with its disputatious factions was classified as "Oppositional." Building on the work of Duverger,[10] Panebianco accepted the importance of the Conservative Party being "internally created" from existing elites in Parliament and that this internal legitimization gave authority and control to those parliamentary elites. He then argued that through strong institutionalization—namely, the way the party structures solidified—the party had strong central command and control of its organization. It was argued that this was a result of "territorial penetration"; however much this central control was easily concealed, all organizational units accepted the party's internal channels of authority, from the top down or from the centre to the periphery. In contrast, Labour, with its externally created and indirectly assembled "units" of trade unions, cooperatives, friendly societies and Fabians etc., fell far short of strong institutionalization. And moreover, like the Liberals, its organizational structure was developed through "territorial diffusion," where many countervailing power bases were left intact that could subsequently challenge the centre: zones of uncertainty that would contribute to such "factious behaviour."[11] Of course, this is a simplistic overview of a wide-ranging theory but nevertheless the adumbration clearly evinces that orthodoxy of informed opinion, which viewed the Conservative Party as the natural party of government. However, as the latter half of the twentieth century wore on, we find more and more challenges to this image of a Conservative Party uninhabited by factions.

Such a trend is discerned in the work of Pat Seyd. In an article on the Monday Club, written in 1972, Seyd accepted "the tendency" as characteristic of the Conservative Party but wished to introduce his own typology of an "Alliance," which he defined as an organized group of persons concerned to replace the policy of the party on a single issue. Thus, the alliance was organized and disciplined like a faction, but it shared similarities with the tendency typology as it was temporary and would dissolve once an issue had been solved. And, for Seyd, the existence of the Monday Club was significant in that it signaled "a slight change in the nature of the Conservative Party" as he believed that "its organization and style is in many ways more appropriate to the Labour Party," and that this was "altering the whole style of conservative intra-party conflict."[12] In a later work, Seyd openly challenged the very idea of "tendency" and wished "to assert that the incidence of factionalism within the Conservative party ha[d] increased since 1964"; although this factional activity, unlike in the Labour party, still provided little guidance to the development of Conservative policies.[13] But, by the 1990s, it became more common, particularly with the issue of Europe in mind, for political historians to disclaim an erroneous characterization of the Conservative Party as a party of tendencies in favor of the view that "factionalism has been endemic in the party."[14]

This chapter confirms the doctrinal nature of Conservative Party politics but it questions, and notwithstanding the issue of Europe, the characterization of the party as factional in Rose's terms. What has changed since the 1960s is not the incidence of factionalism but the increasing public awareness of such intraparty group activity. Indeed, as early as 1964, Rose drew the reader's attention to this: "The Conservatives' unwillingness to divide in public has not sustained continuous harmony in private."[15] And, as late as the 1970s, Norman Tebbit could refer to: "In those more discreet times such clubs were never identified in public, but now the names are common currency in the political gossip columns."[16] Of course, far greater space would be needed to even attempt a comprehensive historical analysis of the extent and number of these Conservative groups; thus, the examination here echoes the familiar academic refrain of such work being by necessity illustrative rather than exhaustive. But, however incomplete the list of Conservative groups, as outlined here, there is no gainsaying their consequent reality in the political recrudescence of the party. And, in the following two sections, we not only see the existence of these intraparty groups, divided in the main along an extended state/limited state axis from the 1940s to the present day, but that they do indeed, contra Seyd, provide guidance to the development of Conservative policies. And, we find, in the supposed era of a postwar settlement, pace E. H. H. Green, that the Conservatives never accepted that anything had been settled. The lines of division are indeed all rather fluid, as expected in a party with a substantive dual nature to its ideology. Thus, section four examines cross cutting dimensions on the limited/extended state spatial context and the many typologies, bordering on *reductio ad absurdum*, that these crosscutting dimensions have given rise to; but, as we shall see, such an analysis merely reinforces the point that, within the party, it is the very issue of the level of governmental intervention or judicious abstinence, which has not been resolved or rendered nugatory by the passage of time. With this left–right ideological continuum in mind, the concluding section comments on the recurrence and the prevalence of One Nation members in these other Conservative groups—on their connectedness and on their "binding role"—leading to a reevaluation and augmentation of the factions and tendencies debate. But, first, we begin with an examination of the postwar years.

## Postwar: Reform and/or Progress?

Around the mid 1970s, there developed a powerful and pervasive myth that characterized the postwar years as an age of consensus.[17] And, as we shall see below, for some Conservatives the portrayal of One Nation as a group exclusively on the left of the party was a critical part of this received wisdom. However, Harriet Jones challenged this unquestioning acceptance—which for at least a decade saw virtually no published work that took issue with Addison's 1975 interpretation of *The Road to 1945* —in contrast, she emphasized Hayek's influence upon the party leadership in 1945 and by the end of the 1940s, the consistent and firm response to Labour of policies that rejected the use of the state as a tool to redistribute wealth and, which at the same time aimed to reduce public expenditure and taxation.[18] This section to a large degree underpins the work by Jones and her colleagues and questions the implicit notion of a "consensus" of common assumptions on the continuity of policy. Indeed, we will see that, on such policy matters, the stance taken in the ranks of the Conservative Party was far from unquestioning. Of course, it is not coincidental that the power of such a myth was derived from its timing; both those who supported the advent of Thatcherism, and those who were resolutely against could utilize it for very different ends. The previous chapter highlighted this very phenomenon where neoliberal Conservatives like Keith Joseph were more than happy to accept such a myth in order to emphasize the ratchet effect of social democracy; while conversely, Gilmour and his allies availed themselves of it to stress the substantive break from, what was for them, the Conservative tradition. For Ben Pimlott, this temporal dimension was crucial to the success of such a conceptual construct as he believed that few ideological strands had been so consistent as the limited state strand of Conservatism, for almost a quarter of a century before Mrs Thatcher came to power; and as the main political actors did not consider themselves to be part of any national consensus at the time, then it was prudent to be circumspect about committing the grievous error of anachronism in any such analysis:

> We need to consider the possibility . . . that the consensus is a mirage, an illusion that rapidly fades the closer one gets to it. We may argue against the popular theory of the consensus, that genuine consensus politics is very rare, further, that we see more agreement in the past than in the present. The heat and passion of current controversy always seems to burn more fiercely while it is actually happening, than later, when tempers have cooled.[19]

Such a possibility may explain why, by the 1980s, the consensus was in such bold relief for Conservatives like James Douglas, or it may well just be the case that the most persistent advocates of the notion that RAB Butler and his young acolytes transformed the party post war, was by, "oddly enough, Butler and his acolytes."[20] For example, by 1983, Douglas speaks of one of the main architects of the Tory policy postwar, viz., RAB Butler, and of how this policy led to the rapid shift towards the middle ground after 1945: signaled so clearly by the publication of the *Industrial Charter* in 1947, before adding an impression that:

> The nucleus of opinion held within the party that already favoured the types of policy advocated in the *Industrial Charter* would have included members of the Tory Reform Committee, the One Nation Group and the not inconsiderable body of industrial and business opinion that favoured the Keynesian approach.[21]

However, we should note that this was the very same James Douglas, of the Conservative research department (1951–1977), who we encountered in Chapter 3, and to whom the galley proofs of *Change Is Our Alley* were passed by Michael Fraser in 1954; "to have a look at in detail" because of the level of criticism from the One Nation group towards the interventionist rationalization policies associated with RAB Butler during and immediately after the war.[22] And, in a 1989 article by Douglas, we find an identical assertion but this time the names of two prominent Tory Reform Committee (TRC) members, Peter Thorneycroft and Lord Hinchingbrooke, are added to those groups "who favoured the type of policies developed during the closing years of the Coalition Government,"[23] although he does admit to their subsequent divergence from such an approach. The evidence accumulated in the previous chapters is quite sufficient to demolish such an assertion from Douglas and further material presented in this chapter will attest to the fact that the One Nation group in the 1950s did not favor polices associated with an extended state. However, an identification of when Hinchingbrooke moved to the right is quite instructive regarding the extent of any "postwar settlement" within the parliamentary Conservative Party. Hinchingbrooke was indeed the first chairman of the Tory Reform Committee. Formed in February 1943, the TRC had 41 MPs listed as members in its first publication of October 1943.[24] Samuel Beer refers to this TRC pamphlet in his treatise "on the politics of a collectivist age" and the significance of it in its encouragement to Conservatives and the coalition government to accept the Beveridge Report.[25] Hinchingbrooke did publish a collection of speeches and articles, in 1944, which not only echoed the Disraelian notion of the need for a national party in harmonious union but that Disraeli's *Coningsby* rather than Marx offered solutions to the young in a period when they could not afford to be indifferent.[26] In this 1944 book, Hinchingbrooke put the case for a "progressive Conservatism," which would see "the modern Tory" rejecting individualism, but he was also well aware that such views would lead to accusations of him merely helping to propagate "Socialist ideas."[27] And, another leading TRC member, Hugh Molson, was also cognizant of this criticism when he published an overview of the work of the TRC in 1945:

> The Tory Reform Committee has been criticised by some Conservatives on the ground that we do not believe in private enterprise and competition . . . .The individualists who protest against controls are anarchists blind to the needs for a planned direction; the Socialists who would put the management of all industry in the hands of the state are aiming at a tyranny of the bureaucrats. The Tory Reform idea is that Government should plan a framework within which industries, shipping and agriculture would have their allotted task both in the home and foreign markets, but that the fullest possible freedom should be left to individuals to exercise their own judgement in the day-to-day management of their business.[28]

Undoubtedly, sentiment of this kind, for such a "planning framework," was resonant in the pages of the *Industrial Charter*[29] but we are fully aware, from Chapter 3, that Enoch Powell and John Rodgers were especially critical of the *Charter,* which for them reeked of *étatiste dirigisme* and that the One Nation group believed the party had only itself to blame for the problems it faced in the 1950s because of the "rationalization/nationalization" policies it was so fond of following in the 1930s and 1940s. Thus, however much planning and copartnership were to be paradoxically the policies the One Nation group wanted to pursue in the 1970s and early 1980s; in the 1950s, such a credo was thoroughly eschewed. Of course, the One Nation group, with hindsight, would see their criticism of planning and controls, and of the Industrial Charter itself, as self evident due to the calamitous state of the economy in the imme diate postwar years. But, there were those who were assertive and compelling critical voices at the time, and remarkably one of them—and publicly—was that of Lord Hinchingbrooke. Hinchingbrooke sent the proofs of a prospective article in which he criticized the Industrial Charter to RAB Butler, with Butler replying that he thought that Hinchingbrooke had "done both the Committee and the Party a good deal less than justice in your description of the way in which the Industrial Charter was prepared."[30] Indeed, Hinchingbrooke believed the Charter was "esoterically prepared" by a small handpicked Committee, which was not representative of the Conservative Party, but later "given the imprimatur of the Leader," that it was "calculated to frighten Conservative supporters in the country more than frighten our enemies."[31] He further believed:

> Conservatives in the years between the wars practised a compromise with modern Socialism. . . . Labour . . . is now doing in full blooded measure what the Conservatives in pre-war years half-heartedly attempted . . . . Conservatives are not providing the balance by allying themselves fully enough to those cells and schools of thought in the country which favour a progressive return to individualism, free trade, the price structure, the rule of law, and society based on contract rather than on status. . . . Large-scale unemployment is inevitable unless we turn from State control towards free enterprise and individualism . . . .[32]

This actual critique is uncannily similar to those views of One Nation found in the 1954 booklet *Change Is Our Ally,* and we know from the previous chapter that Hinchingbrooke attended a One Nation dinner as a TRC representative on June 28, 1951 but such evidence seems to escape those authors, indeed like James Douglas above, who appear to exaggerate the scope of the extended state tradition within the party. Nevertheless, there is no doubt that Hinchingbrooke's conception of "progressive Toryism" had altered dramatically in just three years of the forties decade but as John Ramsden[33] has indicated the TRC's case probably owed more to electoral tactics in the first place. And, moreover, we should note that Hinchingbrooke was wrong about the leader's approval of the document as we now know that Churchill played no part in its formation and that he did not agree with a word of it.[34] Interestingly, and mindful of the lack of sustained harmony in private on any postwar settlement, we should also make ourselves aware of similar criticism emanating from a rather different source, namely from the Progress Trust.[35] It is quite clear from RAB Butler's correspondence that the criticism from this group of Conservative MPs was taken quite seriously. Indeed, David Clarke, the then Research Director in 1947, informs Butler in a memo that the "comments of the Progress Trust on the Industrial Charter . . . are almost word for word the same as those in Hinchingbrooke's article."[36] T. D. Galbraith, the MP for Glasgow Pollok, had written to RAB Butler in July 1947 with comments that "express the agreed views of some twenty members of the Party and not the views of any one individual."[37] A summary of the comments were then compiled for Butler by David Clarke, which included, *inter alia*, the criticism that:

> the faith of the Conservative Party in free enterprise should be explicitly stated . . . the possibility of controls causing scarcity should be kept in mind . . . the belief that it is not possible for any truly Democratic Government to maintain full employment, and that the Party should not be committed to the Coalition White Paper on Employment Policy . . . that the Charter should contain an affirmation that the Party intends to re-enact Section I of the Trades Disputes Act of 1927 . . . that the right to denationalise anything and everything should be specifically reserved.[38]

It is instructive that Galbraith never refers to the Progress Trust; this term is found only in the internal correspondence between David Clarke and RAB Butler. Crocket stresses the secrecy of this select group of around 20 neoliberal MPs, who managed to staff an office in Westminster and, which he believed was still in existence in the mid 1990s—with a recent Chairman being Sir Peter Hordern, a One Nation member who we will encounter again in the next section—but that it was difficult to gauge its influence within the party during the war.[39] However, we find in 1955, in an invitation to Enoch Powell to join, that the Progress Trust had no difficulty at the time in gauging its own influence on Prime Minister Anthony Eden:

> I am very pleased to tell you that you have been elected a Member of the Progress Trust . . . I understand Charles Waterhouse [MP for S. W. Leicester] has had a word with you about us and that your response was sympathetic. The Progress Trust has been functioning for some twelve years and consists of about twenty-one Conservative Members of Parliament, mainly from the House of Commons, but with the addition of some three or four Peers. Our work and activities are strictly private and confidential and it is our hope, at

any rate, that very few people know of our existence outside a few Ministers, etc., who are our Guests at our periodical dinners or luncheons . . . .Last month we had the privilege of entertaining the Prime Minister to a private dinner in the House of Commons. He has long been very friendly to us. [And the following Wednesday the Minister of Defence was to attend]. . . . I would emphasize that our work and activities are very private and confidential. We seek deliberately to hide our light under a bushel. I would be grateful, therefore, if you would say nothing about joining us to anyone or, indeed, about the existence of the Progress Trust, to your friends.[40]

Crocket emphasizes the role of the Progress Trust within a not inconsiderable body of industrial, business and Conservative opinion that, *contra* Douglas, fundamentally rejected the Keynesian approach in this period. With a focus on the outstandingly successful Mr Cube campaign, against the nationalization of the sugar industry, Crocket believed that this network of opinion, that included the Aims of Industry and the British United Industrialists, played a significant part in an "economic counter revolution."[41] And, we find that Crocket's work is indeed corroborated by a rather more contemporary text, which bemoaned the loss of the BBC monopoly with the formation of commercial television in the early 1950s. In this text, H. H. Wilson referred to a "soufflé of interests" within which he placed both the Aims of Industry and the One Nation group, with particular condemnation reserved for the One Nation member John Rodgers[42]:

In addition to the denationalization of steel and road transport and John Rodgers' role in achieving commercial television, members of the One Nation group are credited with taking the initiative in forcing the Government to act in a number of other instances: the withdrawal of the first White Paper on Transportation in May, 1952, when the Minister, J. S. Maclay was forced to resign and a second White paper was produced in July, 1952; the repeal, in November, 1952, of the crucial clause nationalizing development rights in the Town and Country Planning Act. . . .[43]

It is clear then that the Industrial Charter was not the totemic document of a postwar settlement that some, like Douglas, claimed it to be. More poignantly, and rather unfortunately for those advocates of a "consensus era," is the realization that it was more "the final expression of the radical *étatiste* thought of the 1930s"; it closed rather than opened an era.[44] The evidence presented here chimes more with the archival work of Harriet Jones, offering confirmation that the Conservative Party was not transformed postwar in some "progressive" or "extended state" fashion, and thus there was no golden age of consensus to which late twentieth-century Conservatives could nostalgically contemplate as some *ne plus ultra* of Conservative Party politics. "On the contrary, it was the articulation and leadership of a reinvigorated neo-liberal Conservatism, which led the party through the 1950 and 1951 general elections."[45] In the next section, we examine such a reinvigoration—from the 1960s onwards—and of course, the now unsurprising concomitant level of tension found in the intraparty competition of those internal "policy parties."

## No Turning Back to PEST

In January 1974, Patrick Wall was bemoaning the parallels of the present situation with that of the General Strike of 1926; although he was of the opinion that Baldwin had at least made considerable preparations, which were conspicuously lacking for 1974. In his letter of lament to Enoch Powell, he added:

> I am worried about the new defence team few of which know much about the job. Ian Gilmour will not be able to resist cuts as Peter [Carrington] has done, not only is he of the left but lacks the stature to stand up to the Prime Minister. Also I am told he doesn't go down well with the troops as he is too supercilious."[46]

This is the same Patrick Wall, who in 1964, founded the 92 group of Conservative MPs; named after his London address at 92 Cheyne Walk where the group first met and although discrete about its aims and policies, in the manner of the Progress Trust, was seen as distinctively right wing with around 100 members by the time of the 1987 Parliament.[47] Indeed, Norman Tebbit credits the 92 Group with his nascent steps to prominence within the Parliamentary party.[48] Of greater significance is the recurrence of names, which disclose a historical doctrinal linkage between these groups: a connection not only between the groups themselves but to that of One Nation with the likes of the Progress Trust, the 92 group, The Monday Club, The Selsdon Group, The No Turning Back Group, and Conservative Way Forward: to name but a few of the "limited state" groups occupying ideological space on a Conservative left–right dimension. Of particular interest here is the involvement of Nicholas Ridley with the creation of the Selsdon Group in September 1973. In Chapter 1, we encountered members of the One Nation group in the 1960s playing a significant part in the creation of policy, which would eventually manifest itself in the "silent revolution" election of 1970. Of course, by 1972, Edward Heath had embarked upon his U-turns from those neoliberal policy prescriptions adopted by the Shadow Cabinet at the Selsdon Park Hotel in early 1970; thus, symbolically, it was to this venue that Ridley returned to help launch the Selsdon Group:

> The principal speaker last night was Mr Nicholas Ridley, who left the Government after the reversal of its "lame duck" policy. The group's aim is to steer the party back to a free market economy and away from state interventionist excursions, such as pay and price controls . . . ."During the time of

Selsdon policies," he added, "we did well in by-elections, public opinion polls and local elections."[49]

Significantly, one year before, Ridley on his resignation from Heath's Government had also created a parliamentary group, The Economic Dining Club, to uphold and promote the free market policies, which had won the Conservatives the 1970 General Election, and it was claimed that this group played an even greater role in the creation of policy, which would eventually be revealed in the eponymous ideas of Thatcherism:

> Membership was limited to twelve Tory MPs and we dined once a month . . . . She [Thatcher] joined the Club in 1977 and was a regular attender. Most of its members later joined her Cabinet at one stage or another. I like to think we influenced her and ourselves in plotting out the directions in which policy was to go.[50]

John Nott, as a Treasury Minister at the time, was one of the co-founding members of the "Club," and lists some of the others as, John Biffen, Michael Alison (later to be Mrs Thatcher's PPS for four years), Jock Bruce-Gardyne, Cranley Onslow, Peter Hordern (of the Progress Trust, the 92 Group, and One Nation), John Eden, Enoch Powell, and of course, Nick Ridley.[51] We should note that of these nine names, six of them were also members of the One Nation group, and in a 1974 letter from Ridley to Powell, we see that seven of the 12 members listed were of the "Nation."[52] Moreover, when Keith Joseph, with the help of Angus Maude, was coordinating the policy groups, which would shape the "next stage of policy work" for the ensuing Thatcher years, we see that members of the Selsdon group, David Alexander and Stephen Eyre, were invited to participate in such policy discussions as, *inter alia*, the Post Office competition issue, as early as 1975 and the nationalized industries in 1976, respectively.[53] Indeed, of the 10 policy groups listed for 1976, 10 of the 12 Chairmen are members of One Nation.[54] And, *pace* Patrick Wall, unlike 1974, the Thatcher administrations would not lack a level of preparedness in relation to the threat of industrial action; in no small measure due to the work of Nicholas Ridley and his Nationalized Industries Policy Group. In early 1978, this group reported, recommending solutions on how to achieve denationalization, but interestingly the report included a confidential annex on "countering the political threat."[55]

This annex was remarkably prescient, in particular with regards to the resultant industrial relations legislation and the victories over militant trade unionism that would eventually characterize the Thatcher period. Ridley was in no doubt that the "enemies of the next Tory government would try to destroy" the denationalization policy and the *casus belli* would come in the form of either an unreasonable wage claim or over redundancies or closures and that the discontent would likely occur in "vulnerable" industries such as coal, electricity, or the docks. Ridley mapped out five strategies to deal with such a threat and within these we find:

> The most likely area is coal. Here we should seek to operate with the maximum quantity of stocks possible, particularly at the power stations. We should perhaps make such contingent plans as we can to import coal at short notice. We might be able to arrange for certain haulage companies to recruit in advance a core of non-union lorry drivers to help us move where necessary. We should also install dual coal/oil firing in all power stations, where practicable, as quickly as possible . . . .We must be prepared to deal with the problem of violent picketing. This again is a matter going beyond policy for Nationalised Industries. But it is also vital to our policy that on a future occasion we defeat violence in breach of the law on picketing. The only way to do this is to have a large, mobile squad of police who are equipped and prepared to uphold the law against the likes of the Saltley Coke-works mob. It also seems a wise precaution to try and get some haulage companies to recruit some good non-union drivers who will be prepared to cross picket lines, with police protection. They could always be used at the critical point where the result of any such contest is usually determined.[56]

Ridley thought such precautions would enable a future Conservative government "to hold the fort"—particularly when there would be no Incomes Policy against which to strike—until the inefficient units were rooted out in line with the advent of responsible management and incentives to facilitate true worker participation[57]; and the rest, as they say, is history.

Of course, it would be academically remiss not to include a similar continuity and inheritance of views, as well as a connectedness to One Nation that is also to be found on the extended state wing of the party. For example, in Chapter 4, we encountered the group "Pressure For Economic and Social Toryism" (PEST), which was formed in 1963 and, which later metamorphosed as the Tory Reform Group (TRG) in 1975. It was Michael Spicer who was responsible for the formation of PEST and in a press release of 1965, promoting the group's pamphlet "Call an End to Feeble Opposition," he attacked the economic views of Enoch Powell while stressing that "planning" in Tory hands would become a tool of free enterprise.[58] Immediately, there may be some who discern a contradiction in terms inherent in such a claim, not the least of whom is Sir Michael Spicer himself. Spicer resigned from the PEST directorate in 1967, and his views thereafter increasingly began to reflect the position of limited state Conservatism; to an extent, as we shall see in Chapter 7, that by 1992, there is a far closer cooperation between him and the 92 Group of Conservative MPs. However, the TRG is still a very active group and just as we have joint membership of One Nation with the 92 group and the No Turning Back group (for example with David Heathcoat-Amory[59]), there are also those (for example, Alistair Burt[60]) who have joint membership with the Tory Reform Group and with the Lollards and Nick's Diner. William van Straubenzee, a Church of England Commissioner, founded the Lollards in 1972 and its name derives from the Lollards' Tower at Lambeth Palace where the group first met; although only a very small number of Conservative MPs attended the dinners throughout the 1970s and 1980s.[61] Nick's Diner was the eponymous creation of Nicholas Scott who, as we know from the previous chapter, was to become president of the TRG. Indeed, as President of PEST in 1973, Scott wrote to Cub Alport exhorting him to become an honorary member and while pointing out that PEST should not be confused with the BOW Group whose "membership in fact spans the complete Party spectrum," he stressed that "PEST on the other hand is avowedly a pressure group for the sort of Toryism represented by Macmillan, Macleod, Butler, [Edward] Boyle and yourself."[62] But Alport replied: "I am very much out of sympathy with the style of leadership being pursued by the Prime Minister [Heath] and some of his senior colleagues, including Walker, who I see is rather surprisingly the Patron of your organisation."[63]

Thus, not only is there a possibility of tension between different strands of Tory thought, as revealed above in Patrick Wall's opinion of Ian Gilmour, but we also see that some Conservatives can be inclined to dislike even those who putatively are thought to be on the same wing of the party. Indeed, we have the example of the spectacularly bad tempered dinner of the No Turning Back (NTB) group in October 2000 that led to the resignation of Michael Portillo and Francis Maude from the NTB group. Francis Maude was one of the founders of NTB in 1983; formed to safeguard Thatcherite policy and taking its name from the renowned conference declaration of "you turn if you want to. The lady's not for turning." The division in the "Thatcherite" NTB group between those classified as social radicals or "modernisers" and those labeled traditionalists merely exemplified the overall problems for the party—depicted as *Tory Wars* by the journalist Simon Walters[64]—and, which lasted arguably for nearly a decade in the wake of the John Major electoral defeat of 1997. And, we also know from the examples of Hinchingbrooke and Spicer that Conservatives do not feel constrained to maintain consistent ideological positions: in their case, reverting back to the more traditional limited state Conservatism from the so called progressive politics of a resolutely active state.

However, and crucially, such examples merely confirm for us Gamble's notion of "this babel of conflicting voices"[65] within the party. And, we should be aware that there is an argument that the left–right spectrum does not do justice to an in-depth refinement of such clusters of party opinion, with some viewing it, in certain contexts, as "worse than useless."[66] Indeed, Green warned of the importance of avoiding oversimplification as it was "tempting to slip into using a framework of 'Statist' and 'anti-Statist,' but this would draw an overly straightforward divide in Conservative thought and leave too little room for nuance."[67] But, while cognizant of this caveat and with absolutely no desire to impair or detract from the idea of complexity and nuance inherent in Conservative party ideology, we must also recognize that there is a converse pitfall to be conspicuously avoided: "Groups and categories could be further divided and subdivided until one was left only with individual politicians—each divided within himself as well as divided in his sympathies with others."[68] Thus, in the following section, we examine the cross cutting dimensions to the left–right spectrum, while of course, being conscious of the need to avoid such *reductio ad absurdum*.

## Conservative Typologies: Toward "Topsy" Dimensions

Peter Goldman, when director of the Conservative Political Centre, believed the Conservative party was never born but like Topsy "it just 'grow'd.'"[69] In a similar fashion, we now have the perception of an exponential development of Conservative party taxonomies, to an extent that we should be very cautious of this seemingly unremitting subdivision of the party with the consequent potential for producing that absurd category of the individual Conservative politician. Of course, it is much easier to show the weaknesses of the left–right spectrum than to suggest alternatives, as acknowledged by Samuel Brittan when he set out to construct some alternatives to it while utilizing the pioneering work of Professor H. J. Eysenck on the dimensional approach to political classification; this, in reality, meant classifying subjects—in this case MPs—along two axes at right angles to each other.[70] Brittan thought it a great pity that Eysenck's "initial investigations, published as long ago as 1954, ha[d] been so little followed up by others."[71] This is certainly not the case today with such dimensional approaches being so enthusiastically followed up and applied to the ideological categorization of social groups with the Parliamentary Conservative party being no exception.[72] Figure 5.1 gives a flavor of this dimensional approach, listing just three that are seen to "cross cut" our principal dimension of the level of governmental intervention, but of course, with our caveat of subdivision in mind, this dimensional approach could well be applied to the nth degree.

It is from such dimensions, as those illustrated in Figure 5.1, that we derive the taxonomies and typologies of Conservative Party politics. For example, armed with such knowledge as say Ken Clarke's membership of an attitudinal group like the TRG, along with his record in the parliamentary division lists (roll call voting) and of course, his views, as outlined in Chapter 4, on coalition politics with the Liberal Democrats, we can place Clarke in the top left quadrant. Because, there is less circumspection from him in looking to the state to elevate the condition of the people and while having social liberal views on such issues as homosexuality, he is very much in support of further European integration, and we are aware of his views on "concessionary Conservatism." On these same dimensions, we can place Margaret Thatcher diametrically opposite; conversely, she is stridently confident for exclusive Conservative

Figure 5.1: A Four-Dimensional Approach to Conservative Party Politics

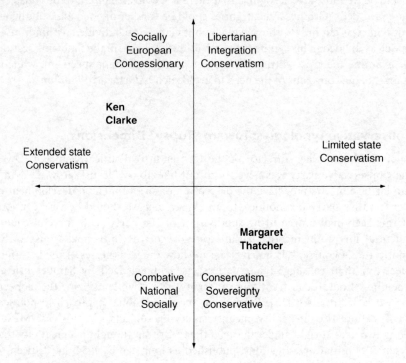

policies that view "the market and/or the voluntary sector" as being the most efficient instrument for the promotion of the peoples' welfare, and while supporting capital punishment, she would view as just as advantageous for Britain the rolling back of the frontiers of the supranationalist state. Apart from the great fun to be had in placing Conservatives into such typological groups, these typologies can augment the academic analyses that attempt to explain the political behavior of the parliamentary parties. The work of Philip Norton[73] has been prominent in this field, particularly, the seminal article on the probable ideological trajectory of the Conservative Party post Thatcher.[74] However, and crucially, there are certain caveats, which have to be acknowledged with regards to this dimensional approach to political analysis. People do change their views on issues; MPs are not necessarily static in their beliefs. Thus, Norton refers to such studies as being snapshots in time, however long and slow the exposure may be; indeed, Peter Riddell's assertion that Thatcher herself did not take a clear-cut or consistent view on a range of matters is quoted to add emphasis to the warning.[75] Moreover, when using the behavioral indicator of voting lists, one can never be sure of what is a truly "principled abstention" where the MP has deliberately not voted as opposed to a number of other reasons.[76] However, we will see in Chapter 7 with regards to the issue of Europe, that we cannot even be sure of the "principled vote" within this "hard data" of division lists. With this in mind, we should make ourselves aware of the importance of the "party faithful" typology wherein Norton classified 217 MPs or 58 percent of the Conservative parliamentary party in his snapshot of 1979 to 1989.[77]

This party faithful group clearly outnumbered the critics within the typological groups of "wets" and "damps" or even those MPs within the supportive Thatcherite groups of "neoliberals," "Tory right" or "populists." And, similar to the "non aligned group" for Rose, which was so important in the cushioning of conflicts and underpinning party cohesion, this party-faithful group ensures that conflict can be contained as it is only when MPs of this group combine with the ideological groups in any numbers that party managers have major problems.[78] Moreover, for Norton and his colleagues, the ideological groupings did not manifest factional behavior and thus, and allied to the idea of the party faithful, it was clear that the Parliamentary Conservative party had not transmogrified into a "factionalised" party with such a view being clearly delineated in an extremely cogent critique of the work of Heppell.[79] Heppell had developed a three-dimensional eightfold typology of the Conservative Party, under the leadership of John Major, 1992–1997 and, which for him showed the extent of factionalism within the parliamentary party.[80] But, as Cowley and Norton demonstrate, he does no such thing:

> Europe may be a whopper of an issue, but it is only one issue. As Heppell concedes, there were few parliamentary rebellions on economic policy. Moreover, Rose argued that factional behaviour required a "group of individuals who seek to further a broad range of policies through *consciously organised political activity*" (emphasis added). This is not an optional extra but an intrinsic condition of factionalism. Heppell does not show any evidence of consciously organised political activity across a broad range of policies.[81]

Indeed, although there is great fun to be had in assigning MPs to particular taxonomies, arguably there is an even greater entertainment to be had in challenging an MP's designated location. For example, Heppell has Michael Alison classified in a group, which is socially conservative but "agnostic" on the economy and Europe. Alison, of course, was a founding member of the neoliberal Economic Club with Nick Ridley and was more than capable of engaging with Enoch Powell in "some very high powered stuff" on the budget and the economy.[82] John Major is also placed in an "agnostic group" on Europe and the economy but is socially liberal.[83] Leaving to one side the idea that any Tory MP could ever be agnostic on such issues and the failed "back to basics campaign,"[84] it will become evident in Chapter 7 that many "Euro-sceptic" Tories would have dearly wished that there were no three line whips on Maastricht or that, there were no bankruptcies or house repossessions in the wake of the prosecution of an ERM policy and its eventual debacle. Importantly, we also find in the Heppell typologies that Michael Portillo and David Davis are in the socially Conservative group, but we know Portillo was to later leave the NTB group over his "socially liberal" stance and that David Davis—of the Conservative Way Forward group, founded in 1991 to defend and build upon the achievements of Thatcherism—resigned as Shadow Home Secretary to fight a by-election on the issue of pre-charge detention of terror suspects for 42 days and which was to include debate on a whole array of other civil liberties issues.[85] Thus, although at a particular juncture, such dimensional studies can give "some shape to the complexity of political configurations within the party"[86] and that importantly, they confirm the conflict and tension over policy provision that is perpetually present in the party debates, they also show that the Conservative Party has not quite reached that "ideal type" of factional behavior where members, across a broad range of policy issues, consistently take the same side in quarrels to the extent that we find the emergence of an alternative leader, one of national stature, due to the actions of that "consciously organized faction."[87]

In this context, we see this lack of consciously organized action illustrated in the 2005 party leadership election contest, where we had the chairman of the NTB group, John Redwood, supporting David Cameron while Damian Green and Ian Taylor, vice-president and patron of the TRG respectively, supported the Conservative Way Forward vice-president, David Davis.[88] Not only is there such fluidity to these lines of division clearly evident in the party leadership contests since 1965, but it is reflected in the overall non-"factional" behavior of the parliamentary party, with the ensuing difficulty of course of finding unequivocal or non contested typological groupings for the party. Europe may well be a "whopper of an issue," where tension can be converted with ease to the malign manifestation of turmoil, but even on this issue, we had a range of Euro-sceptic MPs such as Bill Cash, Teddy Taylor, Francis Maude, and Michael Ancram, along with another 36 of their colleagues, prepared to give support to the Europhile Ian Taylor when he was threatened with de-selection by his constituency party.[89] It might well be the case that there has been far too much emphasis placed upon a "factions and tendencies" dichotomy in the delineation of the architectural structure of Conservative Party group politics and that such behavior, as outlined immediately above, necessitates further explanation as to why we find so much nuance and complexity within that structure. Within the Conservative Party, there are groups, which straddle the party's ideological spectrum, one of which is the One Nation group itself, and as such these groups have an extensive joint membership of those many groups inhabiting "ideological space," thus helping to underpin party cohesion and the "cushioning of conflicts." It is to this "bonding" role of such groups that we now turn.

## "Bondstone Groups"

The list of names in Table 1.1 of Chapter 1 is testimony to the many and varied "typological boxes" that would be needed for an accommodation of One Nation members in any such taxonomy exercise. And, a very good illustration of the extent of the fluidity to the lines of division within the parliamentary party is found with Geoffrey Rippon's and William Benyon's membership of the "Monday Club."[90] Norton had categorized Benyon as a "damp critic" of Thatcherism,[91] and as we shall see in the following chapter Rippon, although in sympathy with much of what may be termed "neo-liberal Powellism," was one of the sternest critics of Enoch Powell's stance on immigration. The Monday Club was formed in 1961 with the stated aims to support the freedom of the individual, the private ownership of property, and the need for Britain to play a leading role in world affairs.[92] However, very quickly it became associated far more in the public mind with support for the crumbling remnants of Empire, particularly with regards to white rule in Rhodesia and notoriously as an anti-immigration group promoting a policy of repatriation. This eventually led to a suspension of its association with the party under Iain Duncan Smith's leadership in 2001, with the party chairman at the time David Davis instructing three MPs, Andrew Hunter, Andrew Rosindell, and Angela Watkins to severe their links with the Monday Club.[93] In its early years, it would clash periodically with members of the Bow Group who took a far more "liberal" line on policy towards Africa and on immigration, and it was from such a policy stance that the erroneous identification of the Bow Group with "left-wing" Conservatism would emanate. However, the membership of the Bow Group, similar to that of One Nation, was drawn from across the full range of the Conservative ideological spectrum. This "bondstone" quality not only helps safeguard those doctrinal debates, so necessary for that creative tension within the party, but crucially, it simultaneously contributes to party cohesion. Just as a bondstone runs through a structure binding one part to another, the *bondstone group* is found running through the structure of the Conservative Party facilitating a cementing of one Conservative ideological face to another; as reflected in the number of conflicting evaluations of the Bow Group.[94]

On the night of November 29, 1950 a "steering" meeting was held in the Bow and Bromley Conservative Club at 149 Bow Road in London to discuss the creation of a "club" for under 35s that would provide for the Conservative Party what the Fabian Society provided originally for the Labour party[95]; with the inaugural meeting of this "Bow Group" being held on the February 7, 1951.[96] Thus, the Bow Group—similar to the extra-parliamentary Monday Club or PEST—was established originally to engage bright young Conservatives in debate on the future of party policy, and it would go on to gain a formidable reputation for the advancement of many a Conservative career.[97] Indeed, in 1960, its Chairman felt the need to emphasize this extra-parliamentary nature due to the fact that:

In 1959 and 1960, the Bow Group has become the subject of extensive press comment . . . In numerous ways we have emphasised that we are a research society, that we never speak with a collective voice, that we are not a particular wing of the Party, that we are in no sense linked to the Party organisation, and that we are merely one among a number of voluntary bodies of Conservatives. We have had considerable success in explaining these points, but erroneous comments still appear, and this must remain a problem which needs attention.[98]

And, as early as 1957, RAB Butler could refer to the "times when, if report is true, you feel morally superior to the Government."[99] In this speech to the Bow Group on its sixth birthday, Butler also joked of the snobbish Romans who boasted about dining with the Borgias but alas the lack of who survived to use the past tense, then added: "In the 20th Century, the Bow Group has come to enjoy a no less distinctive but (fortunately for me) a less brutal renown."[100] In an extremely interesting talk, Butler acknowledged the "restrictive legislation" of the late twenties and thirties which was designed to meet the exigencies of a static or contracting economy, but he was now encouraging the Bow Group to help preach the doctrine of adequate incentives and rewards; in short, to think in terms of a "bias towards opportunity." With this in mind, he believed that it was time for somebody to bring Mallock up to date in order to challenge the egalitarian fallacy and he attacked the Labour party over its revisionist thoughts on taxation and incentives:

But what a piece of bare-faced impudence it is for the Socialists to complain of this now, when *we* have already cut taxation £800 million below the rates at which *they* left it . . . .We believe, and we must have the courage to say and explain, that egalitarianism is bunk. More than that, is national suicide. Our national wealth is not one large slab of pudding, half-baked in the ovens of Transport House, which has only to be cut in equitable proportions and handed round the dinner table. It is something which has to be created all the time. It is something which, in present circumstances, will vanish if it does not expand. And we have to know and proclaim and establish the conditions in which it will be sustained and *will* expand.[101]

However, ten years later in an open letter from the Bow Group chairman Reginald Watts, to the Conservative Party chairman Anthony Barber, we find that although the Conservative faith is firmly pinned to the market place and competition, yet, it stated the party should realize how rough and tough this can be when it talked only about incentives and rewards. And, with regards to housing Watts thought a planning procedure should be adopted and added:

Tory philosophy has always embraced a belief in the continuity of living society, thus:

"Time present and time past
Are both perhaps present in time future."
T.S. Elliot knew the problem and I, for one, don't want my children to inherit
the overdraft as we inherited the non-planning of the 1930s.[102]

Little wonder then at the number of conflicting evaluations of the Bow Group's
ideological position, as just two months earlier, Geoffrey Howe and Norman
Lamont, in a Bow Group memorandum, were calling for cuts in direct taxation
and for a halt to the public sector shouldering any more tasks that the private
sector could cope with: "Education, health, council housing and a whole host
of other social services can and must be brought back to the market place."[103]
Indeed, in 1975, *The Economist* reported that a "once influential forum for left of
centre Tories has become something of a monetarist, free-market-only shrine."[104]
Some of the main influences in bringing about this change were identified in the
persons of "Mr Peter Lilley" and "the new Chairman Miss Patricia Hodgson"
who, it was thought, could be relied upon to keep the organization firmly on its
new path. *The Economist* had 15 years earlier voiced similar erroneous comments
on it being a group of the Tory left[105] but buried within the 1975 article is the
more compelling translation, which shows clearly that the group reflected the
gamut of a Conservative left–right ideological spectrum:

> The Bow group's hallmark has long been a combination of economic real-
> ism (profits, growth, enterprise, reward for initiative and basic belief in
> market forces) with social concern (welfare state, liberal on race and Disraelian
> interest in the "condition of the people").[106]

Patricia Hodgson would go on to have a distinguished academic and media
career, but she was the first woman chair of the Bow Group and edited the group's
periodical *Crossbow* between 1976 and 1980, and it was to Patricia Hodgson and
the Bow Group that Keith Joseph turned in 1975 to elicit some background
research with regards to future policy:

> Would it be possible for the Bow Group to put together a small team of
> suitable people to study, in private, the practicalities of removing the mono-
> poly from the Post Office of the postal services? We would want all the impli-
> cations considered and in particular we would need to know what options
> would be available to protect the interests of the rural community. If you are
> willing to try to do this for us we would be able to help with readings lists
> and PQs. Ideally, we would like a report to reach Michael Heseltine and me in
> about six months.[107]

It would appear then that Michael Heseltine's proposals to privatize all or parts
of the Royal Mail in the 1990s were grounded far more in the recent historical policy goals of the party than in a mere venal attempt to please the right

wing of the party and the NTB group, which was a view commonly held at the time.[108] *Crossbow* was launched in 1957 by the Prime Minister Harold Macmillan who deliberated upon the name's definition, a weapon of great force discharged from the shoulder, but he then asked: "at whom? I am not simple enough to expect that I shall not be—from time to time —one of its principal targets."[109] He was certain of this because the group brought lively and penetrating minds to bear upon the party's problems and ironically in 1981 Keith Joseph became one such principal target. An article in Crossbow called for his removal from the Cabinet because of his inability to curb public spending and pointed to the "fitting irony" of one of the foremost persistent critics of government aid to lame ducks announcing an aid program of £5,300 million[110]; confirming RAB Butler's witty characterization of the group as "the beehive . . . from which we obtain honey as well as the occasional sting."[111]

The Bow Group utilized a sentence from the conclusion to Disraeli's novel *Sybil* for their promotional material: "We live in an age when to be young and to be indifferent can be no longer synonymous."[112] However, there is an even older dining group that occupies every ideological structural nook and cranny of the party and which adopted a Disraeli novel as its name: viz., *Coningsby*. With this Coningsby Club in mind, it is instructive to note that the Backbench analyses of the 1945–1955 and 1955–1959 parliaments found the rather "same strange cleavage" or the "curious cleavage" that was evident between the Oxford and Cambridge "Members", particularly with the signing of Early Day Motions.[113] However, it was in July 1921 that the Coningsby Club was formed under the presidency of Austen Chamberlain, with the aim of promoting a closer unity of interests and more active cooperation between the Oxford and Cambridge Members and to stimulate and encourage the detailed study and examination of foreign, social, and economic questions.[114] RAB Butler, who was "the president for many years" intimated that the party looked to the Club "to provide a good part of our future political elite, if I may still venture to use such a word in the so-called Century of the Common Man."[115] In 1957, Peter Tapsell wrote to Lord Hailsham with an invitation to dine as the members of the club "would very much appreciate the opportunity of having the newly appointed Chairman of the party as soon as possible" particularly as Hailsham was a member of the Club and he further commented:

> The Coningsby Club is, as you know, a dining club of Conservative graduates of Oxford and Cambridge. The majority of our members are Peers, Members of Parliament and Parliamentary candidates. During the last General Election 69 members of the club fought seats and many others were speakers and voluntary workers in the constituencies. We maintain a close liaison with the two Universities. We have, in the past, entertained most of the leading figures in public life and the Prime Minister, Mr R.A. Butler and Mr Selwyn Lloyd are amongst those who have agreed to address us during the next few months.[116]

In a similar vein, four months after becoming chairman of the party in 1965, Edward du Cann attended the Coningsby, with David Howell intimating that:

> I am writing to you on behalf of the Committee of the Coningsby Club to thank you most warmly for your kindness in coming to speak to us last night. All were agreed that it was a most excellent evening, and it was also, incidentally—if I may add a personal note—the first dinner under my Chairmanship at which the speaker has not come under fire from fairly ferocious critics! Either the Coningsby is losing its spirit, or you are already doing all the things to the Conservative party the Coningsby members are usually in the habit of demanding. I very much suspect the latter! Either way it was an excellent evening, and we are all enormously grateful.[117]

One may wonder just how coincidental it was then that the neoliberal "pathfinder" from the Bow Group, Mr Peter Lilley, chose the Coningsby to deliver the so-called clause IV moment u-turn from Thatcherism speech of April 1999 that was to cause no end of consternation and revolt within the Shadow Cabinet of William Hague.[118] The occasional stings from ferocious critics are no doubt part of that necessary process, which facilitates the party's refreshment at the springs of doctrine but importantly such groups also facilitate the bringing together of such diverse and opposite views in a forum that aids party cohesion. Indeed, David Willetts described this in Chapter 1 as one of the greatest functions of the One Nation group, in that over the years it has definitely helped hold the party together.[119] Thus, such an internal policy party architecture has fashioned a political culture that scrupulously tries to avoid any suggestion of rebellion or even lack of discipline, indeed Macleod claimed his wide knowledge of internal Conservative politics led him to the certainty that it would be suicidal for One Nation to attempt the sort of shock tactics, which brought such notoriety to the Keep Left Group[120]; and Simon Walters' *Tory Wars* is a clear illustration of that suicidal effect. And crucially, in Rose's analysis of these internal policy parties, he focused on Enoch Powell as a voice rather than a "factional" leader; he may well have been "a tribune of the people" but such action did not constitute an organized body of opinion.[121] And, it is instructive that we have affirmation of Rose's thesis on Powell's departure from the party with his political sojourn in Ulster, as even in this situation he would still eschew the temptation to create a party within a party. In September 1974, Anthony Kershaw (MP for Stroud) wrote to Powell welcoming him back to parliament and intimating that if Powell was to gather around him "a following" then his admirers, such as Kershaw, should not hear about it first from the press.[122] Powell replied:

> I take on board your admonition but when we worked closely together on defence in opposition it was clear that I regarded teamwork and mutual consultation as the essence of parliamentary action. I still do, circumstances

could only consult very narrowly and privately without creating the inevitable impression and charge of attempting to create a party within a party. This I was determined not to do, at whatever cost.[123]

## Notes

1. Belloni and Beller, 1976, p. 535.
2. Rose, 1964, pp. 33–46; Rose, 1975, pp. 312–328.
3. Rose, 1964, p. 46.
4. Hine, 1985, pp. 36–53.
5. Birch, 1949, pp. 31–32.
6. Berrington, 1973, pp. 181–184; Finer et al., 1961, pp. 110–112.
7. Rose, 1975, p. 313.
8. Ibid., p. 314.
9. Panebianco, 1988.
10. Duverger, 1954.
11. Panebianco, 1988; Rose, 1975, p. 312. Indeed, the Fabian policy of "permeation" of the Liberal Party had failed precisely because the Liberals were too decentralized and fragmented, and this was to play a significant part in the Fabians finally accepting the reality that they would have to become such an indirectly assembled autonomous unit of the nascent Labour Representation Committee; see MacKenzie and MacKenzie, 1979.
12. Seyd, 1972, pp. 467 and 487.
13. Seyd, 1980, pp. 231 and 242.
14. For example, see Barnes, 1994 p. 343.
15. Rose, 1964, p. 36.
16. Tebbit, 1989, p. 122.
17. For example, see Addison, 1975; Kavanagh and Morris, 1989.
18. See Jones, 1996; Jones and Kandiah, 1996.
19. Pimlott, 1989, p. 13.
20. Charmley, 1998, p. 121.
21. Douglas, 1983, p. 60.
22. See note 31 of Chapter 3.
23. Douglas, 1989, p. 420.
24. Tory Reform Committee, "Forward By The Right: A Statement by the Tory Reform Committee," October 1943.
25. Beer, 1976, p. 307.
26. Hinchingbrooke, 1944, pp. 2 and 15.
27. Ibid., p. 24.
28. Molson, 1945, pp. 4–6.
29. See the Conservative Party's *The Industrial Charter*, of May, 1947; in particular, its argument for central administration, copartnership and joint consultation in industry and the Government's responsibility for full employment.
30. "RAB" Butler Papers: RAB H93: 48, "Letter from Mr Butler to Viscount Hinchingbrooke, 7 August 1947," Trinity College, Cambridge.
31. Hinchingbrooke, 1947, pp. 492 and 493.

32. Ibid., p. 490; pp. 492 and 497.
33. Ramsden, 1999, p. 310.
34. Maudling, 1978, p. 45. Reginald Maudling, served on the secretariat of the Charter Committee, and recounts this story of briefing Churchill on the contents of the document.
35. The Progress Trust was also formed in 1943 with a view to aiding the formulation of Conservative policy and had offices at 16 Great College Street London. See, *The Times*, November 6, 1943.
36. "RAB" Butler Papers: RAB H93:47, "Memorandum from Mr Clarke to Mr Butler, 7 August 1947."
37. "RAB" Butler Papers: RAB H93:44, "Letter from Commander Galbraith to RAB Butler, July 24, 1947," and reply from Butler, where we find that he has had discussion with the group on the subject, August 9, 1947, RAB H93:49, ibid.
38. See "RAB" Butler Papers: RAB H93:41–43.
39. Crockett, 1995, p. 68.
40. Powell papers: POLL1/1/11/80, "Letter from Major Sir Guy Lloyd MP, on behalf of the Progress Trust, to Enoch Powell MP, July 18, 1955," Churchill College, Cambridge.
41. Crocket, 1995, pp. 72–73.
42. Wilson, 1961, pp. 129–150 passim and p. 175.
43. Ibid., p. 103. At a dinner on the March 30,1954, The One Nation group did discuss the Television Bill and agreed to vote against Clause 3 if it were not amended; suggesting that they objected to how much control and interference that would be maintained by the state and by the BBC, in Alport papers: Box 37, One Nation Minutes, Albert Sloman Library, University of Essex and see Paulu, 1956, p. 328 on clause 3.
44. Harris, 1972, p. 77.
45. Jones, 1996, p. 242.
46. Powell papers, POLL1/1/22a, "Letter from Patrick Wall MP to Enoch Powell MP, January 12,1974."
47. Brand, 1989.
48. See Tebbit, 1989, pp. 122–123.
49. *The Times*, September 20, 1973.
50. Ridley, 1992, p. 20.
51. Nott, 2002, p. 137.
52. See Powell papers, POLL/1/1/22a: These were: Michael Alison; John Biffen; Tom Boardman; Jock Bruce-Gardyne; Alan Green; Peter Hordern; John Nott, Cecil Parkinson; Enoch Powell; Peter Rees; Nick Ridley and Peter Trew.
53. See Conservative Party Archive (CPA): Keith Joseph papers: KJ/2/1; KJ/8/1 and KJ/8/19; Bodleian Library, Oxford.
54. CPA: Keith Joseph papers, KJ/26/4, "*Economic Reconstruction*: Geoffrey Howe; *The Public Sector*: John Nott; *Public Sector Manpower*: Kenneth Baker; *Taxation*: David Howell; *Industrial Relations*: Jim Prior; *Education*: Norman St John-Stevas; *Social Security*: Patrick Jenkin; *Rates*: Timothy Raison, with Keith Speed and John Nott; *Nationalization*: Nicholas Ridley; and *Town & Country Planning and Environment*: Timothy Raison."
55. This report was leaked to *The Economist*, in full, see Ridley, 1992, p. 67.
56. CPA: Keith Joseph papers, KJ/8/19, "Correspondence with Nicholas Ridley."

57. Ibid.
58. CPA: CCO3/7/43.
59. Interview with David Heathcoat-Amory, House of Commons, June 29, 2004.
60. Interview with Alistair Burt, June 28, 2004. Indeed, Alistair Burt commented on how active the Lollards used to be in backing sleights of candidates for the parliamentary party committees, but after the 1997 election with nearly 60 percent of the party on the "payroll vote," it will not be until the ranks of the Conservative backbenches are replenished at a successful election that such party committees become important again.
61. Brand, 1989, pp. 153 and 156.
62. Alport papers: Box 42, "Letter from Nicholas Scott to Cub Alport, September 20, 1973."
63. Alport papers: Box 42, "Reply to Nicholas Scott, September 24, 1973."
64. Walters, 2001.
65. Gamble, 1974, p. 7.
66. Barnes, 1994, pp. 344–345.
67. Green, 2002, pp. 240–241.
68. Rose, 1975, p. 315.
69. Goldman, 1961, 5.
70. Brittan, 1968, pp. 84–90.
71. Ibid., p. 90.
72. For example, see Heppell and Hill, 2005.
73. Norton and Aughey, 1981; Norton, 1998; Cowley and Norton, 1999 and Norton, 2001.
74. Norton, 1990.
75. Ibid., pp. 52 and 47.
76. Ibid., p. 51.
77. Ibid., p. 52.
78. Ibid., p. 54; Rose, 1975, pp. 314 and 328.
79. Cowley and Norton, 2002.
80. Heppell, 2002.
81. Cowley and Norton, 2002, p. 327.
82. Rodgers papers: OP27/8, One Nation Minutes, April 30, 1969, Centre for Kentish Studies, Kent.
83. Heppell, 2002, p. 316.
84. Evans and Taylor, 1996, p. 266.
85. For example, see the Sunday Telegraph and Sunday Times, June 15, 2008.
86. Norton, 1990, p. 50.
87. See Rose, 1975, pp. 315 and 316.
88. As noted at the time in the leadership campaign websites of David Cameron and David Davis respectively: www.cameroncampaign.org/supporters.html and www.modernconservatives.com/supporters.php; accessed November 16, 2005.
89. For example, see The Independent and Daily Telegraph, December 5, 2000.
90. Seyd, 1972, p. 471; with Patrick Wall of 92 fame a member also.
91. Norton, 1990, p. 54.
92. Seyd, 1972, p. 468.

93. See *The Independent*, October 19, 2001. However, see Seyd, 1972, p. 473, on the attitudes of the respective party leaderships to such groups and that the treatment of the Monday Club would tend to validate the claim that the Conservative Party was a more tolerant party.
94. See Rose, 1961, p. 865.
95. CPA: CCO3/2/62, "Bow Group."
96. CPA: CCO3/3/48: "Bow Group."
97. See Barr, 2001 and note the number of One Nation names involved with the Bow Group. There were close ties between the Bow Group and One Nation right from its inception in 1951 with Cub Alport helping out and with a cross-fertilization of ideas thereafter. See CPA: CCO3/3/48 and Longden papers: Longden Box List, Temporary File Number 31, One Nation, 1950–1990, "Letter from James Lemkin, 21 March 1957, enclosing copies of Bow Group pamphlets and intimating that: 'The members of the Bow Group last night found the first contact with the One Nation group most valuable,'" London School of Economics and Political Science.
98. CPA: CCO3/6/38: "Bow Group—The First Ten years, The Chairman's Annual Report for 1960."
99. CPA: RAB Butler papers, RAB 5/1: "speech to Bow Group dinner 25 February 1957."
100. Ibid.
101. Ibid. And of course, the reference is to W. H. Mallock, a late nineteenth and early twentieth-century "neoliberal" who called for a critical examination of socialism.
102. CPA: CCO3/7/4, "Bow Group press release 18 October 1967."
103. *The Times*, August 21, 1967.
104. *The Economist*, May 17, 1975, p. 17.
105. Rose, 1961, p. 865.
106. *The Economist*, May 17, 1975, p. 18.
107. CPA: Keith Joseph papers, KJ/2/1, "Letter from Keith Joseph to Patricia Hodgson, 15 October 1975 with a reply from Hodgson, on the 13 November 1975, suggesting that the Selsdon Group had greater expertise in this area"; see endnote 53.
108. Critchley, 1995, p. 212.
109. CPA: CCO3/6/38, "Bow Group—The First Ten years, The Chairman's Annual Report for 1960."
110. *The Times*, May 26, 1981. We should note that of the eight Cabinet ministers named as members of the Bow Group six were also of One Nation: Geoffrey Howe, Leon Brittan, Michael Heseltine, John Biffen, David Howell, and Norman Fowler, with the remaining two being Peter Walker and Patrick Jenkin.
111. Quoted in Rose, 1961, p. 865.
112. Disraeli, 1986, p. 497.
113. Berrington, 1973, p. 18; Finer et al., 1961, p. 127.
114. For example, see CPA: CCO 3/6/8, for "the Rules and Members book for the Coningsby Club, for 1964–65 and which reads more like a veritable list of the great and the good in the party, and, of course, note the presence of One Nation names.
115. CPA: Butler papers, RAB 5/1, "Butler address to the Oxford University Conservative Association, 28 October 1960."

116. CPA: CCO3/5/9, "Letter from Peter Tapsell to Lord Hailsham, 30 September 1957."

117. CPA: CCO3/6/8, "Letter from David Howell to Edward du Cann MP, 19 May 1965."

118. See Walters, 2001, pp. 116–117.

119. See Chapter 1, endnote 61.

120. *The Observer*, October 8, 1950.

121. Rose, 1975, p. 319.

122. Powell papers: POLL 1/1/22d, "Letter from Anthony Kershaw MP to Enoch Powell, 4 September 1974." But, interestingly see the obituary for Kershaw by Tam Dalyell in *The Independent*, May 2, 2008, where he speaks of Kershaw's loyalty to Heath in terms of a "supremely loyal Conservative MP."

123. Powell papers: POLL 1/1/22d, "Reply to Kershaw, 6 September 1974," Poll 1/1/22d.

# CHAPTER SIX

# One Nation, but Which?

The preceding chapters clearly show a fundamental aim of the Conservative Party to create an image as *the* Party of the nation and the nation state; a party that could represent the entire British nation, regardless of class or status, due to it being symbolic of the values, beliefs, and customs of One Nation. This Conservative politics of nationhood that had been a central theme for well on nigh two centuries rested upon a patriotic discourse that could paint the Whigs, the Liberals, and then Labour as sectional and of course by extension questioning the very patriotic credentials of such rivals.[1] It has been no mean feat to successfully apply such a strategy for so long to what is in reality a multinational state. Indeed, Bulpitt "points to the obvious: for the Conservative party the United Kingdom is, and always has been, a particularly difficult piece of real estate to manage."[2] But, he found it delightfully droll that on so many occasions the territorial ideas and practices of the party had received so much support from others,[3] a prominent example being the support of Joseph Chamberlain and the Liberal Unionists in the last quarter of the nineteenth century over the issue of "home rule" for Ireland. And, we have also learned that a crucial aspect of the One Nation strategy was to aid a process of depoliticization; the party was contemptuous of the necessity to engage in the shabby realm of ideological political activity because of the belief that it was working on behalf of the whole nation. For Bulpitt, the party's territorial codes not only helped resolve its "real estate" problem but underpinned its strategy of depoliticization.[4]

These operational codes of territorial politics were not static and could indeed mean different things at different times but in essence they contributed to a duality of form in Conservative Party politics between its Westminster and local levels. Although *the* national party, its operational code was to increasingly emphasize, in both constitutional and organizational terms, "the advantages of central autonomy from peripheral forces: the primacy of Westminster politicians and their freedom to pursue 'High Politics', unimpeded by provincial demands."[5] No better testimony to this is to be found than in Scotland where up to 1965 the real power bases in organizational terms were in the dichotomous structures of the Eastern and Western Divisional Councils but this changed fundamentally in light of the centralizing reforms of 1965.[6] And, Bulpitt lists constitutional examples of administrative devolution to Scotland, the reform of local government and the conciliatory or constructive Unionist policies for Ireland and then Northern

Ireland, which were all designed in part to ensure that such time consuming and dreary affairs were hived off to the localities.[7] However, we shall see that such a "duality" and its operational codes would have repercussions for Conservative Party politics and the consequences were to be acutely apparent by the 1960s. By then the One Nation ethos was to face simultaneous domestic and external challenges in the shape of further territorial dissent, questions on immigration, and disagreement over European policy; all issues that would engender deep-rooted and abiding problems for the party. Indeed, speaking at Renfrew in Scotland in 1976 Enoch Powell referred to the upper and nether millstones between which the Westminster parliament had voluntarily offered itself to be ground.[8]

The following two chapters address such abiding issues, Chapter 7 deals with the issue of Europe while the rest of this chapter examines those of devolution and immigration. The latter part of this chapter deals with the increasing focus on immigration which began in the 1950s and early 1960s but by the end of the 1960s had become a truly contentious issue for the Conservative party. "Coloured immigration" quickly provoked hostile reaction from within the party, particularly from local councils and local Conservatives but Bulpitt points out that these peripheral protests were for long ignored because the issue had the potential to interfere with the "high politics" strategy of supporting the United Kingdom's international power pretensions through the role of the Commonwealth.[9] And, the pressures from territorial politics followed a remarkable similar timeframe. As late as the mid sixties a psephological analysis of Scotland could refer to a "case study in British homogeneity"[10] but very shortly afterwards there was no such symmetry to be found in the wake of the increasingly vociferous Scottish aspirations for home rule. In fact Miller, who by the 1970s could allude to "the end of British politics," provided a simple objective measure of the amount of public attention given to the Scottish home rule issue in the postwar period. He recorded the number of lines devoted to the heading "home rule" in the *Glasgow Herald* index published until 1968 and concluded that there was very little until 1946; then, in response to MacCormack's National Convention assemblies on home rule, a swift rise to a peak in 1950, followed by a sharp drop in 1951 and 1952, and a progressive decline until 1960. Interest revived slightly between 1960 and 1966 and exploded in 1967 and 1968.[11] Thus, this first compressive nether force of devolution that exploded in the late 1960s is examined below and of course one that would create an acute problem for a party that claimed to be representative of the "entire British nation."[12]

## The Devolution Dilemma of a Rebounding "Scottish Card"

The Conservative Party, throughout the 1980s and for most of the 1990s, was virtually alone in its position of defending the constitutional status quo while warning against the anomalies that devolution entailed being the slippery

Table 6.1: The Conservative share of the vote in England, Scotland and Wales, 1950–2007.

|  | 1950 | 1951 | 1955 | 1959 | 1964 | 1966 | 1970 | 1974F | 1974O |  |
|---|---|---|---|---|---|---|---|---|---|---|
| England | 44.0 | 49.2 | 50.6 | 50.2 | 44.1 | 42.8 | 48.4 | 38.9 | 40.2 |  |
| Scotland | 46.2 | 49.6 | 50.1 | 47.6 | 40.6 | 37.6 | 38.5 | 24.7 | 32.9 |  |
| Wales | 28.3 | 33.1 | 33.5 | 33.8 | 29.4 | 27.9 | 27.7 | 23.9 | 25.9 |  |
|  | 1979 | 1983 | 1987 | 1992 | 1997 | 1999* | 2001 | 2003* | 2005 | 2007* |
| England | 47.2 | 46.0 | 46.2 | 45.5 | 33.7 | n/a | 35.2 | n/a | 35.7 | n/a |
| Scotland | 31.4 | 28.4 | 24.0 | 25.7 | 17.5 | 15.6 | 15.6 | 16.6 | 15.8 | 16.6 |
| Wales | 32.2 | 31.0 | 29.5 | 28.6 | 19.6 | 15.8 | 21.0 | 19.9 | 21.4 | 22.4 |

*These are the 'devolved' elections for Scotland and Wales and figures represent the 'first or constituency vote' of the Additional Member Electoral system for direct comparability with the Single Member Plurality System used for Westminster elections.

Source: Westminster Elections: data from the series of Nuffield Studies entitled, The British General Election of 1950 – 2005.

Scottish and Welsh Elections: data from Scottish Parliament and Welsh Assembly websites: www. scottish.parliament.uk/ and www.assembly.org.

slope to dissolving the union; in effect opening an inexorable path towards separation, particularly between England and Scotland. In contrast, the Labour and Liberal Democrat parties not only believed that such a policy panacea as devolution was right for Scotland and Wales but that it could be effectively used to attack a Conservative Party garrisoned in its Southern English redoubt. Indeed, for some time now the Conservative Party has had to face the reality of its asymmetrical support and we see this delineated in Table 6.1, where the Conservative share of the vote for England, Scotland, and Wales between 1950 and 2007 neatly encapsulates the reality that the party is now more the party of England than of Britain.

In 1995, the Labour Party's Scottish Shadow Secretary of State, George Robertson declared that "devolution would kill nationalism stone dead"[13] and the former Labour Welsh Secretary, Ron Davies,[14] was fond of identifying devolution as a process and not an event; but, after 2007 with a Scottish National Party government ensconced in Edinburgh (albeit as a minority administration) and with Labour in a governmental coalition with Plaid Cymru in Cardiff, a more convincing argument has this putative nationalist corpse as never before demonstrating such vitality. And, with the nationalist apparition appearing in such conspicuously good health it could be argued that the Conservatives were indeed proven right about the specter of devolution and its anomalous consequences; as the process now appears more the continuous route to secession than any death knell for nationalism. But, there has been no concomitant electoral benefit for the Conservatives and the fact that the Party won a marginally greater share of the popular vote in England than Labour did in 2005 ironically added to its exclusively English image problem, which exacerbates its devolution dilemma. From Table 6.1, we see that the Party had never had a tradition of winning in Wales and its share of the vote there varies from one-third to one-fifth over the period but in Scotland the trend is one of precipitous decline with its marginality very clear from 1997 onwards. But, we also see that this was not always the case as in the 1950s and early 1960s—that age of "British homogeneity in voting behaviour"—the level of success for the Scottish Unionist Party[15] mirrored that found in England for the Conservatives in the 1950s, indeed in some instances outperforming their colleagues south of the border, only for that gap in the level of support to widen adversely for the party in Scotland thereafter; mainly from the 1960s onwards, reaching double digits by 1970. The problems for the Conservative Party in portraying itself as a party of the "whole nation" are obvious from the 1980s onwards; with the party in Scotland polling nearly half the level of the vote achieved in England and obtaining no more than a sixth of the popular vote in Scotland at the start of the new century. However, the Conservative Party's opposition to or indeed support for devolution is a far more complex issue than is commonly recognized, with the party at times not being adverse at "playing the Scottish card" itself.

Although the Party was to have no truck with proposals for legislative devolution for Scotland and Wales between 1979 and 1997, there is an argument that suggests the party was adept at playing "the Scottish Card"; ironically, this is the idea that in practice it had done more than any other party to advance Scottish self-government, to the extent of considering legislative devolution by 1968.[16] As early as 1885, a Tory Government led by Lord Salisbury had set up a Scottish Office (it was 1964 before the Welsh Office was formed) and it also reconstituted the office of Secretary of State for Scotland which was abolished in 1746. In 1939, the Scottish Office was relocated to Edinburgh and it was to be Conservative governments that would increasingly strengthen the structures of administrative devolution. The Party's policy proposals for near on twenty years did not deviate much from those outlined in a 1949 document entitled, "Scottish control of Scottish affairs."[17] This statement of policy, inter alia, proposed a Minister of State for Scotland with Cabinet rank to be appointed, along with a third Under-Secretary for Scotland, which would better distribute departmental duties, along with a proposed Royal Commission to examine Scottish affairs. But, the Royal Commission on Scottish Affairs (The Balfour Commission) which was appointed in July 1952 and reported back in 1954 was precluded by its terms of reference from considering Parliamentary separation.[18] And, it was these immediate postwar years which saw an attack on the socialism of the Attlee Government; the party equating socialism with centralization and London rule. These are the years which provide the material to underpin the "Scottish card" thesis. Undoubtedly much material and rhetoric abound which supports Miller's view that proposing decentralization, in the form of devolution policy, would endear a party to the Scots[19]; although from Table 6.1 we see that there was no appreciable electoral gain for the Tories in Scotland, just point nine of a per-centage point, for proposing a Scottish Assembly in the 1970 Election.[20] But, we should note that Churchill's famous 1950 general election speech at the Usher Hall in Edinburgh, implicitly, if not explicitly, accepted the idea of Scottish home rule if the centralizing menace of socialism could not be thwarted.

> The principle of centralisation of government in Whitehall and Westminster is emphasised in a manner not hitherto experienced or contemplated in the (1707) Act of Union . . . I frankly admit that it raises new issues between our two nations . . . *I would never adopt the view that Scotland should be forced into the serfdom of socialism as a result of a vote in the House of Commons.*[21]

Of course we now have, and arguably from the 1970s, the Scottish Nationalist Party and the Labour Party competing as best facilitators of the right of the Scottish people to that "serfdom of socialism." And, as we shall see, it is remarkable how similar the argument used by Churchill to question how far the concept of parliamentary sovereignty at Westminster should extend north of the border, in the face of Scottish public opinion, mirrors that used by the opponents of the Conservative Party in the 1980s and 1990s. Indeed, typical Tory postwar election addresses evince a similar attitude to that utilized by Churchill, an example being that of Mr. T. G. D. Galbraith's who was the Scottish Unionist candidate in the 1948 Glasgow Hillhead by-election and was to become an under Secretary of State for Scotland in 1959, and who declared under the heading, "Scotland":

> As one industry after another is nationalised we are finding that Scottish affairs are dominated by the control of Ministers and officials in England who are often ignorant of the ways of our Country. Socialist MP's may say that they are good Scotsmen but their whole policy is one of centralisation and control by Whitehall. I will resist this and demand that in each industry which has been nationalised a Scottish Committee shall be set up with full executive powers to deal with Scottish problems.[22]

Moreover, Walter Elliot, the Scottish Secretary of State in the 1930s and a mas-ter at beating the Scottish drum when needed; would explicitly equate the socialist policy of nationalization with the "denationalization" of Scotland. For Elliot, the consequence of such a centralizing policy was London control at the expense of Scottish control. In a 1950, debate with the Labour Secretary of State for Scotland, Sir Arthur Woodburn, he took great pleasure in mischievously castigating Woodburn for having to ring up London for permission to use extra heating from an electric fire. Elliot also criticized Labour in the same debate for having three English born MPs standing for election in Scotland.[23] As we shall see, similar to that of the Labour party for the 1980s and 1990s, stoking the fires of this quasi-nationalism would eventually rebound on the party but from Table 6.1 it is clear that the 1950s were indeed relatively successful years for the Scottish Unionist Party with the Conservatives holding power at Westminster from 1951 to 1964.

However, the "explosion" in the home rule issue in the late 1960s led to Edward Heath adopting a policy for a form of moderate legislative devolution in 1968 that would set up an Assembly which would scrutinize legislation for Scotland. He, like many members of the shadow Cabinet, was concerned about the perceived rise of nationalism. This was the era of the Thistle Group in the Party and the group was formed in November 1967 after the Scottish Nationalist Party's success at the Hamilton by-election. Ironically, its founders and leading members were to later become some of the most prominent and committed unionists of the "Thatcher party": for example, the One Nation members, Malcolm Rifkind and Michael Ancram, along with Lord Fraser of Carmyllie and Alexander Pollock. But, the Thistle Group at the time, in contrast to Heath's moderate proposal, envisaged a Scottish Parliament which would raise its own taxes. And in light of the anxiety over the rise of Scottish Nationalism, Mr. Heath took the opportunity to reverse Party policy at the 1968 Perth Conference.[24] The "Declaration of Perth" may be criticized for being merely grandiloquent posturing, but nevertheless, it was reported at the time as a watershed in Conservative thought on the governance of Scotland.

> Even so, he [Heath] took Tory policy some considerable distance along a new avenue. He rejected separatism; he rejected federalism (which had some sympathy in the party); and, significantly, he rejected the status quo. In its place he virtually committed a future Conservative Government to set up an elected Scottish Assembly, to sit in Scotland.[25]

Although the proposals look pale by the standards of the 1990s, they represented a firmer commitment to change than anything offered by Labour at the time, led as it was in Scotland by the firmly anti-devolutionist, Willie Ross. However, the Heath administration of 1970–74 has been much criticized for reneging on the commitment to set up a Scottish Assembly but extraneous events intervened which led to the failure to implement the policies promised at Perth. The Government believed it necessary to wait on the Kilbrandon Report[26] (set up by Harold Wilson in 1969) expected within a year of the 1970 election because quite simply the Commission threatened to resign if Heath proceeded with legislation on devolution which would have caused the government considerable embarrassment.[27]

By 1975, the Tories were now in opposition under the new leadership of Mrs. Thatcher and she spoke on behalf of a motion calling for a directly elected

Assembly at the Scottish conference in 1976 but by the end of that year her Shadow Secretary of State, Sir Alick Buchanan-Smith, had resigned from the front bench team in protest at the party's policy of opposing the Scotland and Wales Act. The policy was to deprecate Labour's Act as defective while not ruling out the principle of devolution, although Buchanan-Smith believed that ruling out devolution was exactly the attitude being conveyed to the Scottish electorate.[28] It was to be One Nation members, Francis Pym and Leon Brittan, who were chosen to examine the issue and they stressed that the Scotland Act would not remedy the genuine problems of Scotland and would only sow the seeds of discord and friction leading to the breakup of the United Kingdom. Indeed, their pamphlet emphasized the dilemma of the "West Lothian Question,"[29] namely the role of Scots MPs after devolution, and was very prescient in alluding to the resentment that would be felt in England as a consequence of such a policy when after devolution Scots MPs would be able to vote on English housing, education, and health but not on Scots housing, education, and health.

> Even if there were an explicit acceptance of the anomaly in the short term . . . it would be unlikely to survive a Parliament in which the voting patterns of Scottish MPs continuously determined the outcome of non-Scottish legislation. The only logical way in which to overcome the anomaly is to deprive Scots MPs of the right to vote on non-Scottish matters. It is unlikely that would commend itself for long.[30]

The leading proponents of the "New Right" agenda, such as Nigel Lawson, firmly believed that laissez-faire economic policy in tandem with getting government off the peoples' backs was truly devolutionary as it would empower the people directly.[31] Of course, Thatcher eventually took this course and the Party in Scotland loyally followed this unionist approach and her successor John Major, if anything, hardened the stance. So the Conservative Party entered the 1992 and 1997 election battles, deprecating the independence and devolutionary positions taken by the other parties while emphasizing that it was the only true unionist party, with John Major informing his biggest election rally at Wembley in 1992: "If I could summon up all the authority of this office I would put it into this single warning—the United Kingdom is in danger. Wake up. Wake up now before it's too late."[32] But, the present shadow cabinet minister Dr. Liam Fox, and his colleagues, had previously argued that the upsurge in nationalism in the 1960s was merely encouraged by the postwar administrative devolution implemented by the Conservative Party and that such nationalism received a major fillip when Edward Heath proposed the creation of a devolved Scottish Assembly.[33] Thus, crucially, this zigzagging on devolution policy undermined the Unionist case: "The Party of 'positive Unionism' cannot also be the party of legislative devolution. The principles which would be embodied in the former are simply incompatible with the principles on which a system of legislative devolution would be established."[34] However, in the wake of the New Labour victory of 1997 and the setting up of the Scottish Parliament and Welsh Assembly there was again a volte face on such policy; the Conservative Party now wholeheartedly supported legislative devolution while espousing the mantra that only they "could make devolution work." What was meant by this of course was that the Conservative Party would address that major anomalous position that was the West Lothian Question, which was, by the turn of the new century, increasingly referred to as the "English Question"; with the implicit threat of the "serfdom of socialism" of England as a result of the votes of Scottish and Welsh MPs in the House of Commons.

## The "English Question"

There is now an increasing level of resentment to be found south of the border, indeed found within the ranks of both major parties, concerning a putative favorable position for Scotland and Wales, postdevolution, vis-à-vis England; and this has thrown into sharp relief the dilemma that now faces the Conservative Party over its policy on devolution. The main grievances of this resentment concerned the "English question" and the Barnett formula[35] but in developing under William Hague the "English votes for English laws" policy, which was meant to address the anomalous position whereby Scots MPs (and to a lesser extent Welsh MPs) could be the arbiters of legislation for English constituencies while not having the ability to pronounce on such policy for their own constituents merely highlighted the constitutional imbroglio that asymmetrical devolution had now become and the potential for such a policy to further endanger the very union that the party wishes to protect. Undoubtedly the process is one of "unfinished business" and as such its nature is to engender a recurrence of democratic legitimacy questions that have to be addressed.[36] Mitchell examines both a "decline of legitimacy" pre-devolution and what he terms "legitimacy spillover" with regards to the present situation of England: "In essence, one of the predictable consequences of devolution has been to displace rather than remove the legitimacy deficit."[37] Such displacement was ignored by New Labour, to the extent that Derry Irvine, Blair's first Lord Chancellor, declared: "the best way to deal with the West Lothian question was to stop asking it."[38]

Indeed, this opportunistic avoidance of the question was compounded by the existence of a convention acknowledging the West Lothian conundrum, one which was adhered to by the major parties until the rise of New Labour. Even before the Scottish Parliament was constituted but with the existence of the Scottish Office in Edinburgh the convention developed that certain offices of state, notably those of Health and the Home Office, would not be filled by a Scot as such matters relating to Scotland were under the jurisdiction of the Scottish Office. No Scot had occupied such posts since the 1930s but this convention was broken first in 2003 with John Reid's appointment as Secretary of State for Health and then in 2006 when he was moved to the Home Office.[39] Interestingly, at the 1992 General Election, Robin Cook, at the time the Labour Shadow Health Secretary, in an answer to a question about Scots Ministers of State legislating for England while not having a similar authority for Scotland replied: "Absolutely clear and simple answer to this—once we have a Scottish Parliament, handling Scottish health affairs in Scotland, it is not possible for me to continue as Minister of Health, administering health in England."[40]

Although the Conservatives were the most vociferous of the major parties on this English question many within the Labour party shared their concern.[41] The Scottish Affairs committee, with a Labour majority, believed the West Lothian Question was "a time bomb that urgently needs to be defused" and stated that it was "a matter of concern to us that English discontent is becoming apparent."[42] Allied to this discontent was, of course, the issue of funding for Scotland in the Barnett formula. For example, David McLean the former Tory chief whip remonstrated that:

> Not only have we got an unbalanced Parliament in Westminster, with Scottish MPs having more rights than English MPs, we are having legislation foisted on England with the votes of Scottish MPs. We are getting fundamentally greater expenditure on people in Scotland, which is aggravating rural poverty in England. If the Government does not address this, it will find an unstoppable demand in England for separation.[43]

Such attitudes led to the "English votes for English laws" policy, which was included both in William Hague's and Michael Howard's manifestos for the 2001 and 2005 general elections, respectively. The assumption of the policy was that the Speaker of the House of Commons could actually designate which Bills were solely for "English Laws" and thus enable the exclusion of any votes that were not from English constituencies. But in reality it would be very difficult to discern such a clear division to such legislation and for the Speaker of the House of Commons to unequivocally declare when there would be no impact from such laws on the other nations of Great Britain. The complexity of such territorial implications is evident in the parliamentary debates on the two "private member" Bills which were introduced firstly into the House of Lords by the erstwhile One Nation member Lord Baker of Dorking in February 2006 and then into the House of Commons by Robert Walter, the Conservative MP for North Dorset, in March 2007. Speaking on his "House of Commons (Participation) Bill" Robert Walter declared:

> My Bill follows a similar Bill that was introduced in the House of Lords in the last Session by the noble Lord Baker which sought to do very much the same as what I propose. However, a number of anomalies were identified in his

Bill. Therefore, the basic provisions of my Bill are that, in respect of primary legislation, the Speaker may designate whether it should be considered by "all members returned for constituencies in England and Wales"—thus taking account of the fact that Wales does not have primary legislative powers— "all members returned for constituencies in Scotland . . . all members returned for constituencies in Northern Ireland," or any combination of those.[44]

But, as Vernon Bogdanor was to point out such an approach would still create anomalies as it was not that easy to determine which Bills would be precisely English, or English and Welsh, as finance for Scotland and Wales is through a block fund based on that very Barnett formula "the size of which depends on expenditure in England"; thus if education spending was cut back in England this would have a knock on effect to Scotland.[45] Bogdanor warned of the implications of such an approach for the Union as did Labour's Jack Straw, the Leader of the House of Commons, when he warned that "this approach would start to dissolve the glue which binds our Union, and over time would lead to the break-up of the United Kingdom itself."[46] However, both Bogdanor and Straw failed to acknowledge New Labour's part as "catalytic agent" in the attenuation of that constitutional glue in the first place. Something not lost on John Major in 2007, when more than a decade after the 1992 Election where he had warned of devolution being the Trojan horse for separation, he stated:

> If the Union is now unstable, Labour bears the greatest single responsibil-
> ity. It scoffed at all warnings and—for partisan advantage—passed a wholly
> one-sided Devolution Act that gave Scotland all it hoped for with no regard
> to the effect across the United Kingdom. . . . And it would be foolish not to
> acknowledge that a Scottish prime minister with a Scottish constituency will
> highlight afresh the constitutional anomaly.[47]

Indeed, ironically it was Gordon Brown who had previously questioned the right of any English MP to legislate for Scotland:

> In February 1983, Gordon Brown, as vice-chairman of the Scottish Labour
> party, questioned whether Conservative rule of Scotland would be legitimate
> if Labour won in Scotland again. The job of the Scottish Secretary of State
> should be made "untenable," Brown argued.[48]

But with so many Scots in some of the most important UK Ministries, no less in the office of Prime Minister itself, some Conservatives questioned the legiti-macy of Labour rule of England if the Conservatives win in England again and if in such a scenario the position of a "Scottish Prime Minister" is untenable? Of course, the constitutional Pandora's box is now well and truly opened and a major question concerns the ability of the Conservative Party to actually "make devolution work", and if the seemingly inexorable path towards separation can in fact be reversed. To this effect, very soon after becoming party leader David Cameron tasked Kenneth Clarke with setting up the Democracy Task Force, which would address such problems arising from New Labour's constitutional reforms. However, the exchanges in ideas between Kenneth Clarke and Malcolm Rifkind, concerning this "major anomalous position," merely illustrate just how problematic it will be for the party to discover an acceptable solution to this constitutional conundrum. Ken Clarke's democracy task force's latest "English laws variant" proposed the solution of Scottish and Welsh MPs being excluded at the committee and report stage of a Bill that applied to legislation for England only, but then being able to vote again on the Bill's third reading; where of course no detailed amendments could be made. Of course this does not address the problem of how such a Bill would be unequivocally acknowledged as "English." And Rifkind, whose own "English Grand Committee" solution was rejected by the task force, believed such proposals would create for the first time in history two classes of British MPs.[49] Such a split between One Nation members merely confirms the difficulty for the party in finding new operational codes for this compressive force of territorial politics. But, what of the other issue that has implications for a party with an ethos of One Nation; namely that of immigration?

## Civis Britannicus Sum?

The difference of opinion between two such prominent One Nation members, as Clarke and Rifkind, on the composition of future devolution policy, is witness to that perpetual "conflict and tension" that is the internal policy party debate. And, on reading the evidence presented thus far we should by now be little surprised to find a similar disputatious discourse over the issue of immigration and how it may affect the traditions, values, and norms of One Nation. Indeed, as we shall see, it is no exaggeration to make a claim for the One Nation group as the consummate microcosm of party debate on this issue. Layton-Henry informs us that although the Cabinet acknowledged the rising levels of opposition to "coloured immigration" among the ranks of Conservative members and local councilors in the 1950s—with particular regard to the disturbances in Nottingham and Notting Hill—it was never deemed a high priority.[50] Indeed, in these postwar years the dominant sentiment within the Cabinet and the Party was still one of nostalgia for a British Empire which when transformed into a multiracial Commonwealth would help buttress that goal of influence in world affairs. Thus, in 1954 the Conservative Colonial Secretary could say:

> In a world in which restrictions on personal movement and immigration have increased we still take pride in the fact that a man can say *civis Britannicus sum* whatever his colour may be, and we take pride in the fact that he wants and can come to the Mother Country.[51]

A decade or so later and increasingly disappointed with the realization that the Commonwealth had fallen far short of that presumptive influence on the world stage; it was a reference to Roman mythology rather than to a Latin locution which signaled the fundamental change in the consideration of such "priorities." Enoch Powell delivered a speech in Birmingham on April 20, 1968 that utilized the words of the prophetess Sibyl in Virgil's *Aeneid* to assert: "As I look ahead, I am filled with foreboding; like the Roman, I seem to see 'the River Tiber foaming with much blood.'"[52] This was to enter the annals of history as the "rivers of blood" speech but it was also indicative of the intensity and level of debate found within the party on an issue, similar to that of territorial politics that had "exploded" in the 1960s. It was the Conservative Party that had first questioned the very essence of that right to be a "citizen of Britain" and legislated to control the level of immigration from the Commonwealth in 1962; but by doing so they wished to highlight a dual approach which would stress just how conducive such controls were to good community and race relations. However, with the Labour party's proposals in 1968 to introduce further antidiscrimination legislation by extending its 1965 Race Relations Act, the dual approach increasingly came under considerable pressure; opening deep emotional divisions within the party.[53] The One Nation minutes not only reveal the level of such turbulent rifts but with them the concomitant difficulty of maintaining the credibility of the dual approach in light of the emotional rhetoric now surrounding this issue of immigration.

One year before "rivers of blood" the One Nation group had discussed race relations and Commonwealth immigration and enquired after the fate of the policy from the Selwyn Lloyd committee that had recommended the reduction in the number of immigrants if "their passage home was assisted." At this meeting there "was general agreement with the view that it was necessary to make speeches in the country in favor of a complete stoppage of Commonwealth immigration, even in the case of those seeking admission for family reasons."[54] However, at the meeting immediately after Powell's Birmingham speech those present thought it clear that Enoch Powell had no conception of what emotions he was stirring with such inflammatory rhetoric as "it might well be that political life will never really be the same again in this country as a result of Enoch's speech."[55] Indeed, it was considered to be all a populist bid for the leadership of the party in the event of the Tories losing the next general election and they fully supported Ted Heath in asking Enoch to resign.[56] And, when in attendance for the first time since his speech on immigration Powell seemed to be thoroughly enjoying his notoriety and it was also documented:

> Enoch considered that the reaction to his speech was "fantastically greater than he ever suspected." Since circulating the text of the speech he has had a number of letters from Members of Parliament, telling him that having read his speech they could not find anything racialist in it. Enoch confessed

himself that he would have left out the last bit, which included a Latin quotation about rivers of blood, if he had thought more carefully about it. The streets of London over the past ten days had been filled with marchers demonstrating in favour of Enoch's views. . . . Enoch made it plain that he was not a racialist, but was merely expressing the views of his constituents and tens of thousands of people throughout the country, He had no regrets.[57]

But, there were to be many a contrary opinion, from those having read the speech who found much in it that was racist. Indeed, *The Times* found it disgraceful and a deliberate appeal to racial prejudice, classing it: "an evil speech."[58] The racist epithets in the speech, like "wide eyed piccaninnies" or the opinions suggesting that "in 15 or 20 years time the black man will have the whip hand over the white man"[59] are indeed expressed through the views of Powell's constituents. However, in an extraordinary minute of the group for June 1968, quoted at length below, we find a similar sentiment, but on this occasion unequivocally attributed to Powell; importantly we should also note, in the views of those present, the wide acceptance of the party's policy on voluntary repatriation:

Deedes' pamphlet on immigration was nearly complete and a long discussion took place on the subject of immigration. Various views were put forward, but Enoch Powell was convinced that *compulsory* repatriation was the only long term answer. He considered that "without it there will be widespread fighting." All those present appeared to be in favour of a *voluntary* repatriation policy except Deedes, who thought it would achieve nothing. It was also felt that all vouchers should be stopped. It was agreed that the Shadow Cabinet should produce a firm statement in the near future, putting forward the Party's views on immigration. Marcus Worsley suggested that bringing immigrants within the ordinary Aliens Acts might well be a possible solution. Whilst those present agreed with Enoch that it was essential that hope was given to the country that no more immigrants would be coming in and that some would be going out, there were varying views as to how this should be achieved. Enoch stressed that over the period of the next few years, towns and cities throughout the country would come to be dominated by alien groups. These groups, whose faces would be black or brown, and consisting of people who came from either Asia or the West Indies, would be deeply resented by people who were born in this country. "Killing will start," he said, "and I would not hesitate to lead the killing myself." When pressed on this last remark, he repeated it and stated that if an alien force such as Germans were occupying our cities, we would surely fight in the Resistance. The same applied to these immigrants. All members were shocked by Enoch's statement. Later on in the evening the Nation, which had a large attendance due to a running three-line whip on the Prices and Incomes Bill, adjourned to an Interview Room where the discussion continued. During these later discussions, Enoch appeared much more restrained and strove with many of us to try and find some practical solution to the immigration problems which face the nation.[60]

One may speculate on the extent of the worship of Bacchus here but even allowing for such an overindulgence there is certainly no ambiguity to be had with the provenance of Powell's unedifying comments. The One Nation group had been thinking of a pamphlet on immigration for some time and as late as February 1968 it looked as if a pamphlet by Deedes, finally published in August 1968,[61] would be produced on behalf of the whole group[62] but no doubt such "deep emotional divisions" led to its single authorship. However, Deedes argued in the pamphlet that much of the combustible material in Powell's Birmingham speech was not racialism but a resentment that had built up over the lack of candor from the Government on this major issue.[63] Although, such lack of candor was not due to a conspiracy of silence but more to a "native shyness, a nervousness about the subject which has inhibited frank discussion."[64] But, there was to be little evidence of similar indigenous circumspection in the candid exchanges in the One Nation group. In late November 1968 we find:

> Another dialogue on race. Rippon accuses Powell of breach of faith in Shadow Cabinet. Enoch retorts "no such agreement." Tempers under control but not agreement. Then a lot of sound advice to Enoch. "Do you realise the Frankenstein you are arousing"? "Do you think you make things easier for us"? "Do stress the 'no second class citizen' bit in your next speech" and so on. Will he listen? I doubt it—too often a resort to "I am the only person who knows what I am talking about."[65]

Such exchanges illustrate the divide even among the neoliberals on this issue, with Geoffrey Rippon at ease with the more orthodox view that economic benefits accrue with the free movement of labor and Enoch Powell taking a far more "nationalist" line.[66] However, the Rippon accusation that this was a "breach of faith in Shadow Cabinet" does not stand close inspection as the party's policy was one of voluntary repatriation[67] however much the use of inflammatory language by Powell undermined the dual approach; and the 1968 Race Relations Act presented to parliament 48 hours after Powell's speech was condemned by the Conservative Opposition as thoroughly bad law because although there were those who passionately wished to see justice for immigrants there were also those who no less passionately and no less reputably were opposed to the infringement of individual liberty.[68] Indeed, Rippon was present at the One Nation dinner when there was further discussion of the "threatened Race Relations Bill" with unanimous agreement "that it was intolerable to prevent a man selling his own house to whomsoever he chose."[69] And, Deedes believed it wrong to classify such arguments as disreputable as they were deeply felt and expressed by the public at large and thus a party that lays "claim to being a national party must reflect them. To present these matters simply in terms of a 'punch-up' between party factions is less reputable and more damaging to race relations."[70] There may well have been some electoral advantage for the party in its advocacy of tight immigration controls at the 1970 election[71] but it came at the expense of a serious rupture of the dual approach; a political climate that was conditioned by such intemperate and inflammatory rhetoric elicited the impression of a specious association between immigration control and the betterment of race relations. This lengthy exposition of One Nation views in this short period is justified in that it sets the scene for the long-term perception of the party's immigration policy, where at times its advocacy of greater restrictive controls could leave it vulnerable to accusations of racism and to the portrayal by the media of an image—and one normally avoided at all costs—of being sectional.

Of course, there were short-term electoral opportunities to be had as well as the long term dangers in the exploitation of populist strategies and the calculated use of the issue was employed by Mrs. Thatcher in the run up to the 1979 Election; where in a *World in Action* television interview she intimated that the Conservative Party should "hold out the prospect of an end to immigration" because she believed the people were afraid that "the country and the British character might be swamped by people with a different culture . . . [and] if you want good race relations, you have got to allay peoples fears on numbers."[72] However, we should remind ourselves that it was under Mrs. Thatcher's leadership that the party instituted the *One Nation Forum*, which was laudably set up to encourage the recruitment and support from amongst the ethnic minorities; however much it could be presented as mere electoral calculation, as the ethnic minorities were considered to be a political force in around 70 Parliamentary seats.[73] But, arguably William Hague and Michael Howard miscalculated spectacularly with the perception of a one-sided utilization of the dual approach strategy; as conversely both populist appeals were to be labeled racist by significant sections of the media. To give but one of numerous examples, there was *The Times* headline of the "Tories playing the race card" when in fact the actual article referred more to the Labour party intensifying its own hard line on asylum-seekers to the extent that: "the Liberal Democrats said that they were to report both main parties to the Commission for Racial Equality for their language over the issue."[74] Admittedly, the media was not left short of material that could be utilized in this context. In the run up to the 2001 general election William Hague wanted to take the party on "a journey to a foreign land, to Britain after a second term of Tony Blair."[75] This was in direct reference to the single currency but the message eerily echoed the claim of Powell in Birmingham that the existing population "found themselves strangers in their own country" and it was not difficult for the media to conflate this message with Hague's harsh tone on asylum-seekers, with its emphasis that the "next Conservative government will assess the validity of asylum claims within weeks, not years. And, where applications are unfounded, immediate deportation will follow."[76] Hague may well have stressed the role of Britain as a haven for those in immediate peril but unfortunately this message was to be lost in the *non sequitur* that the dual approach was fast becoming.

Around the time of its Conference in 2004, it was argued that the party had returned to its moldy core vote a la William Hague; where the baseball caps had resurfaced with the skinhead rhetoric of endless talk on immigration.[77] This perception of Michael Howard "circling the Tory wagons" around the need to limit immigration and control asylum was not to change right through to the 2005 general election-day itself.[78] Lynton Crosby, the controversial Australian communications strategist, was associated with a "dog whistle politics" strategy which sent out rather controversial messages that, in theory, could only be heard by certain targeted groups of voters, just as the pitch of a dog whistle is not audible to humans.[79] These so-called dog whistle messages, such as "it's not racist to impose limits on immigration," were incorporated into the direct mail, leafleting, poster campaigns, and the election broadcasts. However, in reality it became more a case of "klaxon horn politics" drowning out in the media other less controversial but positive appeals. According to David Davis, the shadow home secretary, "the Tory leadership never intended to major on immigration, but the media 'ramped it up' as Mr Howard's chief message."[80] At best this is an admission of being political communication amateurs and at worst a party in denial. Six months before the election campaign the One Nation member Damian Green—quoting the erstwhile member Enoch Powell that politicians complaining about the press were like sailors complaining about the sea—made the point that a prerequisite for success was an ability to talk to supporters through the media.[81]

Throughout the period of William Hague's leadership there were appeals to One Nation Toryism, with Hague speaking of it in terms of "expressing the instincts of the country"[82]; whereas Rich could stress the Keith Joseph view in the early 1970s of "ourselves as the national party has always meant basing ourselves on what the nation has in common."[83] Rich rightly emphasizes a continuing theme of One Nation Conservatism that can accommodate to a diversity of social groupings and thus that it has the remarkable capacity to adapt towards a more pluralist social make up of the future.[84] With this in mind the next section examines how David Cameron intends to utilize such a capacity in terms of both his devolution conundrum and the knotty issue that immigration has now become for the party.

## Cameron's One Nation Conundrum

After two general elections where the party found it near impossible to rid itself of the racist undertones in those campaigns, Cameron moved swiftly to considerably augment that vital second component of the dual approach, namely improved race relations. He appointed a relatively young but well-known West

Yorkshire Muslim, Sayedda Warsi, the party's vice-chairman in 2005 and on her ennoblement appointed her to the Shadow Cabinet in 2007 with responsibility for community cohesion and social action. Indeed, Trevor Phillips of the Equalities and Human Rights Commission believed Cameron was draining the toxicity from the party on the issue and praised him for "de-racialising the debate on immigration."[85] Moreover, it was apparent that any comment that could be construed as having negative connotations for the party on immigration—however passionately opposed the speaker to the infringement of individual liberty—would be suppressed with alacrity by the Shadow Cabinet. A good example of this was when the candidate for the West Midlands marginal set of Halesowen, Nigel Hastilow, was forced to resign when he refused to apologize for suggesting in a newspaper article that "Enoch Powell was right."[86] But, although no doubt developed with the best of intentions, there were examples of where the policy could go disastrously wrong for the Conservative leader, one being the candidacy of Tony Lit at the Ealing Southall by-election where after joining the party just days before, the Sikh candidate stood as a "David Cameron Conservative" but was then exposed as a former contributor to the Labour party; being photographed with Tony Blair at one such dinner just four weeks before the by-election vote.[87] We shall examine in Chapter 8 if David Cameron has learned lessons from such misjudgments, ridiculed for their egotism and hubris but there is no doubt that he has strived to emphasize the integrative benefits of a One Nation policy for the more pluralist social makeup of a future Britain; which will go a long way to minimize the charges of racism from some sections of the media at the next general election.

However, it is apparent that the party did find itself disadvantaged by the perception of its marginalization on what had become a valence issue for the media; where it received almost universal opprobrium for the racial connotations of its immigration policy. And we can trace a similar eventuality with regards to policy on territorial politics. It may be far more useful to view such issues as devolution for Scotland not in terms of a traditionally "position issue," where the parties take up a distinct political position towards the issue, like most issues of a left–right nature. It may well be that sometime in the 1980s, reinforced in the 1990s, and due in no small measure to Labour exploiting the "Scottish card" in opposition to Thatcherism that it underwent a metamorphosis into one of a valence framework[88]; as this would fit comfortably with the idea of an increasingly vivid portrayal of the Scottish Tories—by a left wing Scottish party consensus and a left wing "Scottish establishment"—as being alien to the Scottish body politic. Stokes differentiates *position issues* that are on our left–right ordered dimension with *valence issues* that are more to do with the degree to which parties are linked in the public's mind with conditions or goals or symbols of which almost everyone approves or disapproves.[89] Adapting Stokes work for territorial politics has us, in this case, viewing devolution for Scotland itself as the valence issue. Thus, such a valence issue acquires its power from the fact that rival parties are linked with the universally approved symbol of Scottishness and the Tories with the universally disapproved symbol of non-Scottishness. The valence framework can also facilitate a venal exploitation of negative campaigning. A valence issue will deliver maximum support for a party if its symbolic content is of high importance to the electorate and there is complete identification of the party with the positive symbol and that of the rival party with the negative symbol.[90] Throughout the last two decades of the twentieth century the left wing parties, Labour, the Liberal Democrats in all their guises, and the Scottish National Party, successfully portrayed the Tories in Scotland with the negative universally disapproved symbol of "un-Scottish."[91] One has only to review the Scottish Press, at the time of William Hague's speech on the need for a solution to the West Lothian Question, for a good example of the use of this negative symbolism. The argument for English MPs having similar rights to Members of the Scottish Parliament (MSPs) was viewed by the other three main Scottish parties as inherently divisive, typical of Tory anti-Scottishness and "the small minded attempt to seek revenge on the voters who rejected them."[92]

This then is the conundrum for "Cameron's Conservative party"; how does it address these views found in Scotland and to a lesser extent in Wales while cognizant of the increasing resentment felt in England over New Labour's "one sided devolution reforms"; and while at the same time not "aiding and abetting" the views of English Nationalists? The party cannot just ignore the English Question, although some left wing commentators do indeed adopt that rather puerile Lord Irvine position of simply advocating the not asking of it.[93] With the Scottish Nationalist Party consistently getting the better of Labour in Scotland, a Scottish Constitutional Commission—the Calman Commission— was set up by the three main Unionist parties to develop cross-party and cross-border proposals that will shore up devolution[94] and this could well form part of the answer for the Conservative Party regarding its valence problem of territorial politics. Thus, the Conservative Party, to its considerable advantage, may well see a cross party acceptance of some form of fiscal autonomy for Scotland. There is no doubt that such an outcome would help immensely with the resentment found south of the border over the putative benefits for Scotland and Wales of the Barnett formula. And, with the attenuation of such resentment Cameron could then address the fundamental issue of "English legislation"; notably in a less febrile atmosphere. But, if nothing else, the Commission facilitates a holding strategy for Cameron; although crucially, in this instance, a cross party one. Of course, one answer to the question of "One Nation, but which" could simply be to accept that the Party is a party of England and move accordingly towards an English Parliament and with it English "self-determination." However, the Party has rejected outright such a notion and remains committed to developing policies that will underpin the Union; indeed the commitment to the Union was reiterated by David Cameron at a Scottish Conservative and Unionist meeting in September 2006:

> Britain has given the world so much and I believe that we still have more to give. Of course, there are some in England, including a few in my own party, who think my pro-Union position is crazy. "Look" they point out, "At the general election the Tories got more votes in England than Labour did. If Scotland split off, you'd find it much easier to become Prime Minister." And so I would. But I have a message for these siren voices. Sorry—not interested. I'm a Unionist and every corner of this United Kingdom is precious to me, including Scotland.[95]

## Notes

1. Lynch, 2003, p. 182 and see also Lynch, 1999.
2. Bulpitt, 1982, p. 144.
3. Ibid., p. 140.
4. Ibid., p. 144.
5. Ibid., pp. 153–154; and see Bulpitt 1986a, for an account of such "statecraft" in the politics of Thatcherism.
6. See Seawright, 1999.
7. Bulpitt, 1982, p. 153.
8. Ritchie, 1978, pp. 135–136.
9. Bulpitt, 1982, p. 161, 1986b; and see Layton-Henry, 1980.
10. Budge and Urwin, 1966.
11. Miller, 1981, p. 24.
12. See also Seawright, 1999, 2002, 2008a, 2008b.
13. Warner, 2007.
14. Davies, 1999.
15. The party in Scotland was known as the Scottish Unionist Party between 1912 and 1965, it readopted the Conservative label in 1965 with an attendant "Anglicised" image problem thereafter; see Seawright, 1999.
16. Miller, 1981.
17. SUA, 1949.
18. Balfour, 1954.
19. Miller, 1981, p. 26 and Miller et al., 1981. p. 205.
20. See Seawright, 1999.
21. Miller, 1981, p. 21.
22. See National Library of Scotland: Acc/10424, "General Election Addresses."
23. Miller, 1981, pp. 22 and 25.
24. However, it would appear that Heath's policy was adopted without much consultation with the parliamentary party and with little acknowledgment of the increasing opposition to it in the Scottish party after the 1968 conference decision, for example, see Bogdanor 1980, p. 81.
25. See *The Glasgow Herald*, May 20, 1968.

26.  Kilbrandon, 1973.
27.  Bogdanor, 1980, p. 85.
28.  Indeed, Alex Douglas Home advised rejecting the Scotland Act because it did not secure proportional representation in the Assembly elections and that the Assembly would not have revenue raising powers, Bogdanor, 1980, p. 90; which ironically were partly the reasons given by John Major for the party opposing the Labour devolution proposals in the 1990s only this time because a Scottish Parliament would have such features.
29.  Enoch Powell coined the phrase after Tam Dalyell asked the question about his role as Member for the West Lothian seat post devolution; see Heffer, 1999, p. 797.
30.  Pym and Brittan, 1978, p. 14.
31.  Bogdanor, 1979, p. 112 and Marr, 1995, p. 155.
32.  *The Scotsman*, April 6, 1992.
33.  Fox et al., 1988, pp. 6–7.
34.  Ibid., p. 11.
35.  It became common for certain newspapers to speak of the £1,500 subsidy, which Scottish people receive each year from the English taxpayers and that because of this the Labour Government had ordered a review of the "controversial Barnett formula" (*Daily Telegraph*, March 5, 2008). Indeed, the New Labour Party's favorite think tank, the Institute of Public Policy Research (IPPR), believed the formula was not fit for purpose and was in fact a source of the increasing tension between England and Scotland (*Daily Telegraph*, July 10, 2008).
36.  Mitchell, 2006.
37.  Ibid., p. 469.
38.  *The Independent*, July 3, 2006. It is instructive that the title of the article is: "Ungrateful Scots have finally awakened the dormant nationalism of the English."
39.  Mitchell, 2006, p. 470.
40.  Harper, 1992, p. 13.
41.  For example, see the articles by the Labour MPs: Frank Field, in the *Daily Telegraph*, June 1, 2008, entitled: "Gordon [Brown] must answer the English Question" and Denis MacShane, in the *Daily Telegraph*, July 27, 2008, entitled: "For Labour, the Scottish years are over."
42.  *Daily Telegraph*, July 20, 2006.
43.  Ibid.
44.  House of Commons Hansard Debates, March 9, 2007: Column 1790.
45.  *Financial Times*, February 10, 2006.
46.  "The Future of Parliament" speech by Rt. Hon. Jack Straw MP, Leader of the House of Commons, to the Hansard Society, London, July 11, 2006: www.commonsleader.gov.uk/OutPut/Page1605.asp.
47.  *Daily Telegraph*, March 9, 2007.
48.  Mitchell, 2006, p. 467.
49.  *The Scotsman*, July 2, 2008.
50.  Layton-Henry, 1980, pp. 55–57.
51.  Ibid., p. 51.
52.  Full text of the speech can found in the *Daily Telegraph* July 17, 2007.
53.  Layton-Henry, 1980, pp. 58–63.

54. Rodgers papers: OP27/8, One Nation Minutes, July 26, 1967: with Mark Carlisle, William Deedes, Charles Fletcher-Cooke, Brian Harrison, Enoch Powell, and John Vaughan Morgan present, Centre for Kentish Studies, Kent.

55. Rodgers papers: OP27/8, One Nation Minutes, April 24, 1968: with Mark Carlisle, William Deedes, Charles Fletcher-Cooke, Ian Gilmour, Brian Harrison, John Hill, Gilbert Longden, Nicholas Ridley, Anthony Royle, and John Vaughan Morgan present.

56. Ibid. Of course this euphemism in the Minutes acknowledges the sacking of Powell by Heath.

57. Rodgers papers: OP27/8, One Nation Minutes, May 1, 1968: with Michael Alison, William Deedes, Charles Fletcher-Cooke, Philip Goodhart, Brian Harrison, John Hill, Enoch Powell, James Ramsden, Anthony Royle, John Vaughan Morgan, and Marcus Worsley present.

58. The Times, April 22, 1968.

59. See full speech in the Daily Telegraph July 17, 2007.

60. Rodgers papers: OP27/8, One Nation Minutes, June 26, 1968: with Michael Alison, William Deedes, Charles Fletcher-Cooke, Ian Gilmour, Philip Goodhart, Brian Harrison, John Hill, Sir Keith Joseph, Enoch Powell, Anthony Royle, John Vaughan Morgan, Marcus Worsley, Paul Channon, Gilbert Longden, and Nicholas Ridley present. The Group agreed with Powell that Jocelyn Hambro should be supported as one should not be pilloried by the Government outside the processes of the law. However, Brian Harrison commented that he "could not wait to see the dockers marching in support of Enoch Powell defending a £4 thousand rise taken by the Chairman of Hambro's Bank," ibid.

61. Deedes, 1968. However, see Rodgers papers: OP27/8, One Nation Minutes, July 17 1968, where we find that: "Immigration, alas, raised its head again as a result of Gilbert [Longden]. Discussion on usual lines. Deedes' paper to be out soon. He is seeming to see the difficulties of a coherent policy to be quite overwhelming."

62. Longden papers: Longden Box List, Temporary File Number 31, "memo from Charles Longbottom to Gilbert Longden, 8 April 1965," and Temporary File Number 30, "idea for proposed pamphlet on immigration 22 February 1968," London School of Economics and Political Science Library.

63. Deedes, 1968, p. 27.

64. Ibid., p. 19.

65. Rodgers papers: OP27/8, One Nation Minutes, November 27, 1968. In the Birmingham speech Powell emphasized Conservative policy of treating all citizens as equal before the law and of Mr. Heath's phrase of having no "first class citizens and second class citizens" but Powell also stressed in the speech that this did not mean that the immigrant and his descendents should be elevated into a special or privileged class.

66. Indeed, see Margaret Thatcher's review—"When Powell was right"—of Simon Heffer's biography of Powell, Daily Telegraph, November 23, 1998 and Casey, 1982, for an academic exposition of such a stance.

67. See Raison, 1990, pp. 61–63, for the work that had gone into policy making for the 1966 Manifesto and its commitment that "immigrants were to be helped to return to their country of origin if they wished."

68. Deedes, 1968, pp. 22 and 28.

69. Rodgers papers: OP27/8, One Nation Minutes, February 28, 1968: with Michael Alison, Mark Carlisle, William Deedes, Charles Fletcher-Cooke, Philip Goodhart, Gilbert Longden, Enoch Powell, Geoffrey Rippon, John Vaughan Morgan, and Marcus Worsley present.
70. Deedes, 1968, p. 28.
71. For example, see Studlar, 1978.
72. Layton-Henry, 1986, pp. 75 and 76.
73. Davies, 1995, p. 160.
74. *The Times*, April 10, 2000.
75. *The Observer*, March 4, 2001.
76. *The Guardian*, March 5, 2001.
77. *Daily Telegraph*, October 8, 2004.
78. See Seawright, 2005b.
79. This was a strategy apparently employed by Crosby in Australia; a subject is picked, which is supposed to send a sharp message that is only heard by the targeted group to whom it is aimed at and in such a manner that it does not alienate the "middle ground voter" in the process.
80. *Daily Telegraph*, May 2, 2005.
81. *The Guardian*, November 17, 2004.
82. *Daily Telegraph*, May 8, 2000.
83. Rich, 1986, p. 67.
84. Ibid.
85. *The London Evening Standard*, November 1, 2007.
86. *The Times*, November 5, 2007.
87. *Daily Telegraph*, July 16, 2007.
88. Stokes, 1992.
89. Ibid., p. 143.
90. Ibid., pp. 144–147.
91. Seawright, 2002.
92. *The Scotsman*, November 14, 2000.
93. For example see Jonathan Freedland, *The Guardian*, July 5, 2006.
94. *The Scotsman*, April 30, 2008.
95. Cameron, 2006. And see the *Daily Telegraph*, July 24, 2008 where under the heading "Historic Tory deal to reach voters in all of UK," we find David Cameron in talks with the leader of the Ulster Unionist party, Reg Empey, to reconstitute the historic understanding where Unionist MPs took the Conservative whip. Stratton Mills was the only Ulster Unionist MP to be a member of the One Nation group before most of the Ulster Unionists broke off the relationship with the Conservative Party over direct rule in the 1970s; with Mills eventually joining the Northern Ireland Alliance party, see Norton, 1978.

# CHAPTER SEVEN

# "One Europe or No Nation"?

The English question then is a conundrum for the Conservative Party the solution of which demands tactful and skilful answers and relatively early in any future term of office; if indeed answers can be found. In the event of no solution being forthcoming, Andrew Gamble had considered the Union issue in terms of its potential for an addition to those famous three concentric circles of foreign policy strategy. Once the automatic identity of England with Britain is broken, the party will still endeavor to be at the centre—if not to the extent of Churchill's "ringmaster" —of not only the Commonwealth, the Anglo/Atlanticist, and the European Union (EU) circles but "making the British Union itself a fourth circle of England."[1] Indeed, the party would be well advised to take cognizance of a nascent but vital "fifth circle" that is Asia, where it is expected that China and India will be influential economic power-houses of the twenty-first-century.[2] Undoubtedly, this calls for a reexamination by the party of the "circular architecture" of its foreign policy, as one "external relations" component could seriously impair, or indeed be completely ruinous of, another. Ironically, with the necessity of such an examination in mind, the New Labour spin doctor and recurrent cabinet minister, Peter Mandelson, when European Trade Commissioner, found himself the personification of that crucial and perennial question that concerns Britain's future prosperity, viz., the extent of protectionism or free trade policy as implemented by a European Commission. In 2005, Stephen Pollard accused the EU Commission of hypocrisy with the level of subsidies to European farmers but he warned: "not only does EU protectionism keep the poor in poverty, it also denies us access to cheaper goods. Everyone loses when Mr Mandelson decides to ban Chinese knickers."[3] And we had the extraordinary spat between Mandelson and the new French president, Nicolas Sarkozy, with Sarkozy blaming him for the Irish No Vote in the referendum on the Lisbon constitution treaty[4]; due to Mandelson's alleged obsession with the issue of free trade in the Doha round of the world trade talks.[5] Thus, arguably there is an even greater issue that needs to be addressed by the Conservative Party, with all the inventiveness and ingenuity the party can muster, and that concerns the extent of further European integration; the issue that will just not go away.[6]

Indeed, past electoral meltdowns for the party in 1846, 1906, and 1997 "emerged over a major strategic choice of Britain's future role in the world economy."[7] The issue of European integration has become the epitome of that "intermestic category," which acknowledges the globalization process blurring the demarcation lines between what is domestic or international. Bulpitt believed we were confronted with the awkward message that Europe was not just another foreign policy game but perhaps the end game:

> The consequence was that Europe could no longer be presented as a foreign policy adventure, like "exporting is fun": rather, it went to the roots of how Britain was governed in the future and, even though most Euro-enthusiasts have sought to downplay this, of the nature of democracy in Britain.[8]

Of course, there are serious implications for a party evoking an ethos of One Nation—claiming to reflect the traditions, values and beliefs of the British people—with any such "end game" of the British state as the "identity of the Conservative party is inseparable from the history of this state. It has been its supremely flexible and adaptive instrument, and also one of the most important articulators of the narratives that have sustained and defined it."[9] Thus, this partly explains the intensity of passion and conflict within the party, which at times can degenerate into pure invective, over just how flexible and adaptive this instrument can be in the face of greater European integration. There are some in the party who believe, as Enoch Powell did, that Europe is that upper millstone inexorably grinding down Westminster and that the British or indeed English identity is eventually lost with the enervation of parliamentary sovereignty. Others believe there is no alternative to Britain's membership in an ever shrinking world due to the processes of globalization and that Britain's prosperity, if not its very survival, depends upon its place at the "heart of Europe," while the most zealous of this group, although very small in number, will enthusiastically acquiesce in the concept of a United States of Europe where "as the European party, we should put Europe first. Nor is there anything to be gained from doing otherwise."[10] Again, or even more so on this issue, all the lines of division within the party will be found to be rather fluid and one would not expect it to be otherwise on such a crucial contested question for the British Nation. This fluidity is as old as the European question itself but there has been a pronounced movement toward Euro-skepticism within the party that has paralleled that indomitable process, which is "ever closer union," labeled, pace Keith Joseph, as "the Euro-ratchet."[11] Sections of the "social liberal-left" media have indicated that this emerging Euro-skeptic strategy represented a "lurch to the right"[12] but as we shall see it is instructive that some of the most European integrationist policies of the 1990s, the Maastricht Treaty and the debacle that was the European Exchange Rate Mechanism (ERM)—which contributed significantly to the worst electoral disaster for the party since 1832—are never explained in terms of a "lurch to the left."

  In this chapter, the emerging Euro-skeptic strategy is examined and explained in terms of an increasingly disillusioned Conservative Party finding itself more and more at odds with the neocorporatist policy regulations and directives emanating from Europe that run contrary to that Conservative Party principle of judicious abstinence in governance. More and more Conservative MPs would come to view Europe (in all its guises from the European Economic Community [EEC] to the EU) as the tenacious trajectory of a federalist leviathan, moving further and further away from the original ideal of promoting the competitive market economy in line with increased trade that the majority of the party thought it had initially signed up to; reflected in the pervasive use by the party of the term "Common Market" and for so long. With an early enthusiasm for the putative benefits of this economic cooperation, the party would utilize the "party of Europe"[13] label but it is also instructive that the party failed to convince enough of its own MPs to accept both the 1972 Accession Treaty and the 1993 EU Maastricht Treaty, relying on "rebels" from other parties for the passage of both Bills,[14] hardly a wringing endorsement from a party of Europe. But, the 1986 Single European Act (SEA) was accepted relatively harmoniously by the Parliamentary party in no small measure due to the sales pitch that stressed the inherent competitive market principles of the Bill while downplaying (or if Mrs Thatcher is to be believed concealing[15]) its significant integrationist clauses. One thing is certain then, and similar to many an issue examined thus far, on the issue of Europe the Conservative Party never fully accepted that anything had been settled. Again, the One Nation group is presented here as a microcosm of party thinking, as we track One Nation members whose reservations on Europe, and in some cases enthusiasm, develop into full blown skepticism; and with such an examination the pervasive myth that equates One Nation with One Europe is comprehensively exposed.

At the time of the 1999 European Election, a number of prominent Conservatives were expelled from the party for their support for an ephemeral rival, the Pro-European Conservative Party; this party was to obtain a derisory one percentage point of the popular vote but amongst those expelled were the former One Nation members: Julian Critchley, Ian Gilmour, and Tim Rathbone.[16] Critchley, in an article on why he could not vote for his local Conservative parliamentary candidate, the Maastricht rebel Christopher Gill, had earlier repeated the commonly held but spurious association between Euro-enthusiasm and One Nation and between Euro-skepticism and "Little Englanders."[17] But, of course, Critchley was exactly the sort of Conservative the One Nation chairman, David Howell, had in mind when in 1996 he referred to "skilled propaganda from ill intentioned friends." And we also saw how contemptible Howell thought the attempts were to either link One Nation to some interventionist vision or to brand One Nation Tories "as a bunch of wets who want a federal Europe."[18] Indeed, it is no coincidence that this is the very year in which Margaret Thatcher famously stated: "As far as I can tell by their views on European federalism, such people's creed would be better described as 'No Nation Conservatism.'"[19]

As early as 1971, it was noted by the press that one visible consequence of the European issue was a schism in the One Nation group of Tory MPs. "Among the few remaining founder members Enoch Powell and Angus Maude voted against the Market. Gilbert Longden and Sir John Rodgers, also founder members and strong Europeans, voted with the Government."[20] But Gilbert Longden, a past Chairman of the Conservative Group for Europe (CGE), would by the 1990s become a member of the Euro-skeptic Bruges Group.[21] Of course, many supporters of further European integration are still to be found in the One Nation group, that is not in doubt, even those like Ken Clarke who support a European constitution and the adoption of the European single currency but it is quite wrong to try to airbrush from contemporary debate the fact that there have always been strong opponents of further European integration from within the "Nation," David Heathcoat-Amory for one:

> The world has moved on, Europe's moved on and the Party has moved on and I actually think that this excessive belief in the European Union, I call it no nation Conservatism, is an attempt to submerge us into an integrated Europe, like a lump of sugar dissolving in tea and you end up with no nation at all, nothing to call One Nation, nothing to call any nation at all, that is a big abdication of our duties because one of the things the Conservative Party is, is a constitutional party, in fact we are often called that and you will see it in our clubs the Conservative and Constitutional club that is in regard to the British constitution and bedded in that is a strong belief in self government.[22]

Such strongly held committed views from both sides of this European divide, on what was best for the British nation, vis-à-vis the level of European integration, would eventually lead to that malign element of political recrudescence coming to the fore in the "parliamentary battle" that was the Maastricht treaty. Indeed, Christopher Gill, to whom Critchley could not countenance a vote, neatly encapsulates the extent of the rigidity of opinion on this issue that was the Conservative Party of the 1990s: "With the passage of time our relationship became somewhat strained because whereas Christopher [Prout], in respect of the European Community, could see no wrong I increasingly find no good."[23] The third section of this chapter focuses on this period when such divisions within the party nearly led to another historical split. The final section sets out to establish by just how much the party has moved on and examines Cameron's approach to future European policy; will it be possible for the party to halt that Euro-ratchet effect as claimed and if not, whether it could seriously contemplate withdrawal? But, in the next section, we examine a time when the party was not so ill at ease with a "party of Europe" image.

## The Party of Europe and "One Europe"?

The historical roots of British ambiguity toward the process of European unity undoubtedly lie with Churchill when, in the fashion of his riddle inside an enigma oratory, he made his Zurich speech of 1946 where he appeared to support the creation of "a kind of United States of Europe" but although Britain would be a "friend and sponsor" to such a "kind" of Europe it should not be a member; famously telling the House of Commons rather less equivocally in 1953 that "Britain was with Europe but not of Europe . . . We do not intend to be merged in a European federal system."[24] This was in effect the British approach, from both the Labour and Conservative parties, to Continental relations throughout the 1940s and 1950s; for all intents and purposes ignoring the Steel and Coal cartel of 1950, the Messina talks in 1955 and foregoing the Treaty of Rome in 1957. It was not until the early 1960s with the loss of Empire and the realization of Commonwealth limitations that Britain seriously looked to Europe for solutions to its slow economic growth and for greater security. The EEC looked to have tremendous prospects but of course these nations were by then reaping their investment in productive capital whereas Britain had frittered away its Marshall Aid on the idealistic myths of maintaining its great power status and of the state as Grand Almoner.[25] But the notion of relative decline led both Harold Macmillan in 1962 and Harold Wilson in 1967 to apply for membership of the European cartel club; with General De Gaulle vetoing both due in part to our history as a free trade nation and our "special relationship" with America. However, this desire by the party to join the EEC in the early 1960s—in contrast to Gaitskell's unequivocal refusal because he believed it to be the end of a thousand years of history and Britain as an independent state—was the creation of its domestic reputation as the "party of Europe"; the party did not discount the electoral benefits to be had in uniting around a pro-European position when engaged in competition for votes with a visibly disunited and increasingly anti-European Labour Party.[26]

Correlli Barnett is incisively critical of the post war government and its lack of willpower in challenging that "primitive industrial tribe ill-fitted for the technological future."[27] The One Nation group had at this time perennially voiced its concern with the pernicious actions of an assertive and powerful trade union movement but mostly privately on the need to develop a coherent policy.[28] Indeed, Geoffrey Howe when writing to Gilbert Longden to praise his 1985 *Crossbow* article that associated One Nation with Thatcherism, added:

> How thoughtful of you to write as you did: many thanks. I quite agree with you about the basic continuity of what we have *all* been trying to do. I think the only major gap in "Nation" thinking—until the mid-sixties—was on the need for trade union reform.[29]

It was certainly not coincidental that both issues of trade union reform and Europe would coalesce at this time. Europe was to be the external structure—or indeed crutch—that would support the implementation of a necessary market discipline into an ailing British economy and this was the line taken by the One

Nation group in the 1960s. Reginald Maudling was one member who was as yet to be convinced of the benefits of the EEC, as indeed was RAB Butler,[30] but following the start of the negotiations for EEC membership in 1961 he dutifully articulated the "cold shower thesis," namely, the intention to shock British industry out of the restrictive practices and outdated methods:

> I think that the great effect of going into a wider European market will be that the efficient firms will prosper and the inefficient will go down. That, surely, is precisely what we must see in this country if our economy is really to expand and our growth is to be more rapid.[31]

The One Nation group published their pamphlet on Europe in 1965. The *One Europe*[32] booklet would most certainly be classified by the present day party as a federalist text—indeed latterly even by its own author Nicholas Ridley[33]—as it stated: "European Unity implies the full economic, military and political union of the free states of Europe, and ultimately of all of Europe."[34] But, the problems with the corporatist sclerosis of the postwar economy was to concentrate the collective mind of the One Nation group and thus the enthusiasm shown for the putative benefits of European integration in the mid-1960s was very much in terms of that "cold shower thesis"[35]; that market disciplines could be enforced at home through the external agency of Europe.

> It was frequently argued during the Brussels negotiations that British membership of the Common Market would interfere with our freedom to plan our own economy. What was really meant by this was that people were not prepared to face seeing petty restrictive practices, the closed shops, the restrictions on trade and competition swept away. The free movement of labour and capital would open up the closed nature of so much of British industrial life; the increased competition from Europe would force businesses to wake up or go under.[36]

After the first veto by the French president the One Nation group believed, with the period of indecision over, that "it must be surely realized that Britain, by her own domestic policies alone, must provide the stimulus which would partly have been provided by membership of the Common Market."[37] However, after the second veto in 1967 and although the One Nation group was of the opinion that the Conservative Party in the country was probably now in favor of the withdrawal of Britain's application in view of the attitude of France, it now thought it was in the interest of Britain to keep the application alive and that "Ted Heath should underline the fact that the Party was still staunchly in favor of joining Europe as soon as possible."[38] But by mid-1969, we find the Group divided on the possibility of future entry: "A split in the Nation between the ardent and rather shocked Europeans and Enoch, David Howell and James Ramsden, who took a more lukewarm line and particularly thought that there could be no question of joining the Communities."[39] Of course the "split" did nothing to stop Britain's eventual accession in 1972, with Edward Heath utilizing so effectively his past experience as chief whip, along with an adept manipulation of the agents in the country, to ensure the success of the "free vote strategy" in getting the Accession Bill through Parliament.[40] However, when the official minutes and papers of the 1971 negotiations with President Pompidou were released to the public domain in 2005, within which we learn of Edward Heath being as keen on monetary union as the French leader and where he also claims that Britain could never have a satisfactory relationship with America, one of those "ardent and rather shocked Europeans" who was present at the One Nation meeting in 1969 intimated that he and his fellow Tories would have been astonished and deeply disturbed if they had known what the prime minister had said in their names in 1971; William Deedes continued:

> It goes to show the depth of his commitment to Europe. But it also shows that all of his critics, especially Margaret Thatcher, who believed he was prepared to give away anything to get us in Europe, and keep us there, were absolutely right.[41]

Mrs Thatcher was seen as a firm supporter of Conservative involvement in the campaign to continue membership of the EEC, when the issue was put to the people in the 1975 Referendum; although "doubts about her own commitment were raised. . . . [but] based on little evidence."[42] However, as early as 1976, we have evidence of such worries among the Euro-enthusiasts that Mrs Thatcher "whenever Europe was mentioned, always said that she 'didn't want to be under the heels of Europeans'" and they wanted it known that we were not under their heel but part of them.[43] And, such a frame of mind was displayed in a memo from Mrs Thatcher to the party chairman on the subject of the appointment of agents by constituencies:

> I am most concerned about one matter in particular. It occurs on page 2, clause 5, where the duties of the agent are set out. You will observe that the interests of the European MP or candidate take precedence over that of the Westminster MP or candidate. I can't think how this clause came to be drafted in that way or approved! Can you secure the necessary changes?[44]

Granted, a rather obscure and esoteric internal organizational matter but it reflects exactly that attitude—which was the exact opposite of Heath's—of a determination to put Britain first as there was nothing to be gained otherwise and which in her first term of government led her to pursue a rebate on the British contribution to the Community's budget although it was not until her second term that Mrs Thatcher managed to obtain a 66 percent refund on the British contribution at the Fontainebleau Summit in June 1984. Geoffrey Howe, as Foreign Secretary after 1983, thought Thatcher's combative approach to European negotiations to be totally wrong headed but she would not accept anything which to her smacked of dreamy federalism. All Thatcher wanted was practical cooperation without the need for Inter-Governmental Conferences (IGCs) or treaty reforms, particularly if it meant opening up the market to greater competition. But to get that greater market competition in the SEA of 1986 Britain did indeed have to face future IGCs and treaty reforms.[45] This was the time, Thatcher alleges, that she came to realize that she was beginning to question both "the fair dealing and good faith in discussions between the heads of governments and with the European Commission."[46] Interestingly, Nigel Lawson dismissed such retrospective justification by Thatcher when reviewing Thatcher's 2002 book *Statecraft*:

> Thatcher refers to "an ugly streak of anti-Americanism" in much European rhetoric. A fair point, but no excuse for the regrettable streak of anti-Europeanism—in particular anti-German and anti-French sentiment—which disfigure this book and notably the key chapter on Europe, the EU and Britain's relationship with it. This is perhaps partly because she feels guilty for having, as Prime Minister in 1985, signed up to the Single European Act, the first substantial amendment to the Rome Treaty, with its commitment to economic and monetary union. She now claims she was misled and betrayed, but this is unconvincing. As Chancellor at the time, I warned her in writing not to agree to an Act which contained anything about EMU, but she chose not to take my advice.[47]

Just to highlight how fluid all the lines of division were on the issue of Europe, we should acknowledge that although Lawson was against Economic and Monetary Union (EMU), the single currency, there was a three-way split between Prime Minister, Chancellor, and Foreign Secretary on the idea of this European Monetary process. Lawson and Thatcher were against the single currency, while Howe and Lawson accepted the ERM but Howe alone of the three was amenable to the single currency. However, Howe, supported by Lawson, argued that accepting Stage One of the Delors plan[48] for monetary union (i.e. showing good faith by joining the ERM) could ward off any necessary link to full blown EMU. But Thatcher had no trust in this approach, and in fact, she was to increasingly circumvent the Foreign Office and rely on her advisers and No. 10 officials, particularly Alan Walters and Charles Powell, for advice and guidance on such issues. This approach led to the distinctly skeptical speech, which was delivered in Bruges in September 1988 and which did so much to "deeply dismay" her Foreign Secretary, Geoffrey Howe.[49] The issue of course led to the downfall of all three but in this denouement the die was cast for the malign element of political recrudescence and the breakdown of those necessary "contingent considerabilities" that were to be so lacking in the relationship that was the Parliamentary party of the 1990s.

## Merchant Shipping with a Malign Form of Maastricht

Thatcher may well have questioned the "fair dealing and good faith" of European officials but throughout the 1990s, there was to be an ever-increasing realization, particularly from within the ranks of the British Conservative Party, that the fundamental questions concerned the structural constraints being imposed by the EU. Not only on the British economy but on the very acts of decision making by Parliament itself and it was this realization that heralded the concomitant expansion of Euro-skepticism within the party. In short, Powell's concept of the upper millstone now became far more readily accepted. Ironically, in the same year that Mrs Thatcher's skeptic Bruges Speech was delivered, Parliament enacted the Merchant Shipping Act of 1988. Basically, the Act was meant to ensure that all companies that operated shipping off the UK mainland would be British, in that 75 percent of their directors and share-holders would have British nationality; in reality, it was intended to put a halt to Spanish fishing vessels using British coastal waters. However, this British Act of Parliament was challenged by the Factortame Company in the European Court of Justice (ECJ) and it was this landmark decision with the ECJ finding in their favor in 1991, striking down statutes of British law, that was to leave no one in the Conservative Party in any doubt of what was now meant by British law being subordinate to the European treaties. And, in 1996 when the 48 hours working time directive was imposed upon the UK economy the Euro-skeptic wing of the Conservative Party knew just how worthless op-outs from treaties really were.[50]

> The disingenuous claim of the Heath government that "There is no question of any erosion of essential national sovereignty" would not now bear rep-etition. The nascent European order now much more directly, overtly and fundamentally threatened British parliamentary sovereignty and thereby the British nation state than previously.[51]

These years then were to be pivotal in that decisive step toward becoming fundamentally a Euro-skeptic party, and when in this period the party did eventually cross the Rubicon the fact that the Labour Party was preparing a crossing of its own but, in the opposite direction, merely confirmed for most Tories that the EU was now inherently at odds with Conservative Party principles. The attachment of the British political elite, particularly from within the Conservative Party, to an open seas policy emphasizing free trade and the free movement of capital and goods had not only endured but was once again to become central to Conservative Party policy, particularly post–John Major, and led many British Conservatives to identify Britain with a global rather than European volition.[52] A strategic goal of those foreign policy circles was to obtain the ideal position where a program of low taxation, low government spending, deregulation, and privatization could be combined with as strong attachment to national sovereignty and the nation-state as the guarantor of national identity and national independence. With the increasing realization amongst Conservatives that the EU would not be such an external facilitator, the national policy-making constraints of globalization were once again welcomed because they ruled out the kind of social democratic and socialist measures,[53] which were viewed as incompatible with British national identity, forcing the government to set the people free whatever its ideological predilections.[54] This approach was to increasingly inform the attitude of many British Conservative Euro-skeptics on the EU and European integration. The survey data in Table 7.1 reveal such attitudes and how such Euro-skeptic sentiment became increasingly entrenched within the parliamentary party.[55]

Whereas the advocates of a more Europhile approach would not baulk at the supranational strengthening of EU institutions, to resemble the typical "executive-legislature" relations of a liberal democracy, the vast majority of Conservative MPs' views are still rooted in the institutions of the nation-state; falling far short of any ideal of a United States of Europe. Indeed, with the example of the 1988 British Merchant Shipping Act to mind, we find a 19 percent rise, to 69 percent in 1998, in the number of MPs who believed that a Supremacy Act should be passed, which would in reality challenge the Treaty of Rome itself (statement, 1.1) and while Europhiles believe the "democratic deficit" in the EU could be addressed by the strengthening of the EU Parliament, in the belief that it would make the EU more accountable to the people of Europe, in contrast an overwhelming majority of Conservative MPs view this democratic deficit as largely due to a lack of scrutiny by the House of Commons (1.2). The antipathy toward the United States of Europe ideal is evident in their views on personal taxation being harmonized within the EU (1.5), a derisory one percent of Tory MPs would accept such a significant path towards unity. After the rout at the 1997 General Election, we should not be too surprised to find that Conservative MPs, once bitten by the ERM debacle, are twice shy about the possibility of rejoining it (1.4) and a similar increase to around two-thirds of them in 1998, from a half in 1996, want no part of a project they see as sounding the death knell on national sovereignty for the United Kingdom (1.3); for them, the single currency would be simply another ERM but without exit. What is not in doubt is the growing uncertainty and dismay over the actual benefits of membership of the EU cartel (1.6) and relative to the future "circular architecture" of foreign relations, a majority of Conservative MPs in 1998, 56 percent, denied that the globalization process made EU membership imperative for the United Kingdom (1.7). To reiterate,

Table 7.1: Attitudes of Conservative MPs Toward Aspects of European Integration
(1994 and 1998)

| | Strongly agree/ Agree | Neither | Strongly disagree/ Disagree |
|---|---|---|---|
| 1.1 An act of Parliament should be passed to establish explicitly the ultimate supremacy of Parliament over EU legislation. | | | |
| 1994 | 50% | 17% | 33% |
| 1998 | 69% | 7% | 24% |
| 1.2 The key to closing the "democratic deficit" is strengthening the scrutiny by national parliaments of the EU legislative process. | | | |
| 1994 | 79% | 11% | 10% |
| 1998 | 84% | 10% | 6% |
| 1.3 Joining the Single Currency will signal the end of the UK as a sovereign nation. | | | |
| 1994 | 48% | 11% | 41% |
| 1998 | 66% | 6% | 28% |
| 1.4 Britain should never rejoin the ERM. | | | |
| 1994 | 48% | 16% | 36% |
| 1998 | 64% | 6% | 30% |
| 1.5 Personal taxation should be harmonized within the EU. | | | |
| 1994 | 3% | 6% | 91% |
| 1998 | 1% | 2% | 97% |
| 1.6 The disadvantages of EU membership have been outweighed by the benefits. | | | |
| 1994 | 60% | 8% | 32% |
| 1998 | 37% | 21% | 41% |
| 1.7 The globalization of economic activity makes EU membership more, rather than less necessary for the UK. | | | |
| 1994 | — | — | — |
| 1998 | 32% | 12% | 56% |

*Source*: ESRC 1994 Survey R000231298 and ESRC 1998 Survey R000222397.

the EU was to become increasingly viewed within the party as a long-term Franco-German project designed ultimately to create a federal super-state, which would impose unacceptably high levels of taxation, spending and regulation on all its component parts, making the UK economy uncompetitive in global markets outside the EU. If successful, it would undo the hard-won market disciplines created during the Thatcher era in the 1980s as an expression of the democratic preferences of the majority of British people and in contrast to that portrayal of the party as "Little Englanders" the reality was more the reflection of a global narrative.[56]

Such tension over the trajectory of the party was clearly evident as John Major struggled to get the Maastricht Treaty through the House of Commons in 1992–3; in fact, he needed to win a vote of confidence to overturn a Euro-skeptic rebellion in order to ratify the Treaty.[57] In 1994, Major felt impelled to remove the whip from eight Conservative MPs who voted against the increase to the EU budget and then he believed it necessary to resign and re-contest a "put up or shut up" leadership contest in 1995. And, it was to be this increasing Euro-skeptic pressure from within the party that further impelled him in 1996 to accept a policy of a referendum on any future decision on a single currency. Two "elder statesmen" of the One Nation group, John Biffen and Michael Spicer, were to rebel on the Maastricht Bill on 30 or more occasions[58] with the resulting divisions edging the party closer to its first major split since the struggle over Tariff Reform in the first decade of the last century.[59] However, the level of rebellion as registered through the division lobbies merely masked the actual level of Euro-skepticism in the party at the time.[60] Ironically, just as John Biffen was to steer the SEA through Parliament in 1986, David Heathcoat-Amory as a party whip in the early 1990s would share collective responsibility for guiding a piece of legislation through the House that he later bitterly regretted was ever enacted. In Chapter 5, we encountered the problem with the "principled abstention" in terms of nonvoting in the division lobby but on the issue of European integration there would seem to be a parallel issue of just when is a vote on European integration a "principled vote"; particularly in light of the extensive use of the whip at the time of Maastricht.[61] Indeed, with this in mind compare the view of Allan Duncan MP: "I voted for Maastricht with a heavy heart. Fearful of the ultimate direction but happy otherwise to put my faith in John Major's stewardship of the next few years"[62]; with that of John Nott twenty years earlier:

> I was one of the last Tory backbenchers to be persuaded for the European Community Act in 1972, because I partly foresaw, under Enoch's influence, the consequences for our independence if we joined this club. But, in the end, I confess that the influence of other friends and colleagues got me through the lobbies behind the government.[63]

Such views are evidence for a large body of opinion in the party, not registered by the official roll call votes, that was increasingly concerned by the direction of events in Europe, which saw the acceptance of rulings from Brussels, which it would have been "hard to imagine ever having been proposed as part of a domestic Conservative programme."[64] Spicer quotes Labour's Roy Hattersley to add emphasis: "Labour has been converted to Europe because Europe has been converted to socialism," and he accepted Hattersley's suggestion that the "last ten years saw capitalism and the pursuit of free trade relegated within the EEC to a secondary position."[65] Thus, Maastricht merely confirmed a long standing trend within the party and which from the late 1980s onward would gather strength, to the extent that within a decade, Euro-skepticism would become the defining characteristic of the Conservative Party's identity and enshrined in its policies. A bewildering variety of Euro-skeptic organizations emerged in that period. The Bruges Group, formed in February 1989 in approbation of Mrs Thatcher's speech at the College of Europe, was the first of this new epoch. It has chiefly served as a Euro-skeptic think tank for the party and together with the European Foundation and the European Research Group accounts for the growing intellectual vitality of Euro-skepticism within the party. In addition, older Euro-skeptic organizations reinvigorated themselves, particularly Conservatives against the Treaty of Rome, which re-launched itself in 1992 as Conservatives against a Federal Europe. Furthermore, both old and new internal party groupings representing broader tendencies within the party made Euro-skepticism central to their positions including the No Turning Back Group, the 92 Group, and Conservative Way Forward. However, perhaps the most remarkable grouping was the Fresh Start Group, which emerged after an attempt to remove Bill Cash from the chairmanship of the Conservative backbench committee on European Affairs in November 1991. This grouping became the organizational core of the Conservative rebellions on the Maastricht Treaty.[66]

Michael Spicer and John Biffen were part of this "Fresh Start" rebellion and it was reported that, with the *Treaty Too Far* manuscript tucked under his arm, Spicer had met with the 92 Group Chairman to coordinate opposition to the Treaty.[67] However, tension and conflict and that fluidity of opinion was not only rife within the ranks of the parliamentary party but was just as common within the Euro-skeptic groups themselves and even within the Fresh Start group. Christopher Gill, one of the "whipless eight" and a leading light in the Fresh Start group, recounts the personal and doctrinal tension within and between these Euro-skeptic groups at the time, indeed he tells of the friction at the 92 group meeting where Peter Hordern was accused by the Chairman, George Gardiner, of using his Progress Trust members to support more Europhile candidates for party committees.[68] Gill's "diary of events" is a good account of such tension and records how the party eventually moves in a more overt Euro-skeptic direction, found even in the behavior of such previous "loyalists" as Peter Hordern and David Heathcoat-Amory, but it is instructive that Gill acknowledges the lack of factional behavior, in Richard Rose's terms:

Now that the battleground is unquestionably Europe some of our members [92 group], Peter [Hordern] and Ray [Whitney] being cases in point, are becoming somewhat "semi-detached" but that is, by the very nature of things, the way life tends to go in Parliament. One coalesces with certain colleagues on certain issues and as the business is disposed of the coalitions thus formed disband as colleagues move on to other issues.[69]

Of course, Gill accepted that the Cabinet at the time of Maastricht was disproportionately Europhile in relation to that changing opinion on the backbenches, suggesting also that Major's actions were strongly influenced and guided by the three One Nation "Euro-zealots": Ken Clarke, Douglas Hurd, and Michael Heseltine.[70] It was no surprise then to find Ken Clarke resoundingly beaten in the 1997 and 2001 leadership contests, by both the votes of MPs and then party members. William Hague's accession to the leadership in the wake of the election of 1997 decisively tilted this balance toward its Euro-skeptic wing with attitudes toward the *euro* being made a test of Shadow Cabinet membership. Indeed, by the 2001 election, the party not only pledged to renegotiate the Nice Treaty to regain British vetoes but also proposed amendments to British law to introduce "reserved powers" protected from the encroachments of EU law. And, following the party's 2001 election defeat and Hague's resignation, the party elected the former Fresh Start group member and Maastricht rebel, Iain Duncan Smith, as leader, who subsequently appointed a shadow cabinet even more Euro-skeptic than his predecessors.[71] On elevation to the leadership in November 2003, Michael Howard maintained the Euro-skeptic trajectory of the party although EU membership was valued the party unequivocally acknowledged "the vital threads that link open markets, free trade, property rights, the rule of law, democracy, economic development and social progress." Indeed, the 2005 manifesto also called for the restoration of Britain's opt-outs and the repatriation of fishing policy, claiming that both the Common Fisheries Policy and Common Agricultural Policy were unsustainable.[72] In such a vision, both democracy and legitimacy are located in the nation-state, which is the basic unit of all legitimate democratic politics and as we find in the next section, the party under David Cameron identifies Britain even more in terms of a global rather than a European volition.

## The Euro-Ratchet Halted or Withdrawal?

In short, where many Conservatives once saw Europe as an acceptable alternative to Empire or Commonwealth, the larger space in which British leadership could be deployed and British interests defended, many more increasingly came to see it as a threat to the preservation both of British sovereignty and national identity, and of the traditional liberal global order, which Britain first created and then sustained through its alliance with the United States.[73] And, in response to Gordon Brown's statement on the Lisbon Treaty, David Cameron echoed the idea of the inherent threat of a Euro-ratchet:

> This Treaty obviously is the constitution. It contains an EU President, a Foreign Minister and an EU diplomatic service. It gets rid of the veto in 60 areas. And it contains a new ratchet clause which allows even more vetoes to be scrapped

without a new inter-governmental conference. When I put that point to him in October, he claimed the measure was already there in the Single European Act. It wasn't. The new clause, for the first time, allows virtually any veto to be scrapped in almost any area. That measure was not in the Single European Act or in any treaty before this one. Once again, he's treating people like fools. So the Prime Minister hasn't been straight about the constitution.[74]

However, a similar accusation could be leveled at the Conservative Party of "not being straight" about their own policy with regards to the postparliamentary ratification of the Lisbon Treaty. William Hague hinted strongly on the possibility of a future Conservative government holding a referendum as it was thought unacceptable that such a treaty could be ratified without being legitimized by the British people. Hague declared: "This would not be acceptable to a Conservative government and we would not let matters rest there."[75] Ken Clarke pointed out that in reality this would mean an attempt to renegotiate the treaty with all the difficulties that would entail but David Cameron insisted that Hague was not giving a "nod and a wink" in any one direction as the party had a range of options if the treaty was ratified but options "he would not discuss at this stage."[76] Such uncertainty and ambiguity clouds most of what now passes for Conservative policy on Europe. Indeed, there was just as strong a suggestion that David Cameron secured his leadership victory with the pledge to withdraw the party from its collaborative compact with the "unremittingly federalist European People's Party (EPP)" but one he was accused "of lying over."[77] What seemed a firm commitment to be carried out in his "honeymoon period, while the media are still talking about the colour of my wife's clothes . . . it will happen within months not years,"[78] is now to happen, if at all, after the European Elections in 2009. However, there was a Movement for European Reform (MER) set up in 2006 for like-minded parties who share the Conservatives vision of a modern, open, flexible, and decentralized EU, as opposed to the EPP's more federalist view.[79] The role of this MER is not yet clear or who might join with the Conservative Party as full partners but what is very clear is the difficulty the party has in finding ideological allies in the European Parliament as relatively few centre-right parties in the EU share the Conservative Party's free market, intergovernmental perspective.[80] From the time of William Hague's leadership, it has been a goal of the party to revisit this collaboration with such a federalist transnational grouping as the EPP. Indeed, as we see in Table 7.2, from as early as 1994 there were 36 percent of Conservative MPs even then who thought the party's association with the EPP more of a political liability than an asset (statement 2.1).

The EPP is deemed to be an overly enthusiastic advocate of the EU's federalist intentions and protectionist practices and thus quite simply is at odds with the Conservative Party's aspiration of Britain in the global marketplace.

Table 7.2: Attitudes of Conservative MPs Towards Aspects of European Integration
         (1994 and 1998)

|  | Strongly agree/ Agree | Neither | Strongly disagree/ Disagree |
|---|---|---|---|
| **2.1 The Conservative Party's association with the EPP is more of a political liability than an asset.** | | | |
| 1994 | 36% | 20% | 44% |
| **2.2 Britain should withdraw from the EU.** | | | |
| 1998 | 26% | 11% | 63% |

*Source*: ESRC 1994 Survey R000231298 and ESRC 1998 Survey R000222397.

The implication of such a view raises the question of the party ever finding ideological allies from within the "cartel of Euro-parties" as:

> Indeed, the British economy can be seen to be the embodiment of a distinctive Anglo-American model of capitalist organisation. This sits uncomfortably with the more dirigiste Rheinisch model of social partnership of most other member states. This allows British Eurosceptics to portray European integration as the imposition of an alien economic model fundamentally inimical to Britain's competitiveness in international markets.[81]

And, it is this position which has come to represent the dominant strand of thinking within the British Conservative Party, particularly over the last decade, as reflected in the analysis of the past One Nation chairman David Howell.[82] There is much to be respected in the European past but a different approach is demanded as the entire edifice of the European unity dream no longer fits the amazing real world, which has rapidly emerged and thus the process of globalization marks a fresh lease of life for nationhood with an emphasis upon the necessity of the nation-state as a cultural anchor in the churning sea of globalization; and for Howell, the EU as presently configured impairs that anchor considerably.[83] What remains central to this perspective is the vision of national political and economic independence, seen as crucial for protecting the economic policy, which can help the economy adjust best to globalization, while leaving the nation-state intact to represent national traditions and proper democratic accountability, it primarily seeks to reverse the federalist tide but if unsuccessful in such a pursuit is not afraid to contemplate withdrawal.[84] In 2002, the One Nation member, Andrew Tyrie, advocated an escape clause for Britain, which would lay the federalist bogy as no federation has an exit clause.

> From such radicals steps [the EU constitution and by extrapolation the Lisbon treaty]—or others in the future—we should at least have the protection of a

treaty clause enabling Britain, or indeed any other country, to withdraw from the EU, if it wishes.[85]

In Table 7.2, we see that over a quarter of Conservative MPs, 26 percent, by 1998 (statement 2.2), were prepared to adopt such a position, a policy line that was diametrically opposed to that of the party's, then and since. Indeed, at the first conference of the MER, David Cameron made it clear that he had no intention of taking the party out of Europe,[86] later emphasizing the possibility of changing the EU to the Conservative Party's view of a "Europe of nation states co-operating where it is in their interests to do so, looking outwards to the world, flexible, competitive, ready to face the challenges of globalization."[87] In government, Cameron may find that there is no possibility of change in such a preferred direction, which will only add to that number who would advocate the trigger of an exit clause. Undoubtedly, the upper and nether millstones, as outlined in this chapter and the last, of the domestic territorial policy of devolution and race relations and the "intermestic" policy of European integration will bear heavily upon a One Nation party. But whereas the identity of the Conservative Party would still be inseparable from the history of England, as much as if not more than that of Britain, and that it could still be a supremely flexible and adaptive instrument as one of the most important articulators of the narratives that have sustained and defined England, it is just so difficult to envisage the EU as presently configured being a fresh lease of life for nationhood. Paradoxically, the dilemma of "One Nation But Which" would not be fatal for a One Nation party but crucially "One Europe, No Nation" needs no further explanation.

## Notes

1. Gamble, 2003, p. 30.
2. For example, see Emmott, 2008.
3. Stephen Pollard in *The Times*, August 22, 2005.
4. There were different estimates to how much the EU Constitution, as voted down by the French and Dutch citizens in 2005, survived to be included in the Lisbon Treaty, an Irish official thought it 90 per cent, see *Daily Telegraph*, June 25, 2007, and we had estimates from between 93 and 95 percent from German and Portuguese politicians. But, whether it was a 10 or 5 percent difference, both the Labour party and Liberal Democrats thought this was enough to renege on their manifesto commitment to hold a referendum on the Constitution.
5. For example, see *The Times*, June 21, 2008. Indeed, the Doha round of talks appeared to have broken down fatally on the July 29, 2008, see *The Sunday Telegraph*, August 3, 2008.
6. Baker and Seawright, 1998.
7. Baker et al., 1993, p. 420.
8. Bulpitt, 1996, pp. 215–216.
9. Gamble, 2003, p. 163.

10. Heath, 1977, p. 21.
11. Bulpitt, 1992.
12. Bulpitt, 1996, p. 252.
13. See Crowson, 2007.
14. See Ludlam, 1996; 1998, for an exposition of the backbench rebellions on Europe.
15. Mrs Thatcher states that she realized too late that in order to obtain the greater market competition of the Single European Act of 1986 Britain would indeed have to face future treaty reforms and this was the time she says, that she began to question both "the fair dealing and good faith in discussions between the heads of governments and with the European Commission" (1993, p. 551).
16. See *The Guardian*, June 23, 1999 and *Daily Telegraph*, August 25, 1999.
17. The *London Evening Standard*, November 15, 1995.
18. See Chapter 4, endnote 3 and Chapter 3, endnote 72.
19. Margaret Thatcher's Sir Keith Joseph Memorial lecture on the 11 January 1996, see http://www.margaretthatcher.org/speeches/displaydocument.asp?docid=108353.
20. Peterborough in *The Daily Telegraph*, October 30, 1971.
21. See Longden papers: Longden Box List, Temporary Number 22, "Conservative Group for Europe, Minutes, 1973–1978" and Temporary Number, 34, "Europe and the Bruges Group, 1992–1996," London School of Economics and Political Science Library. Indeed, in Longden papers: Temporary Number 36, we find that Longden had scribbled on Martin Holmes's Bruges Group occasional paper No. 17, of November 1994, "An excellent pamphlet!".
22. David Heathcoat-Amory, interviewed at the House of Commons, June 29, 2004.
23. Gill, 2003, p. 36.
24. Ashford, 1980, pp. 95–96; Holmes, 1994, p. 11.
25. Barnett, 2001. And see, Macleod and Maude, 1950, p. 19; where in the *One Nation* booklet we find: "Similar evils result from the assumption by the community of the exclusive role of Grand Almoner, which must also follow from the elimination of private fortunes. The expenditure of public money necessarily involves parity of treatment and tends to eliminate discretion. In large things and small, this necessity impoverishes the social services."
26. Baker et al., 2002.
27. Barnett, 2001, p. 271.
28. For example see, Longden papers: Temporary File Number 31, "memo from Keith Joseph to Gilbert Longden 30 May 1957 with 17 page document by Enoch Powell attached on restrictive practices and trade union power, with comments by different One Nation members."
29. Longden papers: Temporary File Number 9, "Letter from Geoffrey Howe to Gilbert Longden, 19 December 1987": Temporary File 9.
30. Ashford, 1980, p. 98.
31. Maudling quoted in Buller, 2000, p. 42.
32. Both the papers of Sir Gilbert Longden and Sir John Rodgers unequivocally establish that Ridley was the author of this pamphlet, having produced a 6,000-word draft of the 6,800-word booklet by January 26, 1965, a subcommittee was then established, with him, Tony Royle, Chris Chataway, and Charles Fletcher Cooke. It was set up to consider points of principle which were then agreed by the "Nation" on the February 12, 1965, with the final draft of the pamphlet produced by Nicholas

Ridley on February 19, 1965. Enoch Powell had agreed to do an explanatory column about the Group for the back of the pamphlet. See Longden papers: Temporary File No. 31, Memoranda from Charles Longbottom to Gilbert Longden: January 26, 1965; February 8, 1965; February 12, 1965, and February 19, 1965, and memo from Ridley to Longden, February 15, 1965. However, Gilmour and Garnett, 1998, make the claim that Enoch Powell had written a quarter of the pamphlet, p. 229.

33. See Ridley, 1991, p. 139 where he recounts the time he was accused of being a "federast" for the extent of his European enthusiasm in the 1960s, but "anyone who has had ten years of experience of the working of the Council of Ministers and the Commission is likely to be converted back again from being a 'federast' and I certainly was."

34. Ridley (ed.), 1965, p. 8. *One Europe* was signed "by the following members of the One Nation Group of MPs: Lord Baniel, Robert Carr, Paul Channon, Christopher Chataway, William Deedes, Charles Fletcher-Cooke, Ian Gilmour, Philip Goodhart, Brian Harrison, John Hill, John Hobson, Charles Longbottom, Gilbert Longden, James Ramsden, Nicholas Ridley, John Rodgers, Anthony Royle and John Vaughan-Morgan."

35. Again see Buller, 2000, pp. 22–47, for an exposition of this "external market solution." When such an interpretation on the One Nation position was put to Lord David Howell at an interview at the House of Lords, June 23, 2004, he agreed that this was "completely the right interpretation . . . we were an over socialised, an over corporatised island and we longed to stretch out and get involved in this better show across the channel, that was an overwhelming feeling in the Tory party, overwhelming, and it remained so until we began to feel that they had changed their tack and began to become too socialistic . . . we didn't change our minds that much, what changed, rather like a rotating scene in the national theatre, was the European scene; one minute we were looking at social and market economics and then it gradually turned round into a huge socialistic outfit, suddenly we had more and more regulations, it was more socialist, we had moved in a totally different direction."

36. Ridley (ed.), 1965, p. 9.

37. Conservative Party Archive (CPA): CCO4/9/400, Letter to *The Times*, February 18, 1963; by the One Nation group entitled: "A Domestic Stimulus," Bodleian Library, Oxford.

38. Rodgers papers: OP27/8, One Nation Minutes, December 6, 1967; note that Powell and Ramsden attended this dinner, Centre for Kentish Studies, Kent.

39. Rodgers papers: OP27/8, One Nation Minutes, June 11, 1969.

40. See Norton, 1978; Crowson, 2007.

41. *Daily Telegraph*, July 25, 2005 and see the Thatcher Foundation Web site for all the released documents and where in session 4 of the negotiations, on May 21, 1971, we find Heath declaring that Britain would be prepared to contribute considerably more to the EEC budget than was originally envisaged, see http://www.margaret-thatcher.org/archive/heath-eec.asp.

42. Ashford, 1980, p. 109.

43. CPA: Keith Joseph papers, KJ/8/21, "Memo from Joseph to Butler 15 December 1976 with attached letter of 29 November 1976" where such views are expressed in a letter between Basil (Boz) de Ferranti and Engineers Employers Federation chairman Anthony Fordsham, and which reported this observation from the

Euro-enthusiast MPs Douglas Hurd and Peter Kirk. The letter was copied to Keith Joseph who forwarded it to Thatcher's PPS Adam Butler so that he could "keep the point in mind if it seems appropriate to bring up at any stage."

44. CPA: CCO20/8/20, "Memo from Thatcher to Peter Thorneycroft, 10 July 1978."
45. Seawright, 2004. This IGC was opened in 1985 and closed with the 1986 Act signed in February 1986.
46. Thatcher, 1993, p. 551.
47. Nigel Lawson, in *The Sunday Telegraph*, May 5, 2002.
48. The Delors Committee was one of a group of central bank heads, set up to enquire into EMU as a result of the Hanover European Council in June 1988 and chaired by the Commission President himself.
49. Seawright, 2004.
50. See Buller, 2000, pp. 152–153.
51. Baker et al., 2008, p. 111.
52. Baker et al., 2002, 2008.
53. It is suggested that governments which attempt to pursue traditional interventionist or social democratic objectives quickly lose the confidence of the financial markets, as the British Government did in the IMF crisis in 1976, the French Government in 1981–2, and the Swedish Government in 1994. In each case, so the argument goes, the massive and sustained outflows of capital, the refusal to extend credits, and the actual or threatened collapse of the currency, forced a swift change of policy. In short, to remain a member of the open and global trading network governments have learnt that they must implement polices which command confidence in the financial markets, see Gill, 1998.
54. Holmes, 1996 and Portillo, 1998.
55. The following data is derived from Economic and Social Research Council surveys of British MPs and MEPs conducted in 1994 (ESRC R000231298) and 1998 (ESRC R000222397) and which employed attitude statements on the various aspects of European integration. These statements elicited Likert-type responses of *strongly agree, agree, neither, disagree* and *strongly disagree*; in Tables 7.1 and 7.2, the responses have been "collapsed" into agree and disagree categories, see Baker et al., 2002.
56. Baker et al., 2002, 2008; Spicer, 1992, pp. 1–2.
57. However see Foster (2002), p. 131; where he points out that: "In this regard, it is interesting to observe that pro-EC MPs have been more willing than sceptics, not merely to disobey their party, but to place loyalty to the European cause before their party."
58. Baker et al., 1999.
59. Baker et al., 1993; Ludlam, 1996.
60. Baker et al., 1999.
61. Gill, 2003; Gorman and Kirby, 1993.
62. Letter from Allan Duncan MP to Gilbert Longden, May 25, 1992: Temporary File No. 9: Londgen Box List, Sir Gilbert Longden papers.
63. Nott, 2002, p. 137.
64. Spicer, 1992, p. 184.
65. Ibid, p. 184.
66. Baker et al., 2008.
67. *The Independent*, October 28, 1992.

68. Gill, 2003, p. 100.
69. Ibid.
70. Gill, 2003. And see Lamont, 1999, p. 250; where, as Chancellor, he was irritated to have the Europhile triumvirate so closely involved with the ERM decision making.
71. Baker et al., 2008.
72. Conservative Party, 2005, pp. 26–27.
73. Baker et al., 2002.
74. David Cameron's response to statement on the EU treaty, December 17, 2007: http://www.conservatives.com/tile.do?def=news.story.page&obj_id=141309&speeches=1.
75. *The Times*, November 13, 2007.
76. Ibid.
77. *Daily Telegraph*, July 14, 2007.
78. Ibid.
79. Ibid.
80. Lynch and Whitaker, 2008.
81. Baker et al., 2008, p. 110.
82. Howell, 2001.
83. Ibid, pp. 251, 262, 276, and 299.
84. Baker et al., 2002.
85. *The Times*, October 25, 2002.
86. *The Times*, March 5, 2007.
87. David Cameron in *The Daily Telegraph*, July 14, 2007.

# CHAPTER EIGHT

# Conclusion: Further Refreshment
# at the Springs of Doctrine

Undoubtedly, the One Nation ethos clearly matters for Conservative Party politics, with the power and longevity of such a conceptual construct crucial to understanding the very essence of the party and its concomitant electoral success. Indeed, whatever date is designated for the party's birth certificate[1]— be it in the era of Pitt or Liverpool, or in the age of Peel or Disraeli— this history of electoral success has been associated with the perennial "cry" of *the national party*, a party which puts Nation first in stark contrast with the sectional interests of other political parties. And, the One Nation ethos is a successful facilitator for its doctrinal aspirations, with the ideological trajectory of the party portrayed as being informed from the politics of the Conservative Nation,[2] which itself is viewed as coterminous with the politics of the British Nation, as the One Nation ethos merely incorporates sets of values that have sprung from the traditions and experiences of the British people. It is instructive, of course, that the very periods when the party struggled to utilize its myth of One Nation and suffered electoral disaster as a consequence was when it appeared split and sectional itself, particularly in relation to the "three great divisive issues" of "Landed Agriculture", "Tariff Reform," and "Europe."

Central to the ideological approach of the Conservative Party then, the One Nation ethos ceremonially shelters those necessary doctrinal debates that are fundamental for the successful renewal of the party's policy program. We have seen that the Conservative Party is by far a more doctrinal party than is commonly thought, as for each successive generation—let alone for that putative era of a post war settlement—it was clear that nothing was ever settled within the ranks of the Parliamentary Conservative Party. However, an intrinsic element of the party's political communications narrative was, and still is, to eschew the very notion of being ideological. Paradoxically, an essential part of the party's ideology is to be seen as nonideological or nondoctrinaire. We are reminded that Freeden believed the absence of absolute boundaries, in the features of ideological systems, was the most important facet of ideological morphology.[3] And there is little exaggeration to the claim that the Conservative Party epitomized this absence in absolute boundaries, due to the inherent "dual nature" or "twin inheritance" of its ideology.[4] This "dual nature" of the party reflected the fact that it contained within itself deposits of political thought that ranged from laissez-faire competition to state collectivism.[5] Indeed, it was to the complexity and importance of this dual character that Eccleshall perceptively traced the success of the One Nation theme:

> There have been two conservative versions of this heroic tale of the endur-
> ing virtues of the people of this land of hope and glory. . . . Each version has
> enabled conservatives to profess membership of a "national" party because of
> its peculiar capacity to preserve or restore features of this great inheritance[6].

Inextricably linked to this "dual nature" was what White[7] termed "the centuries old discussion," which ranged over the whole field of political thought and experience and with which the party was perennially embroiled, namely, the relationship of the state to the individual and with it the question concerning the optimum level of state intervention. The preceding chapters clearly delin-eated a prepotency of concepts that attached themselves to the limited state view of governance and which were utilized by the party in recommended core Conservative texts and by the One Nation group itself in its publications. Indeed, the One Nation group favored the concepts of "individual responsibility" and "competition" in reference to what constituted Conservative principles.[8] Even today advocates of the extended state tradition within the One Nation group are no less cognizant of this emphasis upon individual responsibility when discussing the principles of the Conservative party:

> . . . if Government wasn't to have a purpose at intervening at certain stages
> when either the market couldn't deliver or wasn't delivering then what were
> we in politics for, we may simply be bystanders allowing the process to go on.
> But, we have always been Conservatives at the end of the day and the rea-
> son that we may have a heart but are not socialists is that we just don't think
> socialism worked and unless you have created something, unless you have
> within the mechanism for the sense that people can, by their own efforts,
> make a difference to their own quality of life, then again, we simply would not
> be Conservatives if we didn't have that sense.[9]

As noted throughout this work, such a dual inheritance gave rise to an endur-ing tension within the party over the best way to advance those opportunities for all in society—by free competitive market mechanisms or by a judicious governmental direction to wealth creation—and such tension is found to be a perpetual phenomenon in any analysis of the party's history and also no doubt for its immediate and long term future. We found that such *political recrudescence* was as old as the party itself and was an essential element in the ability for self-renewal. In the early twentieth century Butler perceived it to be, in essence, the "revivifying marrow to Tory doctrine."[10] And, in a 1952 *cur-rente calamo* note to Angus Maude, Enoch Powell sketched out a remarkably similar view—regarding this tension and transformation—when considering "the (real or apparent) contradictions which baffle conservatives today"[11]: the party being seemingly against laissez-faire in favor of control, yet championing competition while retaining nationalization; championing trade unionism but getting the bosses vote while unionists vote for the other side; preaching equality, if not of property, of opportunity but also preaching incentive and reward, if not privilege and rank; conservers of the constitution but the leading exponents of House of Lords reform; liked to be thought of as the creators, if not of the welfare state, yet of the social services, while depending on the votes of those who regard levels of welfare expenditure and taxation as excessive; standing for Empire, unity, sovereignty, but proclaiming self-government to be the goal of colonial policy, while accepting the lowest common denominator of imperial agreement on trade, defense, and policy. Powell considered three explanations for such real or apparent contradictions. It could all be explained by the level of expediency within the party or indeed by that dual inheritance, those historical constituents of laissez-faire and protectionism.

> Or, and here one opens up a new vista—this is one of the historic dilemmas of Toryism (like 1714 and 1832) which can be grasped and met only by a descent into its inner, permanent meaning. . . . It is then possible to survey the apparent contradictions from which one set out, and see how far they are resolved from this standpoint, much as the dilemma of Jacobitism and Whiggism (Nottingham) were resolved in the nationalist loyalist Toryism of the Younger Pitt's era. Conservatism has neither been defeated nor compromised; it has been transformed. But it could not have performed its own transformation and preserved the nation, but for that inner conviction which appeared at first to be in conflict with its doings and sayings in the world about it.[12]

Thus, this perpetual conflict within the party on its direction of progress[13] was the expected norm if the Conservative Party was to continue to be true to itself, as Conservatives should argue with each other about the interpretation of their own tradition.[14] It is through this process of political recrudescence then that the party finds that necessary revival and the ability to perform its own transformation through the resolution of its (real or apparent) doctrinal disputes, with the concomitant claim of course that such generational change is undertaken on behalf of the whole nation and that this has been "the secret of its perennial vitality."[15] Successful parties are indeed forever in need of refreshment at the springs of doctrine[16] and here we have identified the real secret weapon of the Conservative Party—the manner in which it avails itself of such doctrinal refreshment. Political recrudescence was confirmed in the behavior of the groups and committees that make up the Conservative Party, with their debate a prerequisite for the "breaking out afresh" of successful party policy, in short, for such transformation or self-renewal. Moreover, although there is now a greater willingness for the party to divide in public as well as in private, with the names of its internal policy parties or groups now common currency in the political gossip columns, clearly, the lines of division are still all rather fluid reflecting the absence of factions and the overall nonfactional behavior of the Parliamentary Conservative Party.[17] And, it is evident that the One Nation group of Conservative MPs was not only a valuable microcosm in the study of Conservative party politics per se but as a "bondstone group"—facilitating the cementing of one Conservative ideological face to another—it helped underpin party cohesion, cushioning those necessary conflicts and aiding doctrinal resolution, so necessary for that malign element in political recrudescence to be kept at bay. Thus, to reiterate, as a parliamentary group, it helped keep the "conflicting voices" on board and the channels for debate and discussion open.[18]

> If you had been looking at say Nick's Dinner or No Turning Back you would see the ideological coherence there. The great thing about One Nation is that it does not do that. Any group that can have Ken Clarke and David Heathcoat-Amory around the same table tells you its own story; it is therefore much broader and this has always been the sense of the Nation that you had a broader picture represented around the table.[19]

From its very inception the One Nation group reflected this broad range of Conservative opinion from what is in reality the "Conservative continuum." Indeed, it was David Howell, the eminent and distinguished former One Nation chairman, who placed Ian Gilmour "way out on the other wing"[20] of that continuum and yet we saw in Chapter 4 the success of the left's hegemonic project, reflected both in the contemporary mass media and even in much of academia, which fettered One Nation to such a marginal position within the party based mainly on the writings and musings of Ian Gilmour. A clear example of this is to be found in the work of Bevir and Rhodes, where the One Nation narrative in the Tory tradition is based on those views of Gilmour while the Liberal tradition is to be found in the work of the One Nation member David Willetts but ironically "narrated" through the 1954 One Nation pamphlet, *Change Is Our Ally*.[21] At this juncture one has no wish to enter the fascinating "new interpretavist–critical realist" debate[22] but if such an approach, as delineated by Bevir and Rhodes, is to avoid being characterized as "relativist," in the selection of the "best" interpretation, then such a narrative as recited through Gilmour requires closer inspection with regards to its accuracy, comprehensiveness, and consistency.[23] Indeed, with this in mind, Chapter 4 effectively exposed what has erroneously developed as the received wisdom, the portrayal of One Nation as a group within the party that views much in British social democracy as admirable and demonstrated just how distorted and pervasive such an account has become. To reiterate, the capacity for that malign element in political recrudescence could not be clearer in this period, with a small minority on the left of the party aiming to marginalize, or even to eradicate, the free market tradition in the party (which the One Nation group itself had dated all the way back to Lord Liverpool), while, for short-term gain, some of the advocates of that more extensive free marker tradition, in their eagerness to appear radical and to distance themselves from that putative consensus period, willingly acquiesced in this de-legitimization project. Thus, such Thatcherites were to be just as culpable, as some on the left of the party, for the long-term damage to the ideological canopy that is so essential for self-renewal—that *One Nation* ethos.

Such skilled propaganda from ill intentioned friends, from those "way out on both wings of the party," militated against the party's transformation and its renewed refreshment at the springs of doctrine, culminating in the electoral disaster of 1997. As Cecil Parkinson pointed out to Ian Gilmour, in reality, such a gaping lacuna did not exist in the Conservative Party, but the facile exaggeration of this great divide throughout the last quarter of the twentieth century would have consequences for Powell's process of descent into the inner and permanent meaning of the party where apparent contradictions are resolved and Conservatism transformed. However, again it is members of the One Nation group who are involved in that necessary process of self-renewal, evident in the group's contemporary views from both the limited and extended state wings of its Conservative continuum, respectively.

> Thatcherism won, in essence it has now been adopted by our opponents but I think there is now a renewed emphasis on people who get left behind in any system, better still how you help them, but undeniably, call it what you like, social Conservatism is now an important factor; that's not as a reaction against Thatcherism but as an extension of it, in fact Mrs Thatcher was always very aware that there were people who needed help. I don't think Thatcherism was ever incompatible with social provision but it is a question of how it is done. But there is now a drive, and Iain Duncan Smith was very strong on this, to study how it is that some people cannot engage in a market economy and how we as a party can help them to do that and I think in electoral terms this is the battle ground.[24]

And:

> I consider myself to be on the left of the party—however you want to put it—as I believe constructing public policy to help those who are disadvantaged is hugely important. But I also believe that the non-statist approach to it is the best way to do it in the modern world and the whole area of trying to engage voluntary groups and charities in helping disadvantaged people is one of our more creative areas of thought at the moment. So I think the old-fashioned view that the smaller you want to make the state the less compassionate you are actually is not true and in a sense the left of the party has to learn some of the lessons that the right of the party taught it in the 1970s and

1980s about the economy, which is that more state intervention might make things worse rather than better and apply those lessons to the social sphere. You can find a creative synthesis of the various Tory traditions in this area where you will use non state solutions for compassionate ends.[25]

For Damian Green, the idea that you can provide better services if the state is smaller (in relation to use of voluntary groups) was a radical thought that needed explaining and needed developing[26] and it is to this development of the *Responsible Society* under David Cameron that we turn to in the next section.

## Back to the Future: The Responsible Society

In light of the evidence presented thus far, it should by now be no surprise that in the first three years of David Cameron's leadership, the expected ruminative process, concerning the ideological trajectory of the party, is well under way, where ideas are floated in line with that perennial aim of utilizing the "politics of support" for the "politics of power,"[27] which is a realistic goal for the first time in more than a decade. With this aim of power in mind, Cameron developed the interlaced themes of "compassionate conservatism," "progressive ends-conservative means" and "social responsibility", all the while cognizant of course of the need for adaptation to changing circumstances within an ethos of One Nation.

> The British people are looking to see if the Conservative Party has learned the lessons of defeat. The Party has been around for a long time. You could say we're Built To Last. Our history has always been intimately bound up with the history of Britain itself. During every period of social change the Conservative Party has changed too. Sometimes we've led that change. Sometimes we've reflected it. But we have never allowed ourselves to remain isolated from the people of this country.[28]

And, Cameron is no less aware of that "duality" to Conservative Party ideology and the consequent potential for maneuverability that this can give him on the Conservative Party continuum. Just one example of this is to be found in his appeal to attract Liberal Democrat voters, where he describes himself as a "liberal Conservative." He declares that his skepticism of the state led to his strongly held belief in the freedom of the individual pursuing their own happiness with minimum interference from government, while emphasis is placed upon continuity and belonging, which is embedded in the country's institutions and that this historical understanding between past, present, and future generations brings people together to play an active part in their community through social responsibility.[29]

Gladstone, who reduced the tax burden and promoted the freedom of religious conscience. And Disraeli, who legalized trade unions and empowered local government to organize civic action. Liberalism and Conservatism—like Gladstone and Disraeli—are often in conflict. But at a deeper level they depend on each other. On many of the key issues, it is this balance which we need—not state control, but greater freedom and greater social responsibility.[30]

For Cameron, it is the Conservative Party that has been the party of innovation and freedom and thus has not been afraid of utilizing progressive ideals in order to serve Britain best. Thus, the party is the party of Peel, Disraeli, Salisbury, Churchill, Macmillan, and Eden and "the party of Margaret Thatcher, who rejected decline, refused to live in the past and who freed up our economy and stood up for aspiration for all."[31] Cameron makes it clear that just as Thatcher applied the Conservative principles of freedom and enterprise to fix the broken economy, he will utilize similar Conservative values to fix what he terms the broken society.[32] However, there are those from the center-left commentariat who caution Labour paladins in "barking up the wrong tree in charging [Cameron] with crypto-Thatcherism."[33] Such an approach views Cameron as a quintessential Whig imperialist in the semblance of Stanley Baldwin.[34] But, it is not just Labour paladins who bark up the wrong tree. To reiterate, we know that Baldwin placed as much emphasis on the benefits of "independent sturdy individualism" and that he deployed almost as much Gladstonianism as Disraelianism.[35] Indeed, the very balance felt to be required by Cameron and it is in this sense that Cameron follows Baldwin in the "irenic statecraft" of a Conservative Party leader. David Willetts bemoans such caricatured views of the party's history in which the different strands that make the Conservative tradition so rich are not fully understood and thus the result is often the crude model of "first they are wets and then all dries and it is much more complicated than that."[36] A major aim of this work then has been to demonstrate the extent and relevance of such "complexity" to a thorough understanding of Conservative Party politics and the evidence presented throughout its chapters effectively expose the limitations of such "caricatured accounts."

With this in mind, we saw in chapter two the long-standing emphasis upon the individual in Conservative Party politics in both moral and economic terms and the early realization of the unintended consequences of a too active state, namely, "responsibility checked" and "initiative crippled." Thus, it was shown that "Thatcherism" was not some deviation from a "path that had been followed for almost 60 years."[37] Indeed, a comparison of David Cameron's "manifesto for a Responsible Society" with the One Nation group's *The Responsible Society* of 1959 clearly illustrates the continuity in Conservative Party politics, namely, the deployment in both eras of what some may crudely model as Thatcherism. The essays prepared by the One Nation group in 1959 were meant to illuminate the fundamental process of restoring balance between the power of the state and the rights of the individual.[38] In the pamphlet, the group emphasized the

Conservative government of 1951 inheriting a society in whose life the state played a heavy and expanding role, with the heresy of "state parentalism" the accepted creed of the late 1940s.[39] It was argued that with its return to power, particularly since 1955, the party had gone some way to halting and reversing the trend toward state domination and some way toward restoring the balance of individual freedom and the individual's share of initiative. Although by 1959, the party had swept away a vast complex of state authority, it was also argued that much of the work and policy, which had assumed such a coherence and purpose was not widely perceived nor appreciated as such. And, as the One Nation group believed this the most beneficial result of Tory rule, the group thought it their objective to underline the significance of the trend and how it may be developed further for the future; while lamenting the postwar lack of interest with the Conservative warnings on the dangers of establishing a too powerful state and similarly with the lack of inspiration taken from Professor Hayek's *Road to Serfdom*.[40]

The responsible society could never be secured from the work, however well done, of Westminster and Whitehall, thus one had to look further to all society's members, individually, as families, and in other groupings for that fulfillment of social responsibility. Much emphasis was placed upon this role for the family; as the image of settled family life was not just the right of all but the very taproot of a responsible society.[41] Indeed, the words of the Home Secretary, RAB Butler, were utilized in the concluding section to that effect: "Belief in moral obligations, pride in integrity and respect for the rights of others can and should be instilled by the family."[42] There was also to be a conscious effort to encourage voluntary service amongst those other groupings in society, with such service having a great tradition in Britain. And, as the One Nation group noted: "This is as good a place as any to mention the importance we attach to voluntary service in every form. It is the leaven of the Welfare State."[43] However, the phase of Tory government that saw the end of food rationing, the removal of all emergency powers over industry and the individual, the encouragement of house ownership, would not be complete in the eyes of the One Nation group until the taxpayer had more freedom to decide how their own income would be spent. After all, lower taxation passes to the individual from the government power and responsibility, so trust should be placed in the people and in the forces of the market.[44]

A half a century later and David Cameron's conceptual analysis, as well as his rhetoric, is "remarkably" similar to that of One Nation in 1959, as delineated through his modern manifesto for a responsible society.[45] Ten years of Labour government had seen a growing burden of state intervention which was costly, bureaucratic, short-term, superficial, and in the end, counterproductive because responsibility is taken from the people and put in the hands of the state.[46] Cameron does not hide his displeasure at Labour clutching at some sort of intellectual lifeline of the bigger state in both economic and social senses, with particular resentment held for what he terms the extraordinary statist comments of Labour ministers. "David Miliband said that 'unless government is on your side you end up on your own'. 'On your own'—without the government. I thought it was one of the most arrogant things I've heard a politician say."[47] And, despite its 1997 prospectus, Labour had failed to maintain the competitiveness of Britain's economy and had failed to lift the excluded out of the trap of multiple deprivation, mainly because Blair and Brown believed the state to hold the solution to every problem.[48] Thus, Cameron attacks Labour for having no conception of anything between the state and the individual, no family to rely on, no friend to depend on, or charities to work in; no one but the Minister and nowhere but Whitehall. In 1959, the nomenclature used to attack such an approach was "state parentalism" but by 2007, its flip side of "infantilising people" was the preferred term.[49] To counter this Cameron's vision is to build and strengthen the institutions that encourage trust in personal and social responsibility. And, the first and most important of these institutions, which would be at the heart of his vision for a responsible society, is the strong family, which promotes good behavior and the right values.[50]

The other intermediate groupings that make up the voluntary sector are a fundamental part of the visionary ambition to inspire a revolution in social provision, which will see a move from state welfare to social welfare, a big idea that is at the heart of the party's plans for social justice. Cameron is careful to emphasize that the party is explicitly not proposing the privatization of the public services but he believes that the present generation could see a revolution in the social economy comparable to the revolution in the commercial economy of the 1980s, as that is the revolution that Cameron wants to lead.[51] He stresses the existence of over 700,000 nonstatutory, nonprofit organizations in the United Kingdom, which can help develop local responses to local needs.

> To me those 700,000 organisations prove that there is such a thing as society. It's just not the same thing as the state. The term "the third sector" was first coined by the liberal economist Friedrich von Hayek, the intellectual guru of Thatcherism. In Law, Legislation and Liberty Hayek wrote that "it is most important for a healthy society that we preserve between the commercial and the governmental sector a third, independent sector." I mention this not because I want to claim the sector for the Conservative political tradition. That would be quite wrong. But because I want to show that the principles of the free market are not incompatible with the principles of voluntarism and social action which we associate with the third sector.[52]

The utilization of this third or voluntary sector in the party's intended revolution in social provision reflects, for Cameron, a profound philosophical difference between the parties. "Labour thinks that social justice principally means equality, achieved and guaranteed by government. We think it means community, built and maintained by people themselves."[53] This debate on social justice, particularly within the Conservative Party, should not be examined merely in terms of its attributes for a new strategic electoral communications narrative, however important this may be, but crucially, it is a contemporary example of political recrudescence where substantive questions are raised, not only with reference to the actual possibility of a "Conservative social justice" but in terms that concern the very future of the party's ideological trajectory. And, of course, concerning the potential for Powell's process of descent into the inner and permanent meaning of the party where apparent contradictions are resolved and Conservatism transformed. Indeed, the views of Damian Green and David Heathcoat-Amory presented in the first section of this chapter neatly illustrate such a process as does the rhetoric of David Cameron:

> But if you want to know what I really hope we will achieve in government. If you want to know where the change will be greatest from what has gone before. It is our plan for social reform. The central task I have set myself and this Party is to be as radical in social reform as Margaret Thatcher was in economic reform. That's how we plan to repair our broken society[54].

Thus social justice will help mend the broken society. Alistair Burt disclosed that debate had taken place on the use and utility of such a term as social justice, both between the members of the One Nation group and within the party generally and that it first appeared in the speeches of Iain Duncan Smith (IDS) as leader when David Cameron and Tim Montgomerie were writing them.[55] Burt believes it is about the whole concept of "Easterhouse etc" (pace IDS)[56] and that is where he wants the Conservative Party to go and where for him it needs to go: "back into the cities, yes, social justice exists and there are Conservative solutions to it" and thus there is no reason why it should not be part of the Conservative lexicon but he acknowledges that there are others in the One Nation group and within the party who merely view it as a "mechanistic term."[57] Indeed, the debate has been a long-standing one, Alport informed us that Enoch Powell hated the term "because the phrase seemed to him to be waffley and almost meaningless"[58] and in a similar vein David Willetts once classed it as merely "slippery."[59] But, with that process of self-renewal in mind, we note that Willetts now accepts that his position has changed somewhat from that classic Hayekian critique,[60] for him, social justice can now be a good word, which captures the idea that the distribution of opportunities in life are not simply determined by the market. He elaborates:

> I think we Conservatives denied that and came a cropper as a result, so social justice is in some sense trying to get some sense of social obligation back in, it needn't be egalitarian necessarily but it is trying to get that idea back in and I was overly dismissive of that strand of thought in my book about it, so it is a philosophical strand that you can find in Conservatism that I rejected

too forcefully then, and also, at the lowest level of political tactics, we have watched Labour capture so many words from us like community, rights and responsibilities, and the natural Conservative language of enterprise. So part of the revival of Conservatism is to reclaim our vocabulary and if we can press Labour by saying, hold on, we have a different view of social justice than you have and social justice does not just belong to Labour, I think that is an important political task that we have.[61]

## In Conclusion: Cameron Conservatism

Thus, after three successive electoral defeats, the Conservative Party appears to be once again giving serious consideration to that crucial process of transformation and self-renewal. William Hague, Iain Duncan Smith, and Michael Howard no doubt realized that "the loyalties which centre on number one are enormous" but that if the leader "is no good, he must be pole axed."[62] Cameron will be cognizant of such an aphorism with regards to the fate of those who failed the Conservative Party ordinance of climbing to the top of the greasy pole, for both the 2001 and 2005 elections. But, with an eye on the fate of IDS, he should also make himself aware of McKenzie's amendment to A. L. Lowell's statement: "when appointed, the Leader leads, and the party follows, except when the party decides not to follow; then the Leader ceases to be Leader."[63] Cameron places emphasis upon all three of his predecessors opposing a Prime Minister in Tony Blair who claimed that his aims were far closer to those of the Conservative Party and although the party may have won the battle of ideas, there was a fundamental problem as "that victory had left us with an identity crisis."[64] In addressing that fundamental problem of how to tackle New Labour, it is clear that Cameron was also embarking upon that process where apparent contradictions would be resolved and Conservatism transformed. For example, echoing the views of David Heathcoat-Amory above, he asserts that it was Margaret Thatcher and John Major who recognized the need for social justice before Blair, but that it was Tony Blair who preserved the fruits of the Thatcher revolution in making more explicit his aims of a stronger economy and a more decent society—the twin focus on "social justice and economic efficiency." Thus the Tories had to change in line with this twin focus while at the same time avoiding the powerful gravitational pull of its default position, "a move to the right."[65] However, although ten years on, Cameron is careful to lambast Tony Blair and Gordon Brown for neither fulfilling the goal of economic efficiency nor social justice—indeed, stressing that Britain had fallen from fourth to thirteenth in the international competitiveness league and that social mobility was at its lowest level since the 1950s[66]—he needs to be just as alert, with McKenzie's admonition in mind, to the inherent dangers, as well as to the potential electoral benefits, of constructing "Downsian strategies"[67] of "symbolic change."

In recent decades, it has been the parties of the center-left who have been successful in the use of the symbolic sacrifice stratagem in support of such claims for change. Thus, Bill Clinton was advised to make the ultimate sacrifice—in a long line of symbolic sacrifices—in the signing of a workfare bill; in order to show by just how much the New Democrats had actually changed by sacrificing the interventionist welfare policies of old. And, of course, New Labour took the opportunity to construct its own symbolic sacrifice in the shape of re-writing its constitutional Clause IV, which was similarly a device to demonstrate the extent of change from the socialist ideology of old.[68] But, will it be possible for David Cameron to imitate such tactics for the Conservative Party? After all, the evidence presented in this book shows the party was successful in the 1950s by highlighting the differences with Labour and the symbolic sacrifice for both the 1970 and 1979 elections was the "straw man" of the putative consensus period. But, undoubtedly, the party line was initially informed by such thinking and this would explain the "apparent or real" contradictory approaches in the initial period of Cameron's leadership, particularly with some in Cameron's inner circle searching for their own "Clause IV moment." In order to decontaminate the "brand" with its image as the "nasty" and singularly economics party,[69] a number of such strategies were employed by the Conservatives in the first two years under Cameron. There was "the heir to Blair" claim along with the appeals on the environment and crime that were parodied as hugging trees, huskies and even "hoodies." Indeed, one of Cameron's advisers, Greg Clarke MP, went so far as to suggest that Churchill was wrong on the issue of poverty and that the party should now learn from the ideas of Polly Toynbee. In any exercise to appear "counterintuitive" concerning the party's message, for a majority of Conservatives, this example of "drawbridge social democracy" in the hypocrisy of the ex-BBC and *Guardian* journalist Polly Toynbee would be unsurpassed.[70]

In mid-2007, such "counterintuitive" strategies descended into farce with the row over the proposed policy to not create any more grammar schools, with such schools and selection being totemic for much of the party concerning those opportunities for social mobility. Indeed, Greg Clarke, MP, was just one of a number of front benchers who aimed to reverse the policy calling for more grammar schools for his own constituency in Kent, with that county already having more than anywhere else in Britain.[71] In fact, the debacle over grammar schools highlighted a danger that such strategies could be so easily construed as emanating from "Tory toffs" and as such were patronizing and hypocritical. Such a likelihood was manifest in the number of times the now infamous "Bullingdon Club" photograph was produced to indicate the extent of an "elite old-boy network" that it was claimed operated both within and with the Shadow Cabinet.[72] Moreover, a concomitant concessionary approach, in relation to our combative-concessionary Conservative dimension, has the potential for creating further difficulties for David Cameron. As the banking and credit crisis deepened,

Cameron, with indecent haste, called for putting aside party differences, declaring that: "I and this party stand ready to help in whatever way is necessary, to help the Government to do the right thing for the sake of our economy and for our future financial security."[73] But, this approach appeared to corroborate and thus add weight to the strategy being developed by Gordon Brown's advisers, which explained the economic recession in terms of global circumstances rather than as a consequence of Labour party policy. A speedy realization of this led to the just as swift return of responsible fiscal conservatism, "the traditional role of the centre-right."[74] The fiscal irresponsibility and spendthrift ways of Labour were now emphasized. But, had not Cameron's Conservative Party previously participated in such irresponsibility with its counterintuitive message of matching Labour's spending plans? However, the intensity of such counterintuitive hyperbole was toned down considerably and such narratives were as good as dead and buried by the time the party jettisoned the pledge to match Labour spending but there still remains the issue of resolving the real or apparent contradictions in a policy which claims to respect the environment while utilizing the traditional Conservative levers for economic growth.

And, the One Nation ethos, in any future Cameron administration, will still face simultaneous domestic and external challenges in the shape of problems over devolution, immigration, and Europe; those upper and nether millstones between which the Westminster parliament is inexorably ground.[75] A cursory examination of the issue of Europe suggests that the party's Euro-skeptic direction is now its "settled position," with a goal to lead Europe in a new direction.[76] That new direction would see a challenge to a "European constitution," which for the party is effectively the Lisbon Treaty and if this were not ratified by the time of a new Conservative administration, then it would be put to the people in a referendum. But, we have learnt the extent to which "nothing is really settled" within the ranks of the Parliamentary Conservative Party and undoubtedly, for some time to come, that will be the case on such a substantive issue as Europe. It will only take one Euro-enthusiast, with political clout, to question the direction of the party in order to once again raise the specter of division and splits on an issue that will just not go away. And added to the dual strategy of facilitating good race relations by addressing the high levels of immigration is the critique of a cultural apartheid, which has been enhanced by the policies of state multiculturalism. Cameron echoes the words of the Chief Rabbi who challenges the idea of Britain as a hotel, with separate private spaces that have separate cultures living behind locked doors and depending on the hotel management, namely the state, to service them. An alternative vision has Britain as a house with common foundations but which is perfectly capable of alterations and additions so long as they are compatible with the existing architecture.[77] Once again, the party will face the danger of being branded as racist with such a dual approach but the emphasis is upon the integrative benefits of a One

Nation policy that will help develop a society that is held together by a strong sense of shared identity and common values:

> Most of what I've said today comes quite naturally to Conservatives. It's part of the narrative of Britishness—a confidence in the history and the institutions of our country, a basic belief that we're lucky to live here. The narrative is of course an organic thing.[78]

The commitment to this narrative of Britishness and the Union was demonstrated in December 2008 when Cameron visited Belfast to resurrect the historical connection with the Ulster Unionist Party (UUP). The fissure in Conservative–UUP relations began with Ted Heath's imposition of direct rule in the early 1970s but Cameron intended to work toward the restoration of the relationship. "So for me coming here and joining our parties is not a matter of political calculation. It's about strengthening those unbreakable bonds that bind our union."[79] As we saw in Chapter 6, there is no doubting Cameron's sincerity toward that commitment to the union and to making devolution work. But, if it were possible for the party to make devolution work, this could only transpire with a solution to the "English Question," which undoubtedly requires tactful and skilful answers. However, what if the party could not make devolution work? With so few MPs from the UUP to help in the voting lobbies, the political calculation claim has been generally accepted. But, it is the United Kingdom which signs international treaties and which is the constituent member of those supranational agencies, like the UN, NATO, and of course the EU. Thus, it may not be too much of an exaggeration to posit the notion that in this sense Northern Ireland is an essential component of "the United Kingdom state" and with any future secession of Scotland from the UK that it could become even more so. The political calculation, therefore, may not be one solely of numbers in the House of Commons.

Indeed, Powell did not rule out the level of expediency within the party with respect to his tripartite explanation for how the party may deal with its real or apparent contradictions.[80] His second explanation, those historical constituents of laissez-faire and protectionism, the party's dual inheritance, has been a significant factor in those caricatured views of the party's history, so much so that the party periodically feels the need to distance itself from any suggestion of "excess." For example, the One Nation group follows such a line of argument:

> One Nation Conservatism draws on the deep British tradition of safeguarding personal freedom. This is sustained by a suspicion of the intrusiveness of the state. However, the One Nation tradition also emphasises the importance of the need for institutions to restrain the State: the tradition has no home for minimalist laissez-faire.[81]

Of course, the reality is that the party has never advocated positions situated at the uttermost boundaries of its ideological continuum. We have seen that the Conservative principles of individual responsibility with free market competition have a greater prominence in a One Nation ethos that aims to facilitate those opportunities for all and to successfully elevate the condition of the people but at no time has the need for restraining institutions been ignored. One has only to view the case of the bailout of the Johnson Matthey bank in 1985, and with it the legislation to shake up banking supervision,[82] to see just how caricatured the Thatcher era has become and the extent to which such caricatures militate against a thorough understanding of Conservative Party politics. This book has shown that it is indeed "much more complicated than that."[83] It has emphasized the centrality of One Nation to any fundamental understanding of Conservative Party politics and established the party's real secret weapon in the process of how it transforms and renews itself. We have seen that this image of enduring values applied to new challenges, the derivative of which is generational change but within the context of the institutions and culture of One Nation is one of the most abiding myths of Conservative Party politics. We began the book with a quote from David Cameron to that effect but in the effective exposure of the caricatures that have insidiously emerged as the received wisdom, it is apt that we conclude with a quote from Margaret Thatcher:

> Every generation requires a fundamental understanding of human nature, of people's desires and aspirations. Only by appreciating these can we protect our heritage of law and liberty, and promote the virtues of enterprise, responsibility and duty. The task of the politician is to apply these enduring principles to changing circumstances.[84]

## Notes

1. Duverger, 1954.
2. Gamble, 1974.
3. Freeden, 1998.
4. See Gash, 1977 and Greenleaf, 1983a,b.
5. Maude, 1963.
6. Eccleshall, 2001, p. 73.
7. White, 1950.
8. Rodgers papers: OP27/8, One Nation Minutes, 2 November 1966, Centre for Kentish Studies, Kent.
9. Interview with Alistair Burt MP at the House of Commons, June 28, 2004.
10. Butler, 1914.
11. Longden papers: Longden Box List: Temporary File Number 31, "Copy of letter from Mr J. Enoch Powell to Mr Angus Maude, 20 October 1952," London School of Economics and Political Science Library.
12. Ibid.

13. Critchley, 1973.
14. Willetts, 1992.
15. CPA: RAB Butler Papers, "RAB 19: oddments 1952–6, Prime Minister Eden's message to Leeds University Conservative Association, 28 November, 1955."
16. White, 1950.
17. Rose, 1964; Gamble, 1974; Tebbit, 1989.
18. Interview with David Willetts, at the House of Commons, June 28, 2004.
19. Interview with Alistair Burt MP at the House of Commons, June 28, 2004.
20. Interview with Lord David Howell, at the House of Lords, June 23, 2004.
21. Bevir and Rhodes, 1998, pp. 99–103.
22. Bevir and Rhodes, 2006a,b; McAnulla, 2006a,b and see also Marsh and Hall, 2007.
23. Bevir and Rhodes, 1998, p. 99 and see footnote 4, p. 117.
24. Interview with David Heathcoat-Amory MP at the House of Commons, June 29, 2004.
25. Interview with Damian Green MP, by telephone, November 3, 2006.
26. Ibid.
27. Gamble, 1974.
28. David Cameron, speech to the Party's Spring Forum, April 8, 2008. All speeches used in this chapter can be accessed at http://www.conservatives.com/News/Speeches.aspx
29. David Cameron, speech in Bath, March 22, 2007.
30. Ibid.
31. David Cameron, speech to Scottish Conservative party conference, May 23, 2008 and see speech in Bath, March 22, 2007, also.
32. David Cameron, speech following the report of the Social Justice Policy Group, July 10, 2007.
33. See David Marquand: "Labour has got Cameron wrong: this is no crypto-Thatcherite but a Whig," The Guardian, August 29, 2008.
34. Ibid.
35. Williamson, 1993, p. 208.
36. Interview with David Willetts, at the House of Commons, June 28, 2004.
37. David Marquand, The Guardian, August 29, 2008.
38. One Nation, 1959, p. 5.
39. Ibid, p. 5, 6, and 11.
40. Ibid.
41. Ibid, p. 9, 42.
42. Ibid, p. 59.
43. Ibid, p. 58.
44. Ibid, p. 24.
45. David Cameron, speech to the Royal Society, April 23, 2007.
46. Ibid.
47. David Cameron, Conference speech, October 1, 2008.
48. David Cameron, speech on Modern Conservatism, January 30, 2006.
49. David Cameron, speech to the Royal Society, April 23, 2007.
50. Ibid.
51. David Cameron, speech: 'From state welfare to social welfare', December 14, 2006.

52. Ibid. Hayek was in fact quoting R. C. Cornuelle, 1965: "it is most important for a healthy society that we preserve between the commercial sector and the governmental a third, *independent sector* which often can and ought to provide more effectively much that we now believe must be provided by government. Indeed, such an independent sector could to a great extent, in direct competition with government for public service, mitigate the gravest danger of governmental action, namely the creation of a monopoly with all the powers and inefficiency of a monopoly" (1979, p. 50).

53. David Cameron, speech: "From state welfare to social welfare," December 14, 2006.

54. David Cameron, Conference speech, October 1, 2008.

55. Interview with Alistair Burt, MP, at the House of Commons, June 28, 2004.

56. See Iain Duncan Smith's Centre for Social Justice, www.centreforsocialjustice.org.uk, for such fact finding visits to these "inner city"–deprived areas like Easterhouse in Glasgow, where both Iain Duncan-Smith and Alistair Burt had previously visited. Moreover, at this Web site, you can access the reports "Breakdown Britain (2006)" and the "Breakthrough Britain" reports that were presented to the Conservative Party in July 2007.

57. Interview with Alistair Burt, MP, at the House of Commons, June 28, 2004.

58. Alport papers: "The Red Notebook," p. 16, undated in Box 44: Notes for a memoir, etc, Albert Sloman Library, University of Essex.

59. Willetts, 1992, p. 112.

60. No doubt Willetts refers here to Hayek, 1976.

61. Interview with David Willetts, at the House of Commons, June 28, 2004.

62. Winston Churchill quoted in Norton, 1996, p. 142.

63. McKenzie, 1955, p. 145.

64. David Cameron, speech on Modern Conservatism, January 30, 2006.

65. Ibid.

66. Ibid.

67. "Political parties tend to maintain ideological positions that are consistent over time unless they suffer drastic defeats, in which case they change their ideologies to resemble that of the party which defeated them" (Downs, 1957, p. 300). David Sanders, 1998, p. 217 viewed Labour's victory in 1997 as the epitome of such Downsian theory: "Labour's response after its fourth successive general election defeat in 1992 was, quite simply, to cease to be a socialist party. Labour's residual commitment to socialism had been a major factor preventing an electoral breakthrough. In these circumstances, socialism and any belief in challenging the interests of the capitalist class had to be comprehensively abandoned, and new (i.e., old) principles of sound money, private enterprise, tightly controlled state spending had to be warmly embraced. The transformation of socialist old Labour into social democratic New Labour under Tony Blair was not lost on large swathes of the British electorate. The voters showed by way they cast their votes in May 1997 that they were indeed convinced that Labour had undergone a fundamental change. In true Downsian fashion, Labour moved towards them. In equally Downsian fashion, they responded."

68. For example, see Stephanopoulos, 1999; Wring, 2005.

69. The One Nation group's view was that: "The Conservative emphasis on economic and political realities, its scepticism about utopian schemes and critiques of woolly

thinking on the Left—valid and important as they are—can sometimes degenerate into the language of the counting-house or a dyspeptic pessimism about any prospects for improvement" (Tyrie, 2006, pp. 3–4).

70. As a descendent of the ninth Earl of Carlisle Polly Toynbee "dropped out" of her prestigious boarding school, eventually obtaining just one A level at the comprehensive school of Holland Park in the London borough of Kensington and Chelsea, raising the issue of "selection by mortgage" for comprehensive schools in such areas. Indeed, it was described as the "alma mater of the left wing aristocracy" (*Independent*, June 5, 2007). But, nevertheless she was accepted for St Anne's College, Oxford, before dropping out of there after 18 months; such similar career opportunities would be few and far between for present-day children at comprehensive schools but Toynbee was not prepared to take that chance sending her own child to a public school, see *The Sunday Times*, November 26, 2006.

71. See *The Sunday Telegraph*, June 3, 2007.

72. For example, see *The Times*, October 21, 2008.

73. David Cameron, "Together we will find a way through" speech, September 30, 2008.

74. David Cameron, "The Conservative plan for a responsible economy" speech, October 17, 2008.

75. Ritchie, 1978.

76. David Cameron, "Europe needs to be led in a new direction" speech, December 19, 2005.

77. David Cameron, "Extremism, individual rights and the rule of law in Britain" speech, February 26, 2008.

78. Ibid.

79. David Cameron, "A new political force in Northern Ireland" speech, December 6, 2008.

80. Longden papers: Longden Box List: Temporary File Number 31, "Copy of letter from Mr J. Enoch Powell to Mr Angus Maude, 20 October 1952."

81. Tyrie, 2006, p. 2.

82. See *The Times*: "Lawson censures Bank on Johnson Matthey collapse," June 21, 1985.

83. Interview with David Willetts, at the House of Commons, June 28, 2004.

84. Thatcher , 1996, p. xv.

# Bibliography

Addison, P. (1975) *The Road to 1945: British Politics and the Second World War.* London: Jonathan Cape.

Aitken, J. (2006) *Heroes and Contemporaries.* London: Continuum.

Alport, C. (1996) "Forming One Nation," *The Spectator*, March 30, 1996, pp. 15–16.

Annan, N. (1990) *Our Age.* London: Weidenfeld and Nicolson.

Ashford, N. (1980) "The European Economic Community," in Z. Layton-Henry (ed.), *Conservative Party Politics.* Basingstoke: Macmillan, pp. 95–125.

Baker, D., Gamble, A. and Ludlam, S. (1993) "1846...1906,...1996? Conservative Splits and European Integration," *Political Quarterly*, 64, pp. 420–434.

Baker, D., Gamble, A., Ludlam, S. and Seawright, D. (1999) "Backbenchers with Attitude: A Seismic Study of the Conservative Party and Dissent on Europe," in S. Bowler, D. M. Farrell and R. S. Katz (eds), *Party Discipline and Parliamentary Government.* Columbus: Ohio University State Press, pp. 72–93.

Baker, D. Gamble, A., Randall, N. and Seawright, D. (2008) "Euroscepticism in the British Party System: 'A Source of Fascination, Perplexity, and Sometimes Frustration'," in A. Szczerbiak and P. Taggart (eds), *Opposing Europe? The Comparative Party Politics of Euroscepticism: Volume 1, Case Studies and Country Surveys.* Oxford: Oxford University Press, pp. 93–116.

Baker, D., Gamble, A. and Seawright, D. (2002) "Sovereign Nations and Global Markets: Modern British Conservatism and Hyperglobalism," *British Journal of Politics and International Relations*, 4, pp. 399–428.

Baker, D. and Seawright, D. (eds) (1998) *Britain For and Against Europe: British Politics and the Question of European Integration.* Oxford: Clarendon Press.

Baldwin, S. (1926) *On England.* Harmonsworth: Penguin.

Balfour, Lord (1954) Royal Commission on Scottish Affairs: Cmd.9212. Edinburgh: HMSO.

Bara, J. and Budge, I. (2001) "Party Policy and Ideology: Still New Labour?" in P. Norris (ed.), *Britain Votes 2001*, Oxford: Oxford University Press, pp. 26–42.

Barnes, J. (1994) "Ideology and Factions," in A. Seldon and S. Ball (eds), *Conservative Century: The Conservative Party Since 1900.* Oxford: Oxford University Press, pp. 315–345.

Barnett, C. (2001) *The Lost Victory: British Dreams, British Realities 1945–1950.* London: Pan Books.

Barr, J. (2001) *The Bow Group: A History.* London: Politico's Publishing.

Beer, S. H. (1976) *Modern British Politics: Parties and Pressure Groups in the Collectivist Age.* London: Faber and Faber.

Belloni, F. P. and Beller, D. C., (1976) "The Study of Party Factions as Competitive Political Organizations," *The Western Political Quarterly*, 29, pp. 531–549.

Berrington, H. B. (1973) *Backbench Opinion in the House of Commons 1945–55.* Oxford: Pergamon Press.

Bevir, M. and Rhodes, R. A. W. (1998) "Narratives of 'Thatcherism'," in *West European Politics*, 21, pp. 97–119.

—(2006a) "Interpretative Approaches to British Government and Politics," in *British Politics*, 1, pp. 84–112.

—(2006b) "Disaggregating Structures as an Agenda for Critical Realism: A Reply to McAnulla," in *British Politics*, 1, pp. 397–403.

Biffen, W. J. (1961) "Party Conference and Party Policy," in *Political Quarterly*, 32, pp. 257–266.

Birch, N. (1949) *The Conservative Party*. London: Collins.

Blake, R. (1966) *Disraeli*. London: Methuen.

—(1985) *The Conservative Party from Peel to Thatcher*. London: Fontana.

Block, G. (1965) *About the Conservative Party*. London: Conservative Political Centre No. 325.

Bogdanor, V. (1979) *Devolution*. Oxford: Oxford University Press.

—(1980) "Devolution," in Z. Layton-Henry (ed.), *Conservative Party Politics*. Basingstoke: Macmillan, pp. 75–94.

Brand, J. (1989) "Faction As Its Own Reward: Groups in the British Parliament 1945 to 1986," *Parliamentary Affairs*, 42, pp. 148–164.

Brittan, S. (1968) *Left Or Right: The Bogus Dilemma*. London: Secker & Warburg.

—(1992) *There Is No Such Thing as Society*. Swansea: University College of Swansea.

Budge, I. (1987) "The Internal Analysis of Election Programmes," in I. Budge, D. Robertson and D. Hearl (eds), *Ideology, Strategy and Party Change: Spatial Analyses of Post War Election Programmes in 19 Democracies*. Cambridge: Cambridge University Press, pp. 15–38.

—(1999) "Party Policy and Ideology: Reversing the 1950s?" in G. Evans and P. Norris (eds), *Critical Elections: British Parties and Voters in Long-Term Perspective*. London: Sage, pp. 1–21.

—(2001) "Validating Party Policy Placements," *British Journal of Political Science*, 31, pp. 210–223.

Budge, I. Klingemann, H. D., Volkens, A., Bara, J. and Tanenbaum, E. (2001) *Mapping Policy Preferences: Estimates for Parties, Electors, and Governments 1945–1998*. Oxford: Oxford University Press.

Budge, I. and Urwin, D. (1966) *Scottish Political Behaviour: A Case Study in British Homogeneity*. London: Longman.

Buller, J. (2000) *National Statecraft and European Integration: The Conservative Government and the European Union*. London: Pinter.

Bulpitt, J. (1982) "Conservatism, Unionism and the Problem of Territorial Management," in P. Madgwick, and R. Rose (eds), *The Territorial Dimension in United Kingdom Politics*. Basingstoke: Macmillan, pp. 139–176.

—(1986a) "The Discipline of the New Democracy: Mrs Thatcher's Domestic Statecraft," *Political Studies*, 34, pp. 19–39.

—(1986b) "Continuity, Autonomy and Peripheralisation: the Anatomy of the Centre's Race Statecraft," in Z. Layton-Henry and P. B. Rich (eds), *Race, Government and Politics in Britain*. Basingstoke: Macmillan, pp. 17–44.

—(1992) "Conservative Leaders and 'the Euro-Ratchet': Five Doses of Scepticism," *Political Quarterly*, 63, pp. 258–275.

—(1996) "The European Question: Rules, National Modernisation and the ambiguities of Primat der Innenpolitik," in D. Marquand and A. Seldon (eds), *The Ideas That Shaped Post-War Britain*. London: Fontana Press, pp. 214–256.

Burke, E. (1986) *Reflections on the Revolution in France*. London: Penguin Books.

Butler, D. and Kavanagh, D. (1980) *The British General Election of 1979*. London: Macmillan.

Butler, D. E. and King, A. (1966) *The British General Election of 1966*. London: Macmillan.

Butler, G. G. (1914) *The Tory Tradition*. London: John Murray.

Cameron, D. (2006) "I will never take Scotland for granted," speech to the Scottish Conservative and Unionist Party, September 15, 2006, http://www.conservatives.com [accessed March 20, 2007].

Casey, J. (1982) "One Nation: The Politics of Race," *Salisbury Review*, 1, pp. 23–28.

Cecil, Lord H. (1912) *Conservatism*. London: Williams and Norgate.

Charmley, J. (1998) "The Conservative Defeat: An Historical Perspective," *Political Quarterly*, 69, pp. 118–125.

Clarke, D. (1947) *The Conservative Faith in a Modern Age*. London: Conservative Political Centre.

Cole, J. (1996) *As It Seemed to Me*. St Ives: Phoenix.

Conservative Party (1947) *The Industrial Charter: A Statement of Conservative Industrial Policy.* London: Conservative and Unionist Central Office.

—(2005) *The Conservative Election Manifesto 2005: Are You Thinking What We're Thinking?* London: Conservative Party.

—(2006a) *Built to Last.* London: Conservative Party.

—(2006b) *Built to Last: The Aims and Values of the Conservative Party,* 2nd edition. London: Conservative Party.

Cornuelle, R. C. (1965) *Reclaiming the American Dream.* New York: Random House.

Cosgrave, P. (1990) *The Lives of Enoch Powell.* London: Pan.

Cowley, P. and Norton, P. (1999) "Rebels and Rebellions: Conservative MPs in the 1992 Parliament," *British Journal of Politics and International Relations,* 1, pp. 84–105.

—(2002) " 'What a ridiculous thing to say! (which is why we didn't say it)': A Response to Timothy Heppell," *British Journal of Politics and International Relations,* 4, pp. 325–329.

Critchley, J. (1961) "The Intellectuals," *Political Quarterly,* 32, pp. 267–274.

—(1973) "Strains and Stresses in the Conservative Party," *Political Quarterly,* 44, pp. 401–410.

—(1995) *Heseltine.* London: Coronet.

Crocket, R. (1995) *Thinking the Unthinkable: Think Tanks and the Economic Counter Revolution 1931–1983.* London: Fontana Press.

Crowson, N. J. (2007) *The Conservative Party and European Integration since 1945: At the Heart of Europe?* London: Routledge.

Dale, I. (2000) *Conservative Party General Election Manifestos, 1900–1997.* London: Routledge.

Davies, A. J. (1995) *We, The Nation: The Conservative Party and the Pursuit of Power.* London: Little Brown and Company.

Davies, R. (1999) *Devolution: A Process Not an Event.* Cardiff: Institute of Welsh Affairs.

Deedes, W. (1968) *Race without Rancour: A Re-examination of Race and Immigration Problems.* London: Conservative Political Centre No. 414.

De Jouvenel, B. (1951) *The Ethics of Redistribution.* Cambridge: Cambridge University Press.

—(1954) "The Treatment of Capitalism by Continental Intellectuals," in F. A. Hayek (ed.), *Capitalism and the Historians.* London: Routledge & Kegan Paul, pp. 3–29.

Disraeli, B. (1967) *Coningsby, or the New Generation.* London: Everyman's Library.

—(1980) *Sybil or the Two Nations.* Harmondsworth: Penguin.

Douglas, J. (1983) "The Conservative Party: From Pragmatism to Ideology—and Back?," *West European Politics,* 6, pp. 56–74.

—(1989) "Review Article: The Changing Tide—Some Recent Studies of Thatcherism," *British Journal of Political Science,* 19, pp. 399–424.

Downs, A. (1957) *An Economic Theory of Democracy.* New York: Harper & Row.

Drucker, H. M. (1979) *Doctrine and Ethos in the Labour Party.* London: George Allen & Unwin.

Duverger, M. (1954) *Political Parties: Their Organization and Activity in the Modern State.* London: Methuen.

Eccleshall, R. (2001) "The Doing of Conservatism," in M. Freeden (ed.), *Reassessing Political Ideologies,* London: Routledge, pp. 67–79.

Eliot, T. S. (1955) *The Literature of Politics: A Lecture Delivered at a CPC Literature Luncheon by T. S. Eliot, with a Foreword by the Rt. Hon. Sir Anthony Eden.* London: Conservative Political Centre No. 146.

—(1964) "Tradition and Individual Talent," in *The Sacred Wood: Essays on Poetry and Criticism.* London: Methuen, pp. 47–59.

Emmott, B. (2008) *Rivals: How the Power Struggle between China, India and Japan Will Shape Our Next Decade.* London: Allen Lane.

Evans, B. and Taylor, A. (1996) *From Salisbury to Major: Continuity and Change in Conservative Politics.* Manchester: Manchester University Press.

Faber, R. (1987) *Young England.* London: Faber and Faber.

Fielding, S. (2002) "A New Politics?" in P. Dunleavy, A. Gamble, R. Heffernan, I. Holliday and
  G. Peele (eds), *Developments in British Politics* 6. Basingstoke: Palgrave, pp. 10–28.
Finer, S. E., Berrington, H. B. and Bartholomew, D. J. (1961) *Backbench Opinion in the House of
  Commons 1955–59*, Oxford: Pergamon Press.
Foster, A. (2002) *Euroscepticism in Contemporary British Politics: Opposition to Europe in the British
  Conservative and Labour Parties since 1945*. London: Routledge.
Freeden, M. (1990) "The Stranger at the Feast: Ideology and Public Policy in Twentieth Century
  Britain," *Twentieth Century British History*, 1, pp. 9–34.
—(1998) *Ideologies and Political Theory: A Conceptual Approach*. Oxford: Clarendon Press
—(2001) "Political Ideologies in Substance and Method: Appraising a Transformation," in
  M. Freeden (ed.), *Reassessing Political Ideologies*. London: Routledge, pp. 1–12.
Friedrich, C. J. (1955) "The Political Thought of Neo-Liberalism," The American Political Science
  Review, 42, pp. 509–525.
Gamble, A. (1974) *The Conservative Nation*. London: Routledge & Kegan Paul.
—(1989) *The Free Economy and the Strong State: The Politics of Thatcherism*. Houndmills:
  Macmillan.
—(1996) *Hayek: The Iron Cage of Liberty*. Colorado: Westview Press.
—(2003) *Between Europe and America: The Future of British Politics*. Basingstoke: Palgrave
  Macmillan.
Gash, R. (1977) "From the Origins to Sir Robert Peel," in N. Gash, D. Southgate, D. Dilks and
  J. Ramsden (eds), *The Conservatives: A History from their Origins to 1965*. London: George Allen
  & Unwin, pp. 19–108.
Gill, C. (2003) *Whips' Nightmare: Diary of a Maastricht Rebel*. Durham: The Memoir Club.
Gill, S. (1998) "Economic Governance and the New Constitutionalism," *New Political Economy*, 3,
  pp. 5–26.
Gilmour, I. (1969) *The Body Politic*. London: Hutchinson.
—(1978) *Inside Right: A Study of Conservatism*. London: Quartet Books.
—(1992) *Dancing with Dogma: Britain under Thatcherism*. London: Pocket Books.
Gilmour, I and Garnett, M. (1998) *Whatever Happened to the Tories: The Conservatives since 1945*.
  London: Fourth Estate.
Goldman, P. (1961) *Some Principles of Conservatism*. London: Conservative Political Centre No. 161.
Goodhart, P. (1984) *Jobs Ahead: For the One Nation Group of MPs*. London: Conservative Political
  Centre No. 0510-726.
Gorman, T. and Kirby, H. (1993) *Bastards: Dirty Tricks and the Challenge to Europe*. London: Pan
  Books.
Green, E. H. H. (2002) *Ideologies of Conservatism: Conservative Political Ideas in the Twentieth
  Century*. Oxford: Oxford University Press.
Greenleaf, W. H. (1983a) *The British Political Tradition, Volume One: The Rise of Collectivism*.
  London: Routledge.
—(1983b) *The British Political Tradition, Volume Two: The Ideological Heritage*. London:
  Routledge.
Grey, J. (1997) "The Undoing of Conservatism," in Grey, J. and Willets, D. *Is Conservatism Dead?*
  London: Profile Books, pp. 1–62.
Hague, W. (2004) *William Pitt the Younger*. Bury St Edmunds: HarperCollins.
Hailsham, Viscount. (1957) *Toryism and Tomorrow*. London: Conservative Political Centre, No. 181.
Harper, J. R. (1992) *New Unionism*. Glasgow: Society of Scottish Conservative Lawyers.
Harris, N. (1973) *Competition and the Corporate Society: British Conservatives, the State and Industry
  1945–1964*. London: Methuen.
Hayek, F. A. (1954) "History and Politics," in F. A. Hayek (ed.), *Capitalism and the Historians*.
  London: Routledge & Kegan Paul, pp. 3–29.

—(1976) *Law, Legislation and Liberty: A New Statement of the Liberal Principles of Justice and Political Economy, Volume 2, The Mirage of Social Justice*. London: Routledge & Kegan Paul.

—(1979) *Law, Legislation and Liberty: A New Statement of the Liberal Principles of Justice and Political Economy, Volume 3, The Political Order of a Free People*. London: Routledge & Kegan Paul.

Heath, E. (1977) *Our Community*. London: Conservative Political Centre No. 613.

Heffer, S. (1999) *Like the Roman: The Life of Enoch Powell*. London: Phoenix.

Heppell, T. (2002) "The Ideological Composition of the Parliamentary Conservative Party 1992–97," *British Journal of Politics and International Relations*, 4, pp. 299–324.

Heppell, T. and Hill, M. (2005) "Ideological Typologies of Contemporary British Conservatism," *Political Studies Review*, 3, pp. 335–355.

Hinchingbrooke, V. (1944) *Full Speed Ahead: Essays in Tory Reform*. London: Simpkin Marshall.

—(1947) "The Course of Conservative Politics," *The Quarterly Review*, No. 574, October 1947.

Hine, D. (1985) "Factionalism in West European Parties: A Framework for Analysis," *West European Politics*, 5, pp. 36–53.

Hogg, Q. (1947) *The Case For Conservatism*. Middlesex: Penguin.

—(1959) *The Conservative Case*. Middlesex: Penguin.

Holmes, M. (1994) *The Conservative Party and Europe*, Occasional Paper No. 17. London: Bruges Group.

Holmes, M. (ed.) (1996) *The Eurosceptic Reader*. Basingstoke: Macmillan.

Howard, A. (1988) *RAB: The Life of R. A. Butler*. Basingstoke: Papermac.

Howell, D. (2001) *The Edge of Now: New Questions for Democracy in the Network Age*. Basingstoke: Pan Books.

Huntington, S. P. (1957) "Conservatism as an Ideology," *The American Political Science Review*, 51, pp. 454–473.

Jones, H. (1996) "The Cold War and the Santa Claus Syndrome: Dilemmas in Conservative Social Policy-Making, 1945–1957," in M. Francis and I. Zweiniger-Bargielowska (eds), *The Conservatives and British Society, 1880–1990*. Cardiff: University of Wales Press, pp. 240–254.

Jones, H. and Kandiah, M. (eds) (1996) *The Myth of Consensus: New Views on British History, 1945–64*. Basingstoke: Macmillan.

Joseph, Sir K. (1975) *Reversing the Trend: A Critical Re-appraisal of Conservative Economic and Social Policies*. London: Barry Rose.

Kavanagh, D. and Morris, P. (1989) *Consensus Politics from Attlee to Major*. Oxford: Blackwell.

Kebbel, M. A. (1882) *Selected Speeches of the Late Right Honourable the Earl of Beaconsfield*. London: Longmans, Green and Co.

Kilbrandon, Lord (1973) *Royal Commission on the Constitution, 1969–73*, Report: Cmd.5460. London: HMSO.

Kilmuir, Earl of (1964) *Political Adventure: The Memoirs of the Earl of Kilmuir*. London: Weidenfield & Nicholson.

Lamont, N. (1999) *In Office*. London: Little, Brown.

Layton-Henry, Z. (1980) "Immigration," in Z. Layton-Henry (ed.), *Conservative Party Politics*. Basingstoke: Macmillan, pp. 50–73.

—(1986) "Race and the Thatcher Government," in Z. Layton-Henry and P. B. Rich (eds), *Race, Government and Politics in Britain*. Basingstoke: Macmillan, pp. 73–99.

Longden, G. (1985) "The Original 'One Nation'" *Crossbow*, Autumn, pp. 22–24.

Lowe, R. (1996) "The Replanning of the Welfare State, 1957–1964," in M. Francis and I. Zweiniger-Bargielowska (eds), *The Conservatives and British Society, 1880–1990*. Cardiff: University of Wales Press, pp. 255–273.

Ludlam, S. (1996) "The Spectre Haunting Conservatism: Europe and Backbench Rebellion," in M. J. Smith and S. Ludlam (eds), *Contemporary British Conservatism*. Basingstoke: Macmillan.

—(1998) "The Cauldron: Conservative Parliamentarians and European Integration," in D. Baker and D. Seawright (eds), *Britain For and Against Europe: British Politics and the Question of European Integration*. Oxford: Clarendon Press, pp. 31–56.

Lynch, P. (1999) *The Politics of Nationhood: Sovereignty, Britishness and Conservative Politics*. Basingstoke: Macmillan.

—(2003) "Nationhood and Identity in Conservative Politics," in M. Garnett and P. Lynch (eds), *The Conservatives in Crisis*. Manchester: Manchester University Press, pp. 182–197.

Lynch, P. and Whitaker, R. (2008) "A loveless Marriage: The Conservatives and the European People's Party," *Parliamentary Affairs*, 61, pp. 31–51.

MacKenzie, N. and MacKenzie, J. (1979) *The First Fabians*. London: Quartet Books.

Macleod, I. and Maude, A. (eds) (1950) *One Nation: A Tory Approach to Social Problems*. London: Conservative Political Centre No. 86.

Marr, A. (1995) *The Battle For Scotland*. Basingstoke: Penguin.

Marsh, D. and Hall, M. (2007) "The British Political Tradition: Explaining the Fate of New Labour's Constitutional Reform Agenda," in *British Politics*, 2, pp. 215–238.

Maude, A. (1963) "The Conservative Crisis I: Party Palaeontology," *The Spectator*. March 15, 1963, pp. 319–321.

Maudling, R. (1978) *Memoirs*. London: Sidgwick and Jackson.

McAnulla, S. (2006a) "Challenging the New Interpretivist Approach: Towards a Critical Realist Alternative," in *British Politics*, 1, pp. 113–138.

—(2006b) "Critical Realism, Social Structure, and Political Analysis: A Reply to Bevir and Rhodes," in *British Politics*, 1, pp. 404–412.

McKenzie, R. T. (1955) *British Political Parties: The Distribution of Power within the Conservative and Labour Parties*. London: William Heinemann.

Miller, W. L. (1981) *The End of British Politics? Scots and English Political Behaviour in the Seventies*. Oxford: Clarendon Press.

Miller, W. L., Brand, J. and Jordan, M. (1981) "Government without a Mandate: Its Causes and Consequences for the Conservative Party in Scotland," *Political Quarterly*, 52, pp. 203–213.

Mitchell, J. (2006) "Devolution's Unfinished Business," *The Political Quarterly*, 77, pp. 465–474.

Molson, H. (1945) *The Tory Reform Committee*. London: Eyre and Spottiswoode.

Nisbet, R. (1986) *Conservatism*. Milton Keynes: Open University Press.

Norris, P. and Lovenduski, J. (1995) *Political Recruitment: Gender, Race and Class in the British Parliament*. Cambridge: Cambridge University Press.

Norton, P. (1978) *Conservative Dissidents: Dissent within the Parliamentary Conservative Party 1970–74*. London: Temple Smith.

—(1990) "'The Lady's Not For Turning' but What about the Rest? Margaret Thatcher and the Conservative Party 1979–89," *Parliamentary Affairs*, 43, pp. 41–58.

—(1994) "The Parliamentary Party and Party Committees," in A. Seldon and S. Ball (eds), *Conservative Century: The Conservative Party since 1900*. Oxford: Oxford University Press, pp. 97–144.

—(1996) "The Party Leader," in P. Norton (ed.), *The Conservative Party*. London: Prentice Hall/Harvester Wheatsheaf.

—(1998) "The Conservative Party: 'in office but not in power'," in A. King, D. Denver, I. McLean, P. Norris, P. Norton, D. Sanders and P. Seyd (eds), *New Labour Triumphs: Britain at the Polls*. Chatham, New York: Chatham House, pp. 75–112.

—(2001) "The Conservative Party: Is There Anyone Out There?" in A. King, J. Bartle, D. Denver, P. Norton, P. Seyd and C. Seymore-Ure (eds), *Britain at the Polls 2001*. Chatham, New York: Chatham House, pp. 68–94.

Norton, P. and Aughey, A. (1981) *Conservatives and Conservatism*. London: Temple Smith.

Nott, J. (2002) *Here Today Gone Tomorrow: Reflections of an Errant Politician*. London: Politicos.

Oakeshott, M. (1991) *Rationalism in Politics and Other Essays*. Indianapolis: Liberty Fund.

O'Gorman, F. (1986) *British Conservatism: Conservative Thought from Burke to Thatcher.* London: Longman.

One Nation Group (1959) *The Responsible Society.* London: Conservative Political Centre No. 200.

—(1976) *One Nation At Work: By the One Nation Group of MPs.* London: Conservative Political Centre No. 585.

—(1992) *One Nation 2000.* London: Conservative Political Centre No. 0510/833.

—(1996) *One Nation at the Heart of the Future.* London: Conservative Political Centre.

O'Sullivan, N. (1976) *Conservatism.* London: J. M. Dent & Sons.

Panebianco, A. (1982) *Political Parties: Organization and Power.* Cambridge: Cambridge University Press.

—(1988) *Political Parties: Organization and Power.* Cambridge: Cambridge University Press.

Patten, C. (1983) *The Tory Case.* Essex: Longman.

Paulu, B. (1956) "Britain's Independent Television Authority (Part I)," *The Quarterly of Film, Radio and Television,* 10, pp. 325–336.

Pimlott, B. (1989) "Controversy: Is the Post-War Consensus A Myth?" *Contemporary Record,* 3, pp. 12–15.

Portillo, M. (1998) *Democratic Values and the Currency.* London: Institute for Economic Affairs.

Powell, E, and Maude, A. (eds) (1954) *Change Is Our Ally: A Tory Approach to Industrial Problems* London: Conservative Political Centre No. 133.

Pym, F. (1985) *The Politics of Consent.* London: Sphere Books.

Pym, F. and Brittan, L. (1978) *The Conservative Party and Devolution: Four Viable Options.* Edinburgh: Scottish Conservative Party.

Raison, T. (1964) *Why Conservative?* Middlesex: Penguin.

—(1990) *Tories and the Welfare State: A History of Conservative Social Policy since the Second World War.* Basingstoke: Macmillan.

Ramsden, J. (1987) "'A Party For Owners Or A Party For Earners?' How Far Did the British Conservative Party Really Change after 1945?" in *Transactions of the Royal Historical Society,* 5, pp. 49–63.

—(1999) *An Appetite for Power: A History of the Conservative Party since 1830.* London: HarperCollins.

Rich, P. B. (1986) "Conservative Ideology and Race in Modern British Politics," in Z. Layton-Henry and P. B. Rich (eds), *Race, Government and Politics in Britain.* Basingstoke: Macmillan, pp. 45–72.

Ridley, N. (1992) *My Style of Government: The Thatcher Years.* London: Fontana.

Ridley, N. (ed.) (1965) *One Europe: By the One Nation Group of MPs.* London: Conservative Political Centre No. 314.

Ritchie, R. (ed.) (1978) *Enoch Powell: A Nation or No Nation? Six Years in British Politics.* London: Batsford.

Roberts, A. (1995) *Eminent Churchillians.* London: Phoenix.

Rose, R. (1961) "The Bow Group's Role in British Politics," *Western Political Quarterly,* 14, pp. 865–878.

—(1964) "Parties, Factions and Tendencies in Britain," *Political Studies,* 12, pp. 33–46.

—(1975) *The Problem of Party Government.* Harmondsworth: Pelican.

Sanders, D. (1998) "The New Electoral Battleground," in A. King, D. Denver, I. McLean, P. Norris, P. Norton, D. Sanders and P. Seyd (eds), *New Labour Triumphs: Britain at the Polls.* New Jersey: Chatham House, pp. 209–248.

Scruton, R. (2001) *The Meaning of Conservatism,* 3rd edition. Basingstoke: Palgrave.

Seawright, D. (1999) *An Important Matter of Principle: The Decline of the Scottish Conservative and Unionist Party.* Aldershot: Ashgate.

—(2002) "The Scottish Conservative and Unionist Party: The Lesser Spotted Tory," in G. Hassan and C. Warhurst (eds), *Tomorrow's Scotland.* London: Lawrence and Wishart, pp. 66–82.

—(2004) "Geoffrey Howe, 1983–89," in K. Theakston (ed.), *British Foreign Secretaries since 1974*. London: Routledge, pp. 157–181.

—(2005a) "One Nation," in K. Hickson (ed.), *Conservative Political Thought since 1945*. London: Palgrave, pp. 69–90.

—(2005b) "'On A Low Road': The 2005 Conservative Campaign," *Journal of Marketing Management*, 21, pp. 943–957.

—(2008a) "The Conservative Party's Devolution Dilemma," *Textes & Contextes*, 1, pp. 1–24, http://revuesshs.u-bourgogne.fr/textes&contextes/sommaire.php?id=22.

—(2008b) "The Cameron Conundrum: The Union and/or 'the English Question'," *Babel: Langages-Imaginaires-Civilisations*, 17, pp. 27–44.

Seldon, A. (1981) *Churchill's Indian Summer: The Conservative Government, 1951–55*. London: Hodder and Stoughton.

Seyd, P. (1972) "Factionalism within the Conservative Party: The Monday Club," *Government and Opposition*, 7, pp. 464–487.

—(1980) "Factionalism in the 1970s," in Z. Layton-Henry (ed.), *Conservative Party Politics*. London: Macmillan.

Shepherd, R. (1994) *Iain Macleod: A Biography*. London: Pimlico.

Skelton, N. (1924) *Constructive Conservatism*. Edinburgh: William Blackwood & Sons.

Smith, P. (1967) *Disraelian Conservatism and Social Reform*. London: Routledge & Kegan Paul.

Southgate, D. (1977) "From Disraeli to Law," in N. Gash, D. Southgate, D. Dilks and J. Ramsden (eds), *The Conservatives: A History from Their Origins to 1965*. London: George Allen & Unwin, pp. 109–270.

Spicer, M. (1992) *A Treaty Too Far: A New Policy for Europe*. London: Fourth Estate.

Stephanopoulos, G. (1999) *All Too Human: A Political Education*. London: Hutchinson.

Stokes, D. (1992) "Valence Politics," in D. Kavanagh (ed.), *Electoral Politics*. Oxford: Clarendon Press, pp. 141–164.

Studlar, D. T. (1978) "Policy Voting in Britain: The Colored Immigration Issue in the 1964, 1966, and 1970 General Elections," *The American Political Science Review*, 72, pp. 46–64.

SUA (1949) *Scottish Control of Scottish Affairs: Unionist Policy*. Edinburgh: Scottish Unionist Association.

Talmon, J. L. (1957) *Utopianism and Politics*. London: Conservative Political Centre No. 180.

Tebbit, N. (1989) *Upwardly Mobile*. London: Futura.

Temple-Morris, P. (1996) "Still the Party of One Nation?" *Reformer Spring*, 1996, pp. 9–10.

Thatcher, M. (1993) *The Downing Street Years*. London: HarperCollins.

—(1996) "Foreword," in K. Minogue (ed.), *Conservative Realism: New Essays in Conservatism*. London: HarperCollins, pp. xiii–xv.

—(1999) *Margaret Thatcher: Complete Public Statements 1945–1990 on CD-Rom*. Oxford: Oxford University Press.

Tyrie, A. (2006) *One Nation Again*. Surrey: 4 Print.

Vincent, A (1995) *Modern Political Ideologies*, 2nd Edition. Oxford: Blackwell.

Walsha, R. (2000) "The One Nation Group: A Tory Approach to Backbench Politics and Organisation, 1950–55," *Twentieth Century British History*, 11, 183–214.

—(2003) "The One Nation Group and One Nation Conservatism, 1950–2002," *Contemporary British History*, 17, 69–120.

Walters, S. (2001) *Tory Wars: Conservatives in Crisis*. London: Politico's Publishing.

Warner, G. (2007) "How Bulldog Brown Could Call Braveheart Salmond's Bluff," *The Scotsman*, May 6, 2007.

White, R. J. (1950) *The Conservative Tradition*. London: Nicholas Kaye.

Willetts, D. (1992) *Modern Conservatism*. Middlesex: Penguin.

—(1997a) "Civic Conservatism," in Grey, J. and Willets, D. *Is Conservatism Dead?* London: Profile Books, pp. 67–139.

—(1997b) *Why Vote Conservative?* Middlesex: Penguin.

Williamson, P. (1993) "The Doctrinal Politics of Stanley Baldwin," in M. Bentley (ed.), *Public and Private Doctrine: Essays in British History Presented to Maurice Cowling.* Cambridge: Cambridge University Press, pp. 181–208.

Wilson, H. H. (1961) *Pressure Group: The Campaign for Commercial Television.* London: Secker and Warburg.

Wring, D. (2005) *The Politics of Marketing the Labour Party.* Basingstoke: Palgrave Macmillan.

Young, H. (1990) *One of Us.* London: Pan Books.

# Index

Lightning Source UK Ltd.
Milton Keynes UK
UKOW040827090812

197278UK00004B/10/P